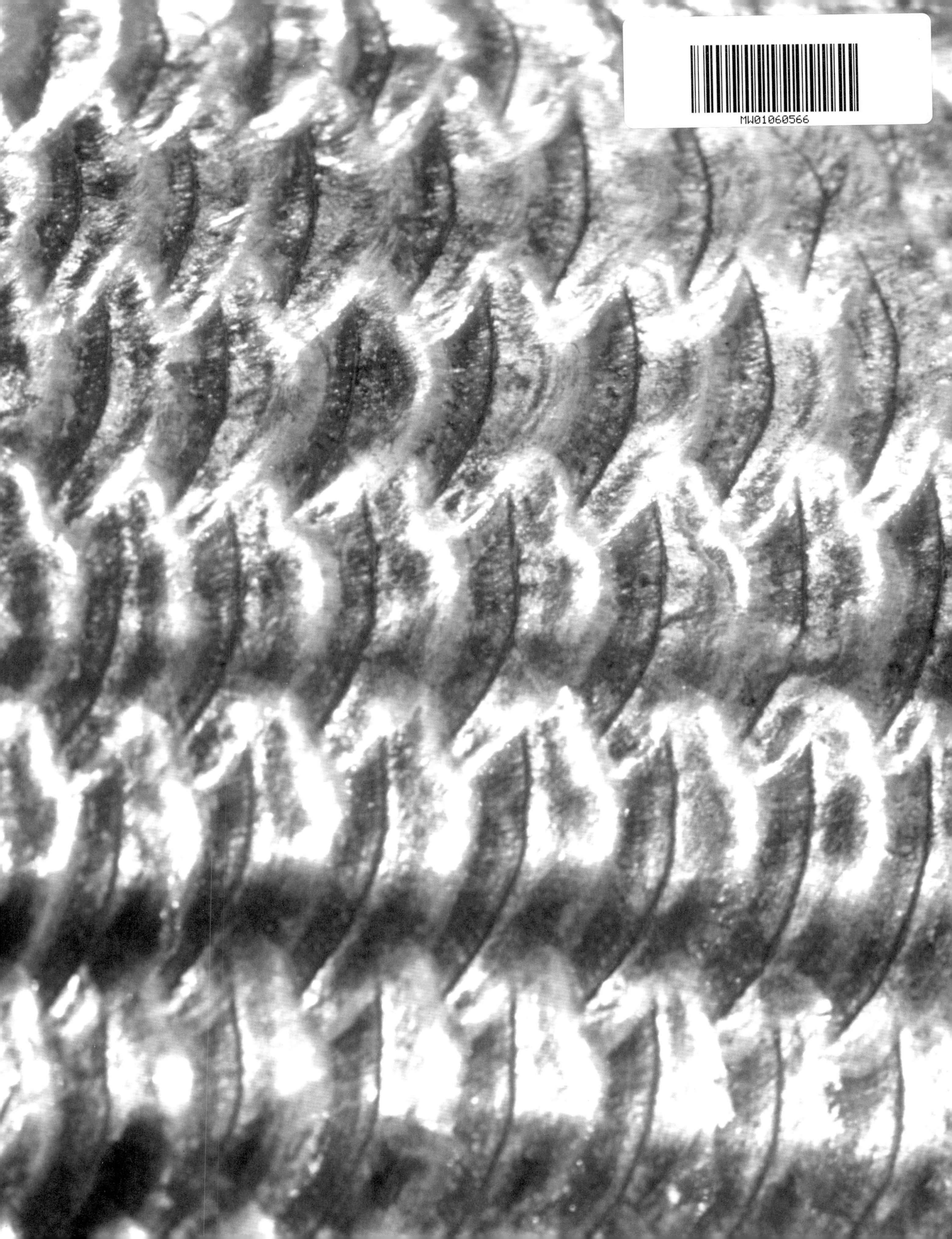

Fly-Fishing for Bonefish

Fly-Fishing for Bonefish

CHICO FERNÁNDEZ

STACKPOLE
BOOKS

Published by
STACKPOLE BOOKS
5067 Ritter Road
Mechanicsburg, PA 17055
www.stackpolebooks.com

Printed in China

First edition

10 9 8 7 6 5 4 3 2 1

Photographs by the author unless otherwise credited
Watercolor paintings by Millard Wells

Library of Congress Cataloging-in-Publication Data
Fernández, Chico.
Fly-fishing for bonefish / Chico Fernández ; with biology by Aaron J. Adams.—1st ed.
p. cm.
Includes bibliographical references (p.).
ISBN 0-8117-0095-X (hardcover)
1. Bonefishing. 2. Fly fishing. I. Adams, Aaron J. II. Title.
SH691.B6F47 2004
799.17'43—dc22

2004001991

To my wife, Marilyn,
for her support and enduring patience.

To my father,
who first took me fishing,
and lit the flame.

And to my son, Stephen,
my favorite fishing partner,
who will keep the flame lit.

Contents

Foreword

I have been eagerly waiting for my friend Chico's book on bonefishing ever since he let me know it was in the works. Actually, at my first meeting with Chico Fernández back in 1973, he asked me to wait for a bit. I'd gone to his home to pick up an ample ration of his personally tied bonefish flies, which he sold to help make ends meet. Even for an excited and impatient newcomer to saltwater fly fishing, I knew it was okay to wait for Chico because he had already achieved a reputation as one of south Florida's finest bonefish anglers.

I waited because Chico's life was in transition away from a career as the budget director for Miami-based Burger King. I waited because I was learning that Chico was meticulous when it came to bonefish flies or anything else that he set his mind to. He had just decided to leave the day-to-day, coat-and-tie lifestyle to pursue his dreams. Those dreams were to build a life around the people he cared about and his passion for fly fishing, especially bonefishing.

Thirty years later, it's easy to joke about how he and his wife, Marilyn, were more than a little apprehensive over the idea of abandoning a regular paycheck and benefits of the corporate world. Over the years, Chico has certainly succeeded in relieving those initial financial anxieties, and together he and Marilyn have raised a fine son, Stephen, who has become an exceptional angler in his own right.

That Chico would mature to become one of the planet's most dynamic, talented, and knowledgeable anglers and authorities on bonefish says even more about his ability to follow those dreams and turn them to reality. Few people knew very much about bonefishing back in the early 1970s, but I knew that I had to have a good supply of Chico's Bonefish Specials and Honey Shrimp in my fly box when I fished in a tournament. I had to have them simply because they worked better than any other bonefish flies I had used. I knew they worked better than other flies because I kept catching more and larger bonefish than most other anglers fishing the same areas on the same days. Chico's flies were worth waiting for.

During the late 1970s and early '80s, our paths crossed frequently on the flats, at boat ramps, at environmental forums, and at various angling events or seminars. I read his many articles and always learned something new and significant. Chico was always returning from new destinations with wonderful stories. At the same time, he was planning another trip to another exotic destination in pursuit of bonefish. Again, I found myself waiting for Chico to return with more stories and new information. He created a new fly here and a modification of one there that seemed to work a little better.

I realized that day by day, week by week, and year by year he was sorting out the myths from the facts on catching bonefish with a fly rod. Chico was finding out details like what prey bonefish preferred and what actions to impart to flies to imitate that prey. Sink rates, hook sizes, hook setting, fly-line tapers, rod actions, and fly-reel capacities seemed to be boiling in him like a great chef's recipe. There was a passion in him to learn more. Chico developed confidence in the knowledge he had and a willingness to share with others and an openness to learn more from others as well. His career and reputation as a writer, photographer, innovative fly designer, and fly-rod, fly-line, and fly-reel consultant grew by leaps and bounds. Mostly, though, Chico was an angler.

Throughout those years I had done more than a little bit of bonefishing myself. In 1989 we began teaching saltwater fly fishing together at the Florida Keys Fly Fishing School in Islamorada half a dozen weekends a year. It wasn't too slouchy a faculty that included Flip Pallot, Stu Apte, Rick Ruoff, Steve Huff, and Steve Rajeff. Since then I have spent over 300 days with Chico, many on the water in pursuit of bonefish.

Since 1990, I have spent many days listening to Chico explain the details of fly-line tapers and weights. More days were spent listening to his explanations of rod materials, actions, and tapers. Even more time was spent hearing his ideas about flies, presentations, fishing techniques, boat characteristics, fish habits, and habitats. He offered history, personal experiences, diagrams, outstanding photography, and lots of humor with his presentations. Chico could break subject matter down to the basic beginner level or take it to the highest level of technology. We debated minute details and broad theories of fly fishing. He always had research, facts, and experience to draw from. Most times we came to the same conclusions, but sometimes not. Many evenings were spent discussing why his preferred Scotch whiskey was inferior to my preferred sour-mash whiskey, and I am still waiting for Chico to yield on that issue.

What we always seemed to agree on was that there are no tricks, no gimmicks, and no instant-pudding mixes for catching bonefish. It was in the mid-1990s that Chico told me he was going to write a book on bonefish. I was very excited for him and for me, because whatever Chico writes is well worth reading. To put into print what he so wonderfully presented in discussion would be his greatest challenge. When I asked him when it would be published, he told me I would have to wait just a bit. That was okay because after knowing Chico for thirty years, I knew that it would be worth the wait.

In October 2003, Chico gave me the manuscript of *Fly-Fishing for Bonefish,* and I could not put it down. It is the most complete work on bonefishing I have ever seen. Information on tackle, destinations, presentation skills, stomach contents, fly selections, fish-fighting techniques, guides, and on and on—Chico was able to put into print what he so aptly delivered in person. His talented photography puts icing on the cake. *Fly-Fishing for Bonefish* is surely required reading for any bonefish angler at any experience level, and it is the standard by which books on the subject will be measured for years to come.

Chico, my friend, it was worth the wait.

Sandy Moret
Islamorada, Florida

Preface

I first knew bonefish as *macabi*, their common name in Spanish, and caught my first one with a fly rod on the northwest coast of Cuba around 1956, near then-remote Jibacoa Beach. That morning is still fresh in my memory. Walking along the beach at dawn, I blind-cast into the calm surf, hoping that something would take my small yellow streamer. The day before, I had taken a couple of small jacks and a mangrove snapper before a barracuda had cut off my only fly. But this morning, armed with several flies, I felt I was prepared. As I cast, I concentrated on making a slow, steady retrieve. I could not buy flies in Cuba in those days, so I would buy spinners, keep the fly attached to the tail of each one, and throw the rest away. Those light, little streamers were all I had during my first year as a fly fisher.

My concentration was broken when a pod of four to six fish went by me, swimming steadily only twenty feet from the beach. Their backs were bright green, almost iridescent, and they looked chunky but agile. I had no idea what they were, but I remember that in my excitement to cast, I ended up with the fly line inexplicably tangled all over me, the fly stuck in my shirt sleeve with the hook buried past the barb.

By the time I untangled the line and ripped my shirt sleeve to recover the precious fly, the fish were gone. I looked for them as I walked to the end of the beach area more than a mile away, but they had disappeared.

Then they reappeared, though in a different setting. At the end of the sandy beach there was a cove, beyond which the shoreline became rocky. This cove was very shallow; its flat bottom was part sand, part grass. The pod of strange fish were in the cove with their noses to the bottom, producing a cloud of mud while their long, translucent tails occasionally showed above the water.

I waded toward the fish and cast as accurately as I could. If memory serves me right, the fly landed about ten or fifteen feet from the mud. I started to strip and suddenly the fly line was plucked from my left hand, then all the slack line in the water disappeared through the stripping guide with a sound like a sword slicing through the air, and then my reel started to scream and vibrate as it had never done before.

I used to think that run was 100 yards long, but it probably was closer to 40. By the time I landed that 5-pound dynamo, I knew what he was. I had seen his kind in magazine photos and the nets of commercial fishermen. This was a *macabi*, or bonefish, and I was so excited that I could think of only one thing as I rode home on my bicycle: Where can I find other shallow areas like the little basin?

I still ask myself the same question today.

In the years since, I have taken thousands of bonefish on flies, but none is so vivid in my memory as that first one. I can still see those bright green bonefish swimming along that deserted beach. How often I have relived those few seconds of my life!

This book is about the world and the ways of a fabulous fish, the bonefish.

Fishing for bonefish consists of hours of hunting and a few minutes of catching. To become a bonefisherman, you must be at a point in your fishing career where you truly enjoy the hunt, and not just the moment of the strike. Yes, there are days when you may take many bonefish, but such days are the exception, a bonus.

And a good hunter you had better be, because in no other sight-casting situation will you find a 10-pound fish that can disappear in just a few inches of crystal-clear water. "Impossible," you may say to yourself as you look for him all over, but it's true. Puff, he is gone. And then you know why he is called the ghost of the flats.

If you hook him, you will enjoy runs that are improbably long for a fish his size. And when you finally land one, still struggling in your hands, you are rewarded with the sight of a beautiful fish, perfectly tapered for speed and extraordinarily graceful.

A day's hunting in an area that has big bones is all about taking one fish. That's it! It's not about numbers. If you can take one big bonefish that day, you've had a great day. I feel that you must see and understand bonefishing in that light.

As extra entertainment while you hunt, you experience the incredibly complex and beautiful environment in which you are hunting—the bonefish's neighborhood. It is a neighborhood of big spaces. You can see the horizon all around you, interrupted by a few or many keys of different sizes and shapes. Often, you will not see another boat for hours or even all day. Visually, bonefish flats have not changed much from a century ago.

The warm, tropical salt air cleanses you and gives you strength. Little by little, the preoccupations and complexities of the city, while not totally forgotten, fade to their proper significance. This is why I can't stand a cellular telephone ringing in a skiff. It depresses me. It wakes me up from my reverie and brings me back to the city. Although I do bring a phone these days, it's only for emergencies, and it's turned off until an emergency happens. Even so, the phone's mere presence bothers me. It makes the day too safe, I guess, less of an adventure. I did not need it years ago, but now I'm not safe if I don't bring one. Does that make sense?

Life is all around you on the flats—rays, sharks, barracudas, sea grasses, the bonefish themselves—but for all the sounds you may hear, the flat is still more tranquil than dead silence in a city, because each city has its own beat, and your heart beats to that rhythm. You never really rest from it. But the flat does not force you to its rhythm; it lets you keep your own.

The flats also require a special type of skiff that must be propelled as quietly as possible during the hunt. No push-button entertainment here. Poling a boat is as natural an activity as walking along a beach. If your only experience with bonefish has been catching them, then there are still great things in store for you. Poling a truly great, light skiff is a joy. With the pushpole in your hands, you are not just the fish catcher up front; you are the hunter. You decide where to fish on the flat, selecting depth, direction, approach. A great guide may look relaxed while he poles you down the flat. But if he is truly great, he is thinking, he is looking, he is feeling the wind, he is calculating tides. He is hunting. Some of my great experiences in flats fishing have been poling a friend or my son, Stephen, while hunting, both of us blending in the same intense purpose, becoming one hunter. This is fishing at its best. If you've never done it, you've got to pole a bonefish skiff sometime.

And then there are the charts. There is a certain fascination in reading a chart full of flats, channels, bays, and creeks. You get to the point where you can visualize what an area might look like or calculate if it would have good fishing or not. For me, a nautical chart has always represented the hope of a new adventure. Hanging in my office is a three-by-four-foot chart that my wife, Marilyn, framed for me. It shows the area of Florida Bay, and it's full of drop-offs, creeks, flats, basins, and dreams. I look at it every day I'm home.

Finally, I must tell you that I don't think that you have fully graduated as a bonefisherman until you wade alone after a tailing fish, rod in hand, minimal tackle with you, hunting in the most basic, primitive style, one on one, *mano a mano*. And if it happens to be a really big bonefish that you are hunting, you will learn that fishing doesn't get any better. I want your heart to be pounding, your throat to be dry, and your palms to be sweaty. Then, even if you don't get him, you will be a bonefisherman!

Miami, Florida
October 2003

Acknowledgments

Among the greatest trophies of fly fishing are the many friends that one makes along the way and the great fountain of knowledge that they bring with them, if one takes the time to listen. I have been very fortunate in having met many wonderful fly fishers.

When I came to this country from Cuba in the very late 1950s, I brought my bamboo fly rods with me. Miami was then a very small town, and within a few weeks I had found three other young fly fishermen who were as crazy for the sport as I was: Norman Duncan (of the Duncan loop), John "Little John" Emery, and Flip Pallot. Together, we were the Four Musketeers. We experimented, tied flies, made our own fly rods, made some of the first clear fly lines by sanding 300- or 500-pound monofilament, modified reel drags, and swapped information.

Norm Duncan became an engineer. Little John became a great fishing guide but, tragically, passed away far too young. Flip became a guide and later a celebrity in the fly-fishing world. And I, well, I continued to fly fish and eventually started teaching the sport and writing about it.

I learned a great deal of what I know today about fly fishing and bonefish from the other Musketeers—not only techniques, but also the soul and the essence of the sport. I think of them often and can't thank them enough.

Capt. Bill Curtis also played an important part in my development as a bonefish angler. Bill often took me bonefishing in the very early 1960s, when I did not have a boat. Many years later, he took my son, Stephen, fishing many times. I've learned a lot from Bill over the years.

Many friends contributed to this book in one way or another. My thanks to:

Artist and master fly tier Tim Borski. As an artist, Tim contributed two drawings of bonefish looking for food. As a tier and an angler, he gave me several of his flies and much information about bonefish flies and how he fishes them.

Bruce Richards, an old friend and one of the great fly casters. Bruce has designed fly lines for Scientific Anglers for many years. His input on lines and leaders has been invaluable.

Jorge Martinez, fly fisher and fine artist. Jorge drew several knot, loop, and clock-system diagrams for this book.

Sandy Moret, of Florida Keys Outfitters in Islamorada, a dear friend and one of the best fly fishermen I have ever known. Sandy actually volunteered to write the foreword, and I quickly accepted. He also contributed a great deal of information on bonefish behavior and how to fish for them.

Sue Moret, Sandy's wife and a close friend. Her insistence that I go fishing on a windy afternoon because she had landed a 13-pound bonefish the day before produced my biggest bonefish to date, a 14-pounder. Sue took the photo, too.

Bob Stearns, whom I have known for forty years. Bob is a master at rigging leaders and fly lines and the creator of the Bob Stearns Snapping Shrimp. During our long friendship, we have swapped a huge amount of bonefish information, some of which is in this book.

Frank and Liz Steele, for offering so much help and encouragement during their years in the fly-fishing business. Frank is as good at rigging a fly line as anyone else I know. Thanks, guys.

Tom and Karl Schmuecker, of Wapsi Fly Company, for many years of advice on fly-tying materials.

This book could not have happened without help from my friends who are guides. I would like to thank:

Capt. Craig Brewer and Capt. Geoff Colmes, both from Islamorada, for much fishing information over the years.

Capt. Chris Dean, Miami, a great guide and saltwater fly tier, for the many trips we have taken looking for bones, and a great amount of information on bonefish flies.

Capt. John Donnell, Plantation Key, for guiding me to a 14-pound bonefish, my largest.

Capt. Steve Huff, Everglades City, a friend of more than thirty years and one of the best guides in the world. I have learned much about the bonefish and his ways from Steve, and I always look forward to our next trip.

Capt. Steve Kantner, Fort Lauderdale, who gave me information on bonefish caught out of their normal range.

Capt. Tim Klein, Islamorada, for sharing with me his knowledge of bonefish and their environment in the Keys. His TK Special took my biggest bone ever.

Capt. Joel Moxey, Mangrove Cay, the Bahamas, one of the best guides in the Bahamas, for the big mutton snapper that we took on the flats and all his information about the area.

Capt. Dale Perez, Grassy Key, for our days of fishing in Key West and the knowledge he shared.

Capt. Tom Rowland, Key West, for his wisdom on fly fishing for barracudas and permit.

Capt. Rick Ruoff, Islamorada, another friend of many years, for his input on bonefish, sharks, permit, and especially mutton snapper.

Several well-known fishing camps gave me the use of their facilities, allowing me to do the necessary fishing, research, and photography, which often resulted in long days. I am very grateful for their generosity. My thanks to:

Bob and Karen Hyde and the crew of Peace and Plenty in Exuma, the Bahamas, for many trips over the years. Many underwater photos came from Peace and Plenty. The different trips that Bob planned also produced a 27-pound 'cuda on fly, a 40-pound dolphin for my son on fly, and a beautiful tiger shark that I'll never forget, even though it would not take my fly.

Bobby Settles and Steve Spencer and the rest of the crew at Casa Blanca in Mexico, for supplying me with two skiffs and three guides to complete my photography, and for their help on past trips. The tough part was bypassing many tailing bonefish and permit while we shot the photos on the list. The fishing was great, and we shot seventy rolls.

Judy and Ben Rose, club managers of North Riding Point Club, Grand Bahamas, for all their help, the great hospitality, the use of an extra skiff, and an open offer to come and shoot photos any time. I took many beautiful shots here, caught some nice bones, and saw the largest school of bonefish I can remember in recent years.

Photography is an important part of a book such as this. I owe five gentlemen my gratitude:

Dr. Alfred Forns, a friend of many years, for his technical photo help, especially in the "dry lab."

Marcus Haugg, for spending a whole week with me and my son just to shoot photos; lots of good images came out of those days.

Pat Ford, for his photo contributions.

Marc Vaughn, for contributing several photos and for his technical advice.

Brad Miller, for taking the photos of Millard Wells's paintings and for years of photo advice.

Several friends offered publishing advice and warm encouragement that really helped:

Capt. Jeffrey Cardenas, owner of the Saltwater Angler in Key West.

Joe Healy, editor of *Vermont Magazine* and, formerly, *Saltwater Fly Fishing*.

Gary Borger and Trey Combs, two great anglers, who encouraged me to do this book.

For their help in the actual making of this book, I want to thank:

Dr. Aaron Adams, a fly fisher himself, who wrote the first four chapters on bonefish, the flats environment, tides, and bonefish foods, and did a great job from an angler's perspective. It was fun and easy to work with you, Aaron.

Art Scheck, a great angler, editor, and fly tier, and a friend of many years. Art has endured the editing of dozens of my columns and articles over many years and knows me well. Thank you for your help and advice, and for taking the time to edit this long manuscript. No one could have done better.

Judith Schnell, my publisher, for her warm encouragement, her help, and her valuable advice in organizing and producing this book.

The folks at several fly shops encouraged me to write this book and provided great information on tackle, flies, local guides, and more. I am very grateful to them. I have already mentioned some of these anglers, but I also want to thank:

John Holmer, of the Saltwater Fly Fisherman, for being so persistent and supportive of my book. Thanks, John.

Franco Zamboli and Ashley Cornelius, of Biscayne Bay Fly Shop, for lots of information on bonefish flies and bonefishing.

My son, Stephen Fernández, who has fished with me since he was about six, was immensely helpful in encouraging me to finish this book. We spent many days shooting photos, catching bonefish food with fine-mesh nets, and, of course, fishing. Stephen also shot many of the photos, including all the underwater photography in this book. The most exciting times in the making of this book were those I spent with him. I'll never have the words to express my gratitude. Thanks, son.

At IGFA, biologist Glenda Kelly and librarian Gail Morchower have been of great help in looking up information for many years. Many thanks.

My association with Bonefish & Tarpon Unlimited (BTU) has also exposed me to much information about bonefish. A special thanks to Dr. Jerry Ault for his input on releasing bonefish, and for a clear view of the state of bonefish populations worldwide.

A very special thanks to the gang at Scott Fly Rod Company, for their many fine saltwater fly rods, and to the Scientific Anglers crew for hundreds of fly lines and no end of information over the past thirty years.

After so many years of fly fishing for bonefish, I am bound to have forgotten someone important who helped me become a better angler. So, to those I have inadvertently left out, I am truly sorry, and thank you for your help.

PART I

The Bonefish's World

The aim of this section is to describe the factors that make up a bonefish's world, including temperature, habitat, food, predation, and tides. Over the ages, the bonefish has found strategies that have proved successful in navigating the challenges encountered in this world where weakness, mistakes, and just plain bad luck can mean failure. What to eat and when to eat it, how to avoid predators, and which habitats are best at different times of year, at different times of day, and on different tides are all variables that influence the daily life of a bonefish.

The strategies that bonefish use to tackle these challenges are reflected in what they eat and when and how they use habitats. Correctly interpreting these strategies leads to catching more bonefish. The information in this four-chapter section will, I hope, lend additional meaning to the fishing strategies and techniques explained by Chico, and should help explain how Chico knows when and where to employ the various techniques that he uses.

Aaron J. Adams, Ph.D.
St. James City, Florida

Chapter 1

The Bonefish and Its World

On the evolutionary tree, bonefish are members of the family Albulidae. Research continues in this area, but as of this writing there are thirteen or more genetically distinct species in this family of fishes that are found in tropical marine environments throughout the world, and eight of these species are in the genus *Albula*. Additional genetic research may reveal more species of bonefish. Interestingly, many of these species are incredibly difficult to distinguish from one another without genetics. Based on the research conducted so far, these bonefish species have very similar life cycles and diets, and can be virtually identical in appearance. In fact, researchers have found different species of bonefish overlapping in their habitat use.

The most common bonefish species in the Caribbean is *Albula vulpes*. Indeed, *Albula vulpes* is limited to the Caribbean and nearby western Atlantic waters. At least one other species of bonefish is also found in the Caribbean; recent genetics research lists this species as *Albula* type B. Other species are limited to other regions, such as the Gulf of California or the Indo Pacific. For example, *Albula glossodonta* is the species found in the Seychelles. In any case, the similarities among these species mean that our strategies for stalking bonefish in the shallows is equally applicable to whatever species we may find. This is why an angler who learned to fly fish for bonefish in the Caribbean can use the same fishing techniques and catch bonefish in the Seychelles.

Bonefish can be found in estuaries, especially when they are young, but are best adapted to the salinity of marine environments. Much of the information presented here is based on studies of *Albula vulpes*, because this is the most studied species, but if an angler were to encounter one of the other species of bonefish in his or her travels, the knowledge gained here would be just as applicable.

TEMPERATURE

Although bonefish can be found in temperate waters during the warmest months of the year, these occurrences are rare and incidental. Bonefish are a tropical species, and are limited in their range because they prefer water temperatures that center around 78 degrees Fahrenheit.

In the western Atlantic, bonefish have been recorded as far north as the Bay of Fundy, Nova Scotia, and as far south as temperate Brazil, but bonefish are not able to remain in these areas because they cannot tolerate the cold temperatures of autumn, winter, and spring. During the summer, adults might occasionally migrate along the coast from tropical to subtropical areas, but they return as soon as the water cools because extended exposure to water temperatures below 60 degrees can be lethal.

More often, however, the bonefish found in temperate waters are the result of wayward larvae that have been transported by currents and transformed into juveniles far from their parents' home. These juveniles are likely to be eaten or die from cold when water temperatures drop because they are too small to migrate to the tropics, so they never join the adult populations farther south. Every summer, rocky reefs off the Northeast coast of the United States are temporarily home to juvenile bonefish and other tropical fish, including coral reef fish. The larvae are transported north by currents, and are able to survive on these reefs as juveniles in the summer, but will die as temperatures drop in the fall. In fact, juvenile tropical fish are so abundant off the Northeast coast that the New England Aquarium and other aquariums make trips every fall to rocky reefs off Rhode Island to collect reef fish.

In the Florida Keys, bonefish juveniles have been captured in water temperatures ranging from 61 to 83 degrees, which may be a good indicator of juvenile temperature preferences. In any case, the frigid winter waters of subtropical and temperate climates are not suitable for juvenile bonefish.

Immersed in the bonefish's world, these two anglers are joined by the lure of the hunt, an instinct that is in most of us.

MARC VAUGHN

Within the bonefish's normal geographic range, environments at the northern and southern limits are likely to have the most extreme temperatures at both ends of the scale. For instance, wintertime cold fronts in the Florida Keys can drop the water temperature considerably. In contrast, these same areas can experience very warm water temperatures in the summer, in part because the location of the sun near the Tropic of Cancer means that the days are longer, which helps to warm the water. More tropical latitudes experience day lengths and sun exposure that are similar throughout the year, and experience a narrower temperature range.

The target preferred temperature for bonefish seems to be around 78 degrees, with a temperature range of 70 to 85 degrees the favored range. When water temperature drops below 70 or above 90 degrees, bonefish head elsewhere or alter their behavior. In southern Florida, which is in the northern part of their range in the western Atlantic, bonefish will migrate to avoid the cold temperatures associated with a winter cold front. Many bonefish that live on the Florida Bay side of the Florida Keys during the summer migrate to the Atlantic side of the Keys for the winter because Florida Bay can become too cool for them. Florida Bay is very shallow, and it changes temperature more quickly than deeper water. When a cold front drops air temperatures into the 50s, the shallow waters of Florida Bay are not far behind. In contrast, bonefish on the Atlantic side of the Keys can use shallow flats during warm periods and retreat to nearby deeper water when cold fronts pass through. Like the shallow waters of Florida Bay, the ocean-side flats will also cool quickly during a cold front, but temperatures in the deeper nearby waters will remain more stable. Once the weather improves after the cold front, the shallows will warm quickly and the bonefish will return to the ocean-side flats.

Even within their tropical range, bonefish have a preference for water that is not too warm. When the water temperature in the shallows passes the upper 80s, bonefish will usually search for deeper, cooler water, or will adjust their feeding patterns to feed in the shallows when temperatures are slightly cooler. This is because shallow areas warm more quickly and to a higher temperature than deeper water during the summer. When the shallows get too warm, bonefish might start to feed at dawn, dusk, and even at night.

Like most fishes, bonefish are cold-blooded, and their physiology is adapted to operate most efficiently in their preferred temperature range. Even if temperatures are bearable, bonefish might not be up to speed in water at the low or high end of their tolerable range. This is why bonefish might seem sluggish or lethargic at times, even when you find them on the flats; the water temperature is near one extreme of their tolerances.

HABITATS

The image most often depicted in magazines is of bonefish feeding on shallow sand or sea-grass flats, but they can also use deeper sea-grass beds, mangrove lagoons, coral reefs, and even the deeper edges of cuts through coral reefs or drop-offs on the outside of reefs. Some of the reasons for changes in habitat use are due to temperature, but tides, predators, food, spawning, and age are other reasons.

Because they use so many different habitats, bonefish see a wide variety of prey. The potential prey list for bonefish includes crabs, shrimps, fishes (gobies, blennies, toadfish, silversides, anchovies, and others), worms, urchins, sea stars, brittle stars, clams, and more. From a fly fisher's perspective, bonefish adaptability is great, because they can be caught on a variety of flies. I will address bonefish diet in detail in chapter 4, but it is important to briefly mention the variety in their diet here because what bonefish eat is so closely tied to the habitats they use.

Despite their ability to use a wide range of habitats, bonefish are best adapted to using shallow areas. This is fortunate because when bonefish are using these shallow habitats they are most accessible to fly fishers. But why are bonefish so well adapted to shallow habitats? This simple question requires a long, complicated answer, but I'll summarize only the main points here.

In basic terms, a bonefish is faced with a couple of main challenges and goals in its life. On the one hand, a juvenile bonefish wants to grow as fast as it can because smaller fish are more likely to be eaten than larger fish; the faster the fish can grow, the lower its chances of being eaten. A second goal comes as the bonefish reaches maturity—it needs to reproduce to pass its genes on to the next generation. Even though a mature fish doesn't grow as fast as it did when it was smaller, it still needs enough food to have the energy to spawn. The requirements of growth and spawning would suggest that a bonefish should be out foraging as much as possible.

On the other hand, the more time a bonefish spends out in the open searching for food, the greater its chances of being eaten by predators such as sharks and barracudas. So a bonefish is faced with a tradeoff—it needs to eat so it can grow and reproduce, but it has to avoid predators.

The bonefish's strategy for making this tradeoff is to spend most of their time in shallow water. In the shallows, bonefish are able to use a variety of habitats that provide access to a variety of prey. This gives them the energy they need to grow and reproduce. And by specializing in shallow habitats, they are out of reach of most of the predators they would encounter on coral reefs and other deep-water habitats. Of course, they can't escape all predators, but the list of predators bonefish encounter in shallow water (such as barracudas, sharks, and birds) is much shorter than in deeper water or near reefs.

During its life, a bonefish will live in a handful of habitat types and will encounter different types of prey and different risks from predators in each of these habitats. This translates into differences in bonefish behavior because each habitat has different advantages and disadvantages. The part of the bonefish world experienced by fly anglers (the shallows) can be divided into seven broad habitat types: sea grass, algal plain, open sandy bottom,

MARC VAUGHN

During hot summer days, early or late in the evening is the best time to find tailing bonefish in the flats.

open muddy bottom, rubble, mangroves, and shoreline. The following general descriptions illustrate how these habitats might be perceived by bonefish. These descriptions also lay the foundation for the following three chapters, which address how bonefish interact with these habitats. How fly anglers can use this information to become better bonefish anglers is Chico's expertise, and is what this book is all about.

Sea Grass

The habitat that probably supports the most organisms that a bonefish would consider potential meals while providing protection from predation is sea grass. Tropical sea-grass beds encountered by bonefish and bonefish anglers are composed primarily of turtle grass (*Thalassia testudinum* in the Caribbean and Atlantic, and its relatives in the Pacific). Manatee grass (*Syringodium filiforme*) will be mixed with turtle grass in deeper water; shoal grass (*Halodule wrightii*) and a handful of other grasses may be mixed in shallow areas. But most of the areas where fly anglers pursue bonefish have turtle grass.

Turtle grass grows best in shallow areas that are protected from excessive current and wave action. Once established, one important ecological function of the broad blades of turtle grass is to reduce the velocity of the currents that flow over grass beds so that sediment particles suspended in the water can drop to the bottom. This acts as a filter, keeping sediments from reaching reefs, and provides food for shrimps, worms, snails, and numerous other organisms that feed on the microorganisms attached to the sediments and on decaying plant and animal matter in sea-grass beds (this collection of sediments, plant, and animal matter is called detritus). In addition, turtle grass supports a diverse array of algae and invertebrates that attach to the surfaces of the grass blades (the algae attached to the surface of the grass blades are called epiphytes, and the invertebrates are called epifauna). In turn, these organisms fall prey to grazers and predators, and in this way the productivity of the sea-grass beds supports the food web that supports bonefish in these shallow waters.

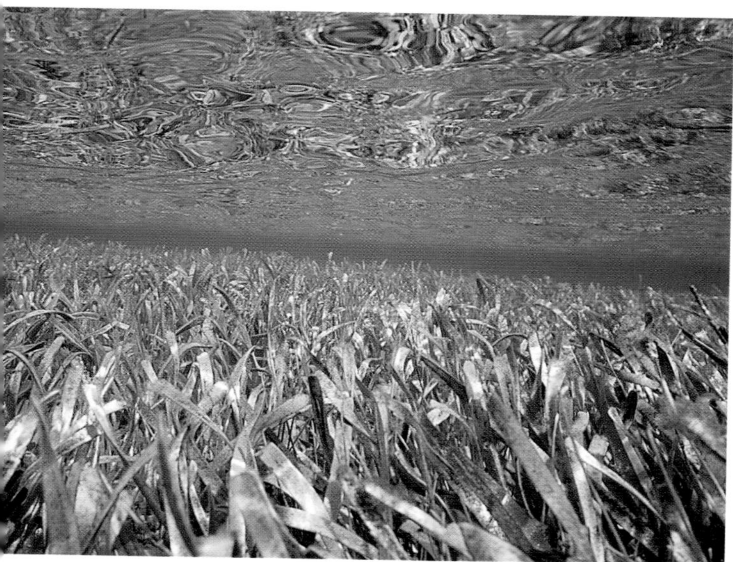

Turtle grass supports a great variety of bonefish foods.

STEPHEN FERNÁNDEZ

Since sea-grass beds are shallow and very productive areas that provide food for many species, they are attractive areas for numerous small organisms, many of which are well camouflaged to match their surroundings or very adept at using the sea-grass blades for shelter (they are cryptic, in the parlance of biologists). The ins and outs of bonefish prey in sea-grass beds are discussed in more detail in chapter 4. In addition, bonefish have devised strategies for using sea grass to hide from predators, which will be discussed in chapter 2.

Algal Plains

An algal plain consists of open sand or mud bottom with scattered calcareous algae, which are algae that can incorporate calcium carbonate (limestone) from the water into their tissue. The types of algae most common in these areas are disk algae (Halimeda), shaving brush algae (Penicillus), and fan algae (Udotea). These algae can also be mixed within sea-grass beds, but algal plains are areas where sea grass is largely absent and algae is the dominant growth. This habitat is not nearly as complex as sea-grass habitat, and it doesn't have the abundance of prey found in sea grass. However, a bonefish foraging in algal-plain habitats will still find an assortment of crabs, shrimps, and small fishes.

Although a bonefish might not find as many prey in algal-plain habitats as in sea grass, its success at capturing prey is probably greater on an algal plain. Unlike dense sea-grass beds, the algae provide little in the way of shelter for prey, so when a bonefish does find prey, it has a better chance of catching its food. This also gives an angler an advantage because a fly will have less chance of fouling and the bonefish has a better chance of seeing the fly than in sea grass, where a fly can get snagged or disappear among the grass blades.

Algal-plain habitats occur in areas protected from wave action and usually experience little in the way of current, and the still, shallow water often results in high temperatures during summer. Given the temperature preferences of bonefish, these areas will be visited by bonefish only at certain times of year or times of day. During the summer, you might expect bonefish to feed in algal-plain habitats early or late in the day, while in winter the shallow waters will warm quickly on a sunny day, and so may attract bonefish at midday.

Open Bottoms

The type of open bottom reveals the typical wave and current conditions that an area experiences and can tell you whether it is a good feeding area for bonefish. Sandy bottom occurs in areas with more wave or current energy than mud bottom, or in locations far removed from a source of soft, fine sediments that make muddy bottoms. Rivers, streams, estuaries, or lagoons with currents that might carry sediments are potential sources of soft-bottom material. Stable bottoms tend to harbor the most prey for bonefish. Sandy areas with ripples or ridges are frequently exposed to waves or currents that shift the sand, and shifting sands tend to have fewer prey organisms than more stable sediments.

STEPHEN FERNÁNDEZ

A sandy bottom supports a different community of creatures than does a sea-grass bed or a mud bottom.

Sandbars are the results of currents produced by waves or tides, and occur in areas where the currents slow enough that suspended sediments fall to the bottom. This may occur where opposing currents meet, such as where incoming ocean currents meet outgoing river currents in estuaries, where currents that flowed strongly through a constricted area (an inlet or cut, for example) are dispersed over a large open area, and where waves lose energy as they approach land or shallows (like a beach) and crash onto themselves.

Sandbars exposed to wave-induced currents will usually be parallel to the waves, with the deepest water on the side opposite the direction from which the waves approach. Regardless of how they are formed, once sandbars are large enough they can exert an influence on water flow by deflecting waves and channeling currents. The abrupt changes in currents help to create areas with shallow and deeper habitats immediately adjacent to each other. The deeper areas next to shallow, sandy flats are used as refuges by bonefish during low tides and as pathways onto and off flats during changing tides.

Sand and mud bottoms don't have as many prey creatures as sea grass, but, as on an algal plain, a bonefish's chance of catching prey is much higher on the open bottom. However, because shallow, open bottoms don't provide any shelter, bonefish usually stay on the move and are skittish when feeding in these habitats. As you will see in chapter 3, bonefish use these open-bottom habitats at particular stages of the tide.

Rubble Bottoms

Many tropical islands have rubble flats located on the shoreward sides of coral reefs. The shallow reefs break up the surf coming in from deeper water offshore, and, over time, the wave energy has pushed coral debris and sand onto the back side of the reef. Eventually, sea grass and algae take hold in the back-reef and spread into the lagoon, which results in a further slowing of currents and more deposition of debris and sand. In some spots, small colonies of finger coral grow among the sea grass. When everything works out just right, a shallow, rubble flat results.

The mixture of rubble bottom, sea grass, and scattered corals supports a mixture of prey species. Many of the usual suspects found in sea-grass beds are present on rubble flats that have sea grass. In addition, the many crevices among the pieces of rubble are good hiding places for an assortment of other prey species. Bonefish love to feed on the crabs, shrimps, urchins, brittle stars, small clams, and other prey found on these shallow flats, and the hard bottom makes these areas perfect for wading. Since incoming waves constantly push water over the reef, rubble flats rarely get as warm in the summer as nearby shallows with less water flow, and they can be good places to fish throughout the summer.

Tidal range in the Caribbean, and most of the tropics, is generally small, the water level changing a foot or less through a normal tidal cycle, so water depth on rubble flats doesn't change much. Bonefish respond to even minor tidal fluctuations, and are particularly sensitive to the extreme changes in water depth (perhaps as much as two feet) associated with spring tides. During low-tide periods, bonefish will be completely absent from a rubble flat, but during high-water periods they may venture far onto the flat in search of food.

Wave energy can vary on rubble flats. If the reef and flat are shallow, little wave energy carries over the reef and onto the flat. But if the reef or flat is deeper, the remnants of larger waves might roll across the flat, which can dislodge prey hiding among the rubble.

STEPHEN FERNÁNDEZ

Mantis shrimp are often found around the scattered coral on a bonefish flat.

Whether the reef and flat are shallow or not, extended periods with strong surf can increase the water depth more than tides will. The constant surf will actually push more water onto the flat than can escape back to sea through cuts and channels in the reef, which can result in higher than normal water depth for days. Bonefish take advantage of these high-water periods just as if the high water was due to an extended high tide.

All of these factors combine to make rubble flats great places to find bonefish on islands because bonefish get access to a variety of prey and avoid predators on a flat with stable temperatures.

Mangroves

Although numerous species of mangroves occur in regions where bonefish are found, anglers in search of bonefish almost always encounter only one species, the red mangrove (*Rhizophora mangle*). One of the most important adaptations of red mangroves that allows it to grow in salt water is the support structures, called prop-roots, that elevate the plants above the water and allow the mangroves to take advantage of submerged areas that other land-based plants can't use. Since many of these areas are exposed at low tides, they aren't suitable areas for sea grass to grow, so mangroves are the only source of shelter and food.

Throughout their range, mangroves are found in similar conditions—along low-energy shorelines, in protected embayments, and on wide, shallow flats that dampen all but the most intense waves and currents associated with hurricanes. Locations that are consistently buffeted by high energy from waves and strong currents are not suitable for these plants.

From a bonefish angler's point of view, the most important aspect of red mangroves is that the prop-roots provide a labyrinthine habitat for fishes, crabs, shrimps, and a host of other organisms in shallow water, making mangroves an important part of the food web in coastal environments. The combination of sediments trapped by the prop-roots, the continual dropping of leaves from the mangrove trees, and activities of organisms within the mangroves form the center of the food web known as detritus, which is fed upon by fungi and bacteria. In addition, an extensive community of algae, sponges, barnacles, oysters, clams, mussels, and other organisms grows directly on the prop-roots. In turn, small organisms such

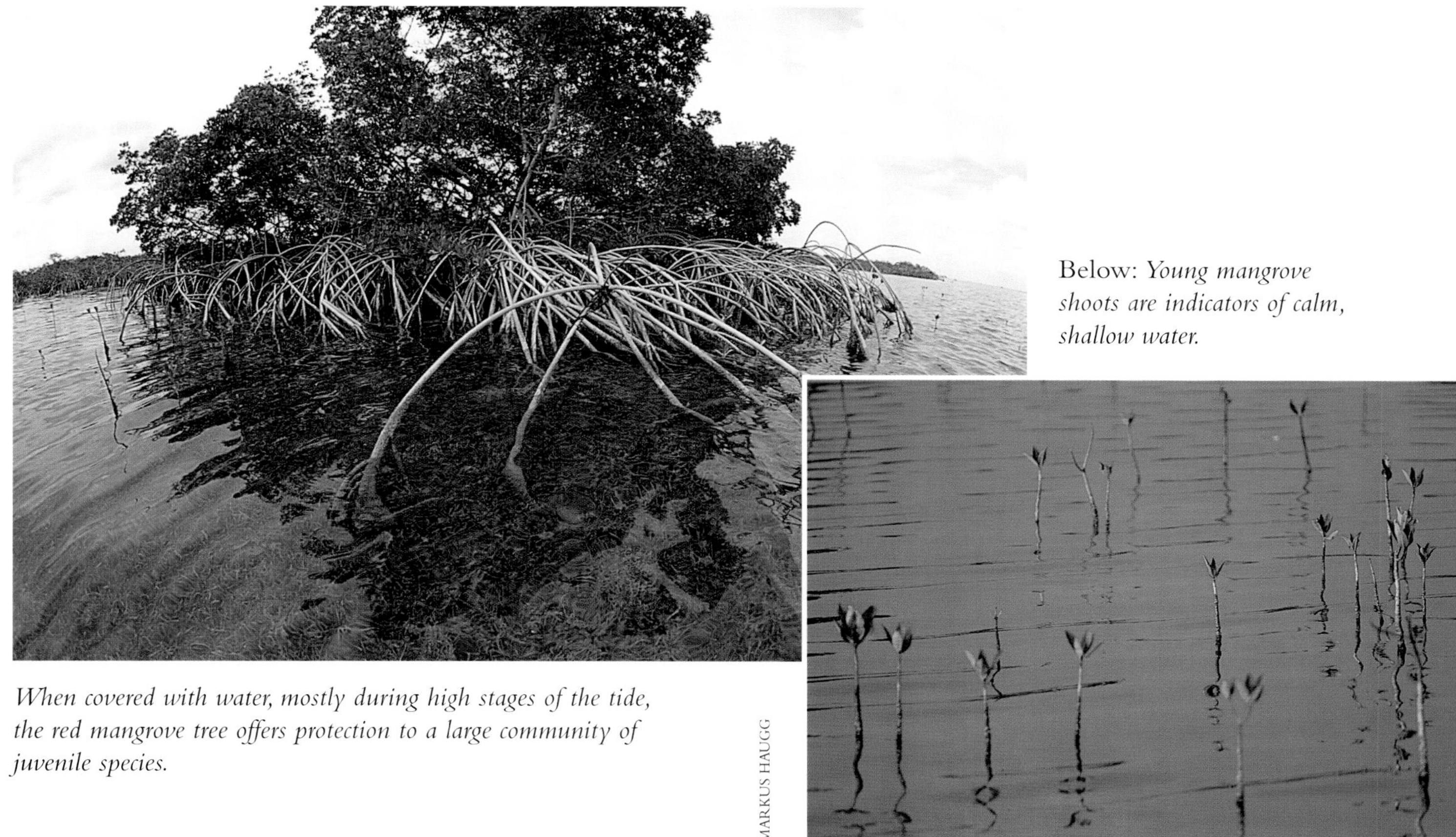

Below: *Young mangrove shoots are indicators of calm, shallow water.*

When covered with water, mostly during high stages of the tide, the red mangrove tree offers protection to a large community of juvenile species.

MARKUS HAUGG

as shrimps, crabs, worms, and fishes feed on the detritus. The structure of the mangrove prop-roots and the abundant food combine to make these great habitats for small fishes and invertebrates that bonefish eat.

Mangroves growing in very shallow or intertidal areas will be accessible to bonefish only during times of deeper water, such as high tide or when wind pushes additional water onto the flats and shorelines. And shallow, protected areas may be warmer than surrounding areas in the summer and on sunny winter days but may cool quickly when a winter cold front passes through. Tides and temperatures combine to restrict the bonefish's access to these extra-shallow mangrove habitats.

Bonefish may find different choices in prey according to the location of the mangroves. The composition of fish and invertebrate communities depends on the immediate environment (semienclosed lagoons, shorelines exposed to open sea, flats, a backwater estuary, or a creek), the habitats adjacent to the mangroves (sea grass, sand, or mud), and the depth of nearby water. Mangroves along creeks often have more total species and a greater number of individuals than those in shallow areas. Those growing next to sea grass tend to support more species than mangroves bordered by mud or sand. This is especially true for the small organisms that bonefish prefer as prey. For example, small juvenile fishes prefer locations with sea grass adjacent to mangroves, but as they grow, the larger juveniles often move to areas with open bottom next to mangroves.

Mangroves on flats exposed to the open ocean are likely to harbor high numbers of small juvenile coral-reef fishes during the summer. In contrast, mangroves that are more removed from the ocean (such as those in lagoons connected to the ocean by a narrow channel) or are deep within estuaries will be more dominated by the core group of resident species that are associated with mangrove habitats.

Many prey species use the mangrove prop-roots as shelter during the day and venture out at night to feed in the adjacent open areas of sea grass, sand, or mud. The different types of prey a bonefish is likely to encounter in each of these habitats are described in chapter 4.

In addition, bonefish use mangroves at high tide to hide from predators. You may occasionally find bonefish resting in the shade of mangroves at high tide, taking advantage of the protection provided by the prop-roots. As the tide drops, the bonefish return to the flats adjacent to the mangroves. If you find a mangrove shoreline

Aerial view of bonefish flat adjacent to deep water

where bonefish are resting under the mangroves, be sure to return to that spot on the dropping tide to intercept the fish as they move onto the flat. And make a note of this spot, too—these fish may shelter in the mangroves on a regular basis, and you may be able to intercept them on a rising tide as well.

Shorelines

Sandy tropical beaches where you might find bonefish are of two general types: exposed and protected. The exposed beaches are usually the windward coasts, and they receive high wave energy. The grain size of the sand is large on exposed beaches, the beach slope is often steep, and since so much sand is moved by waves and associated currents, the diverse bottom community (sea grass, clams, shrimps, etc.) that is often found in more protected areas is replaced by a short list of more hardy species, including mole crabs and coquina surf clams. On calmer days, bonefish will cruise just outside the surf zone along exposed beaches searching for these hardy creatures.

Protected beaches receive little wave energy because they are sheltered from the wind or from waves by an offshore reef, by extensive shallows, or are on the lee side of an island. The stable bottom allows the establishment of bottom (sea grass) and intertidal (mangrove) organisms that support more diverse prey communities than do exposed beaches. Protected beaches often have lush seagrass beds ending right at the shoreline. Bonefish will sometimes use the sea grass as cover to search for small crabs feeding in the sand at the water's edge.

Beaches that are semiprotected—they are occasionally exposed to waves during storms or especially high winds—often support an even more diverse prey community than completely protected beaches. This is because the occasional wave energy mixes the water column and keeps the bottom waters from becoming depleted of oxygen, maintaining a diverse benthic community. This does not imply that low-energy areas are not healthy ecosystems, only that a wider variety of species is able to take advantage of semiprotected areas.

Semiprotected beaches often have a thin strip of sand between the beach and the beginning of the grass bed. Although these aren't the kind of beaches that resorts prefer, these shorelines are fantastic for fly fishing because bonefish can cruise in these strips of sand and surprise prey that ventures from the safety of the sea grass. And bonefish will ride the small surf into the wash zone in search of prey such as small crabs, shrimps, and small fishes.

In some locations, you will find that the water remains shallow a greater distance from shore, providing wading access to large areas of sea grass. In general, very shallow sea-grass beds have a less diverse community of prey species than deeper grass beds. This is partly because the shallower areas are harsher environments and can become very warm and very low in oxygen during calm summer periods. During extremely low tides, these areas can be completely exposed to the air.

Although bonefish are most often associated with sandy shorelines, they may venture onto beachrock shorelines in search of urchins, brittle stars, and crabs. Beachrock is hard limestone pavement, actually the solidified remains of old coral reefs and sediments. Low-lying beachrock shoreline may be bordered on one or both ends by sandy beach, and this is the type most frequently visited by bonefish. Beachrock that drops abruptly into the water and is undercut by wave action is less often used by bonefish.

If we combine the temperature requirements of bonefish with their need to eat and avoid being eaten, and add their ability to use a wide range of habitats, we can begin to understand some of their behavior and movements. Many factors go into the bonefish's strategy to succeed in their environment, including what they eat, when they eat it, where and when they can be found, why they are found there, and how they behave at different times of the day, year, and tide.

The perfect situation for a bonefish is to have access to a mosaic of habitats that provide the most shelter and the most prey. A mixture of sea grass and open bottom is one example. Dense sea-grass beds hold a lot of prey but can be difficult places for bonefish to find and capture food. In contrast, open bottoms don't hold as many prey creatures, but a bonefish is better able to see and catch them. The next three chapters will elaborate on the strategies bonefish use to take advantage of their world.

Even with all that we know about bonefish, we must realize the limits of our knowledge. Most of what we know comes from studies conducted in the Florida Keys, with a few other studies in the Bahamas and Puerto Rico. These studies have provided valuable information about bonefish diet, growth, and habitat use that allow us to formulate fishing strategies that should be applicable anywhere we find bonefish. But differences in latitude that change environmental factors, differences in habitats, and even differences in prey and predators may cause bonefish to act differently in various locations. These differences are all important to a scientific understanding and proper management of this gamefish. From an angler's point of view, we must be ready to adapt to local nuances in the places where we pursue bonefish with a fly rod.

Chapter 2

The Bonefish's Life

The bonefish is uniquely adapted to its environment. The diet, habitat use, temperature requirements, and life cycle of *Albula vulpes* are the cumulative results of natural selection over millions of years. With such a long history, the strategies employed by bonefish clearly have proved successful. Our fishing strategies will prove more successful if we understand the bonefish and its environment. The life cycle and morphology (shape and form) of bonefish can help us better understand how bonefish have adapted to and use their environment.

LIFE CYCLE

Bonefish follow a life cycle similar to those of most other shallow-water marine fish. Adults reproduce through a behavior known as broadcast spawning: females and males (either as pairs or in groups) release their eggs and sperm into the water column, where fertilization takes place. That is, they "broadcast" the eggs and sperm into open water rather than lay eggs in a nest. Research in the Florida Keys suggests that bonefish spawn in groups between November and May, while data from the Bahamas indicates an October through January spawning period. Research suggests that spawning occurs in water deeper than what we consider typical bonefish habitat. The bonefish eggs hatch into clear, ribbonlike larvae, called leptocephali, that float in open water as plankton for months. Research in the Bahamas indicates that bonefish larvae live as plankton for forty-one to seventy-one days, but data from the Gulf of California suggest that bonefish larvae may live as plankton for up to six months.

The leptocephali that survive the larval stage ride incoming flood tides on moonless nights back into the shallows, where they metamorphose into juveniles. Juvenile bonefish are most abundant from winter through early spring. Which habitats are used by juvenile bonefish remains unclear. Juveniles in the middle and lower Florida Keys appear to use shallow beach habitats, but no juvenile bonefish were captured in extensive sampling of beach habitats in Belize. Juveniles have been captured in mangrove lagoons in the U.S. Virgin Islands and the Gulf

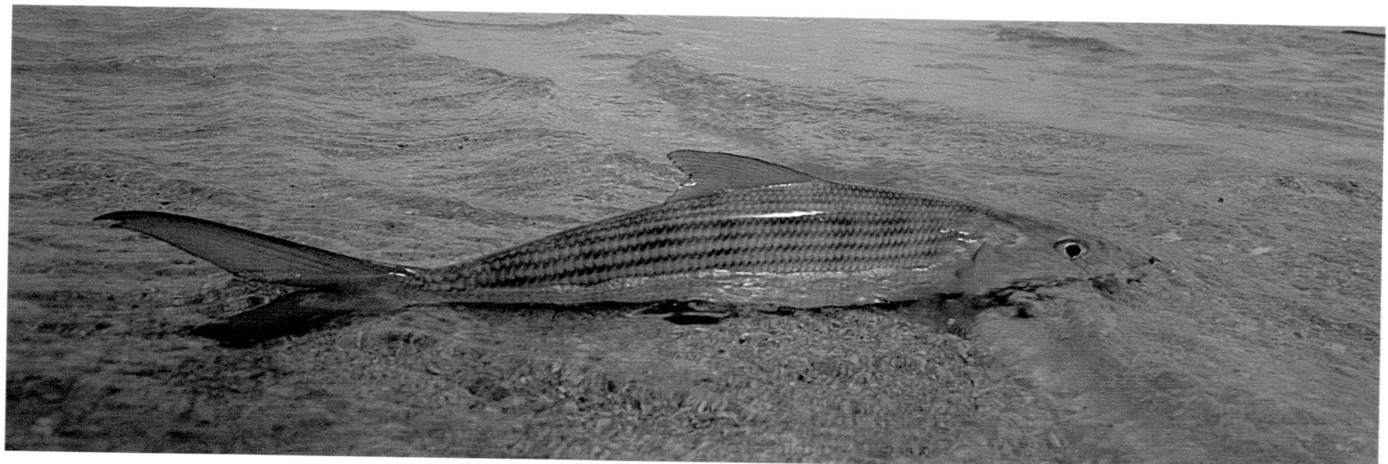

MARKUS HAUGG

Bonefish are uniquely adapted to cross the shallowest of waters.

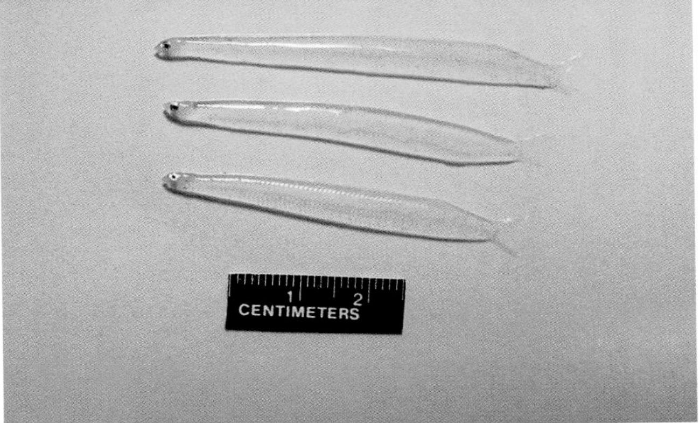

DERKE SNODGRASS

Bonefish leptocephalus. Shortly after adult bonefish spawn, the fertilized eggs hatch and leptocephalus larvae (shown here) emerge. Leptocephali live in the open ocean for many days before transforming into juveniles. Except for their eyes, they are completely clear—a perfect camouflage for the clear waters of the open ocean.

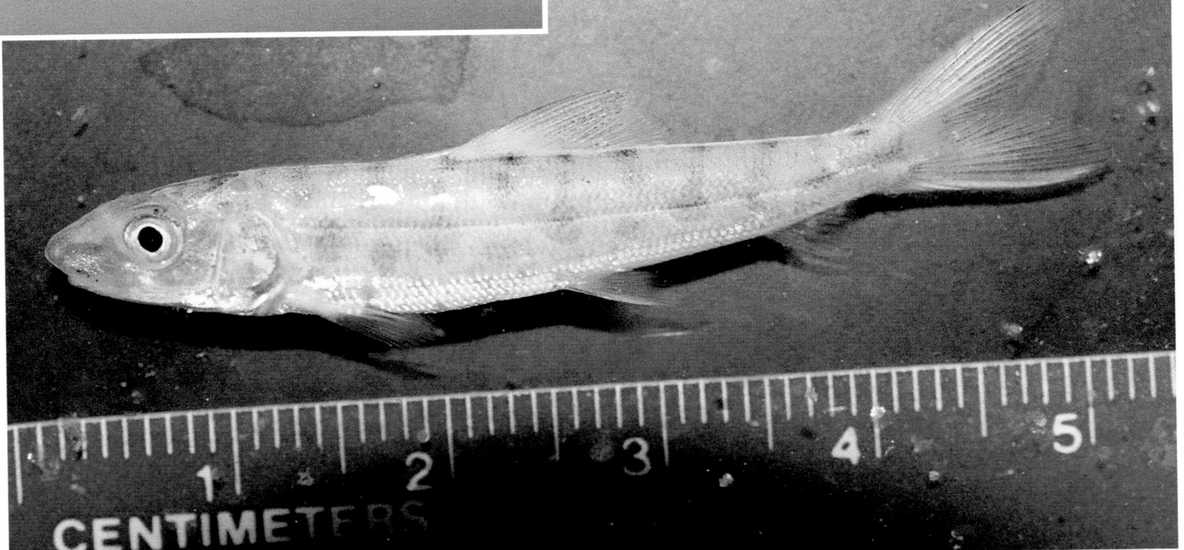

DERKE SNODGRASS

Bonefish juvenile. After living as plankton for many weeks, the leptocephali transform into miniature bonefish (shown here). Juvenile bonefish grow rapidly, about 3/4 of an inch per month. The juvenile shown here is approximately one month old; that is, it has been a juvenile for one month, after spending a long time as a leptocephalus larva.

of California. In all cases, though, the important juvenile habitats were shallow areas where the immature bonefish could avoid predators. Juvenile bonefish can grow rapidly, at a rate of almost ¾ of an inch a month (based on Florida Keys research). As they grow, juvenile bonefish begin to use a wider variety of habitats and become less common in or even absent from the nursery habitats used by early juveniles.

As bonefish grow and increase the suite of habitats they use, they also undergo changes in diet. While the most drastic changes in habitat use and diet occur in the juvenile and adolescent life stages, the bonefish's diet continues to shift with size and age, and these habitat and diet changes are accompanied by changes in behavior. For example, smaller specimens usually live in schools, while large bonefish tend to be solitary foragers. The specifics of diet and habitat shifts with age are discussed in detail in chapter 4.

In the Florida Keys, bonefish grow rapidly until they reach about six years of age, when growth rate slows. On average, a six-year-old bonefish will have a 19- to 22-inch fork length (the length from the tip of the nose to the fork in the tail). Male and female bonefish grow at slightly different rates and become mature at different ages—females grow more rapidly but mature at a larger size and later age than males. On average, 50 percent of males are mature by the time they reach a 16-inch fork length and 3.6 years of age, while females don't reach the 50-percent maturity level until around 19-inch fork length and 4.2 years of age.

The differences in growth rate and age at maturity might be explained by differences in energy requirements for male and female bonefish. In general terms, it takes more energy for a female to produce eggs than for a male to produce sperm, and the number of eggs is related to body size (a larger fish has more eggs). It pays for females to be larger when they reach maturity.

Bonefish in the Florida Keys can live at least nineteen years, but little is known about their life span in other areas. Likewise, most of the research on the life cycle of bonefish has been conducted in the Florida Keys, and little is known about bonefish in other locations, but any variations are expected to be slight. For

Age (years)	Male Fork Length (inches)	Male Total Length (inches)	Female Fork Length (inches)	Female Total Length (inches)
1	11.34	15.93	11.18	15.75
2	14.58	19.67	14.98	20.14
3	17.12	22.60	17.86	23.46
4	19.11	24.91	20.04	25.97
5	20.68	26.71	21.69	27.87
6	21.91	28.13	22.93	29.31
7	22.88	29.25	23.88	30.40
8	23.64	30.12	24.59	31.22
9	24.23	30.81	25.13	31.84
10	24.70	31.35	25.54	32.32
11	25.07	31.77	25.85	32.67
12	25.35	32.10	26.08	32.94
13	25.58	32.36	26.26	33.15
14	25.76	32.57	26.39	33.30
15	25.90	32.73	26.49	33.42
16	26.01	32.86	26.57	33.51
17	26.09	32.95	26.63	33.57
18	26.16	33.03	26.67	33.62
19	26.21	33.09	26.70	33.66
20	26.25	33.14	26.73	33.69

(Data from Crabtree, Harnden, Snodgrass, and Stevens. 1996. Research conducted in the Florida Keys.)

example, spawning may occur at a slightly different time at lower latitudes, which would influence the time of year juvenile bonefish are most abundant. Since bonefish in more tropical latitudes than the Florida Keys do not experience the extreme seasonal changes in temperature that Keys bonefish endure, their growth rates might differ.

The table above shows the average lengths of bonefish in the Florida Keys by age. On average, females are larger than males.

Fork length is measured from the tip of the nose to the fork in the tail, and is generally used in fisheries science to measure the length of fish. This is considered more reliable than total length because fish may be missing the end portions of their tails, and the lengths of the forked extensions may vary. An even more reliable measure of fish length used by fish biologists is standard length—the tip of the nose to the base of the tail.

The next table correlates the length of bonefish to their average weight. It is based on data from the same group of researchers. You might find it helpful in estimating the weight of your catches.

MORPHOLOGY

Morphology is the study of shape and form. A bonefish has a fusiform (tapered at both ends) shape and a forked tail, which translate into speed. The fusiform shape creates very little drag as the fish speeds through the water, and the forked tail provides strong thrust with less drag than a larger, fan-shaped tail. This escape speed helps bonefish avoid being eaten by large and speedy predators such as barracudas, sharks, dolphins, and birds.

Bonefish Fork Length (inches)	Bonefish Total Length (inches)	Average Bonefish Weight (pounds)
10	11.82	0.48
11	12.97	0.65
12	14.13	0.86
13	15.28	1.11
14	16.43	1.41
15	17.59	1.75
16	18.74	2.15
17	19.89	2.62
18	21.05	3.14
19	22.20	3.73
20	23.35	4.39
21	24.51	5.13
22	25.66	5.95
23	26.82	6.86
24	27.97	7.86
25	29.12	8.95
26	30.28	10.14
27	31.43	11.44
28	32.58	12.85
29	33.74	14.37
30	34.89	16.01

(Data from Crabtree, Harnden, Snodgrass, and Stevens. 1996. Research conducted in the Florida Keys.)

Bonefish also use camouflage to avoid being eaten. Their small, mirrorlike scales reflect the colors of their surroundings, which amounts to a mobile type of coloration. The ability of bonefish to mirror their surroundings explains in part why they can use such a variety of habitats: whatever the surroundings, they can blend in. But bonefish have an additional talent in their repertoire of camouflage. They have a limited ability to change their coloration.

You've probably noticed that many gamefish can change color. Depending on the species, fish can gain or lose stripes and bars, or become lighter or darker in color. Flounder are some of the best at changing color—some species can change color to match the bottom almost as quickly as they swim from one spot to another. And anyone who has fished for mahi mahi knows that a feeding mahi changes color and "lights up"—a sure sign of fishing action.

Bonefish aren't as adept at color change as flounder or mahi mahi, but they can change their hue and pattern of markings. To do this, fish use chromatophores, specialized pigment cells in their skin. By contracting or expanding the chromatophores, bonefish are able to disperse or concentrate pigments to become darker or more closely mimic their surroundings, and to make their vertical bars become darker or disappear. This is why bonefish feeding over sea grass will have a green hue and darker bars on their backs, while bonefish feeding over pale sand will have almost no coloration at all. The combination of color changes and mirrorlike scales can make the bonefish almost impossible to see in any habitat.

STEPHEN FERNÁNDEZ

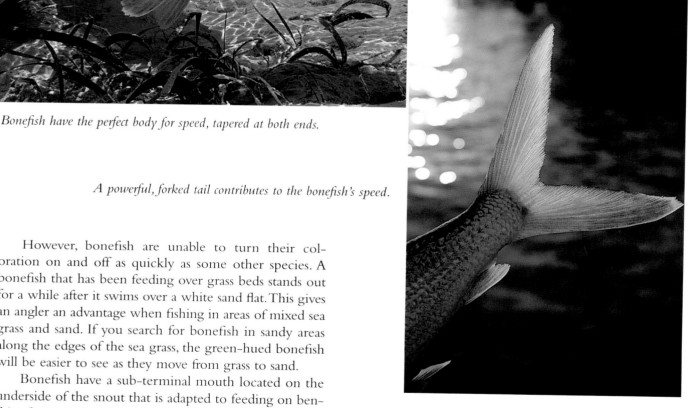

Bonefish have the perfect body for speed, tapered at both ends.

A powerful, forked tail contributes to the bonefish's speed.

MARKUS HAUGG

However, bonefish are unable to turn their coloration on and off as quickly as some other species. A bonefish that has been feeding over grass beds stands out for a while after it swims over a white sand flat. This gives an angler an advantage when fishing in areas of mixed sea grass and sand. If you search for bonefish in sandy areas along the edges of the sea grass, the green-hued bonefish will be easier to see as they move from grass to sand.

Bonefish have a sub-terminal mouth located on the underside of the snout that is adapted to feeding on benthic (bottom-dwelling) organisms. But they are agile enough to take advantage of midwater prey like baitfish. A bonefish's mouth is designed to grab, suck in, and crush prey. This is a different approach from a species like a barracuda, which has large teeth to grab and cut prey, or a grouper, which vacuums in whole fish with its huge mouth.

The typical feeding strategy of a bonefish is to grab prey with its lips, suck the prey into its mouth, and then crush the prey with bony plates within its mouth before swallowing. Sometimes it simply slurps the prey into its mouth and then crushes it. Their mouth structure and feeding strategy explain why bonefish are able to eat things with hard shells such as clams, crabs, and urchins. This also explains why bonefish can slurp in, crush, and spit out a fly before an angler can react.

Bonefish find prey with vision, smell, and their lateral-line system. They have good vision, and their eyes are protected by a clear outer covering. (Other species found in shallow water, such as crevalle jacks, have a similar clear covering over the eyes.) The outer covering

MARKUS HAUGG

This bonefish is camouflaged well for the turtle-grass environment.

Inside flats are often not as clear as ocean-side flats, but bonefish often mud as they feed on them, and the muds help you locate the fish.

protects the eye from being scratched by debris or clogged with sediment while the bonefish is digging for prey. In addition, bonefish lack scales on their heads, which reduces the risk of snagging scales on bottom debris. These are great advantages for a fish that makes its living with its nose in the bottom.

A bonefish's good sense of smell is essential for finding prey such as clams, crabs, worms, and shrimps that live in or burrow into sediments. Clams, some species of worms, and numerous other species that live in the sediment are filter feeders—they draw water in one opening of their burrow, filter plankton and other food from the water, and expel the water out another burrow opening. Bonefish can smell the outflow from these species, which is a great advantage for feeding on animals that are nearly or completely buried.

Even organisms that don't filter feed aren't safe. Just as terrestrial animals have to pass air through their lungs to obtain oxygen, marine animals have to pass water over their gills to breathe. And just like air breathers, marine organisms leave a scent on the water that leaves their gills—underwater bad breath, in effect. Bonefish use it to track down prey as they grub along the bottom. The bonefish's keen sense of smell is one reason knowledgeable anglers don't use head cement on their flies and make sure that they wash their hands after applying sunscreen or bug repellent.

When searching for buried prey, a bonefish can blow a jet of water out of its mouth to excavate a hole in the bottom to expose clams, shrimps, worms, crabs, and other food. This behavior is what causes the telltale "muds." The excavating technique can be used in pursuit of a specific prey (such as a single mud by a bonefish chasing a crab that has buried itself in the bottom) or can be a more general sweep for prey (such as a mud made by a school of bonefish jetting water into the bottom over a

Because sound travels faster and farther in the water than in air, you must approach bonefish slowly and very quietly.

large area that contains clams). The "blow en masse" strategy used by schooling bonefish also dislodges a host of prey that might otherwise escape notice.

Bonefish have stomachs that are especially adapted to their diet and foraging strategy. Crabs, clams, and urchins all have a lot of hard parts that are difficult if not impossible to digest. And slurping so many prey from sandy and muddy bottoms means bonefish suck in sediments along with their meals. Rather than limit how much they eat because they quickly fill their stomachs with nondigestible items, bonefish have a large stomach to make room for more of everything—digestible and not.

Sound in water travels about 4.5 times faster (and also travels farther) than in air. Sounds (or vibrations made by things moving through the water) travel through water in waves. At close range, the waves are felt as changes in pressure in the bonefish's lateral-line system, which is best at picking up low-frequency sounds. The fish's inner ear can pick up both nearby and far-off sounds and is best at detecting high-frequency sounds. So a crab scurrying for cover from an approaching bonefish may give itself away by its own movements. Perhaps this is one reason many prey species employ a strategy of diving for the bottom and remaining motionless rather than fleeing.

Given how well sound travels in water, bonefish can detect even the slightest sound over a considerable distance. Thus, in addition to detecting prey, the lateral-line system and inner ear can also detect sound waves from anglers and vibrations created by predators. Anyone who has watched bonefish flee a flat after he dropped a rod in the boat can attest to the acuity of their hearing.

The combination of the life cycle and morphology of bonefish results in a species that is highly adapted to its environment. Through its life, a bonefish exploits the variety of habitats that give it the best chances of survival, and within these habitats the fish's shape helps it avoid predators by allowing it to achieve incredible speeds in extremely shallow water. To top it all off, the bonefish's mouth and digestive tract are adapted to take advantage of the many types of prey it finds in shallow water. The bonefish is highly attuned to its environment, and an angler who is also in tune with that environment is more likely to be in the right place at the right time, with an appropriate fly tied to the tippet.

Chapter 3

Tides

When asked about the influence of tides on bonefish, the conventional answer is something like, "Bonefish move onto the flats with the rising tide, and do most of their feeding on the incoming tide. When the tide falls, the bonefish leave the flats until the next incoming tide." To a novice, this implies that a rising tide is the only worthwhile time to be on the flats stalking bonefish. But while bonefish do follow the tides, experienced anglers know that the whole answer is a lot more complicated. This chapter incorporates information from the previous two chapters into a description of how tides influence bonefish. Let's start with a basic overview of tides, and then look at how bonefish use tides to their advantage.

TIDE BASICS

A full treatment of how tides work is available in other texts (*The Fisherman's Ocean*, by Dr. David Ross, provides an excellent description of tides), but a brief summary will help explain how bonefish use tides to their advantage. Tides are the result of gravity and inertia. The gravitational pull of the moon creates a bulge of water on the side of the earth facing the moon. The inertia of the water on the side of the earth opposite the moon creates a second bulge of water that is kept from leaving the earth by the planet's gravitational pull. These two bulges of water, one on the side of the earth closest to the moon and the other on the opposite side, correspond to high tides. Halfway between the bulges are areas of extra-low water on opposite sides of the earth from one another, which correspond to low tides. As the moon revolves around the earth, the bulges of water remain aligned with the moon, so the areas of high and low water rotate around the earth. The changes in water height that correspond with the passing of the high and low water are called tides.

These bulges of water can be envisioned as waves that move around the earth, with troughs (low tides)

STEPHEN FERNÁNDEZ

Bonefish can often feed in less than six inches of water.

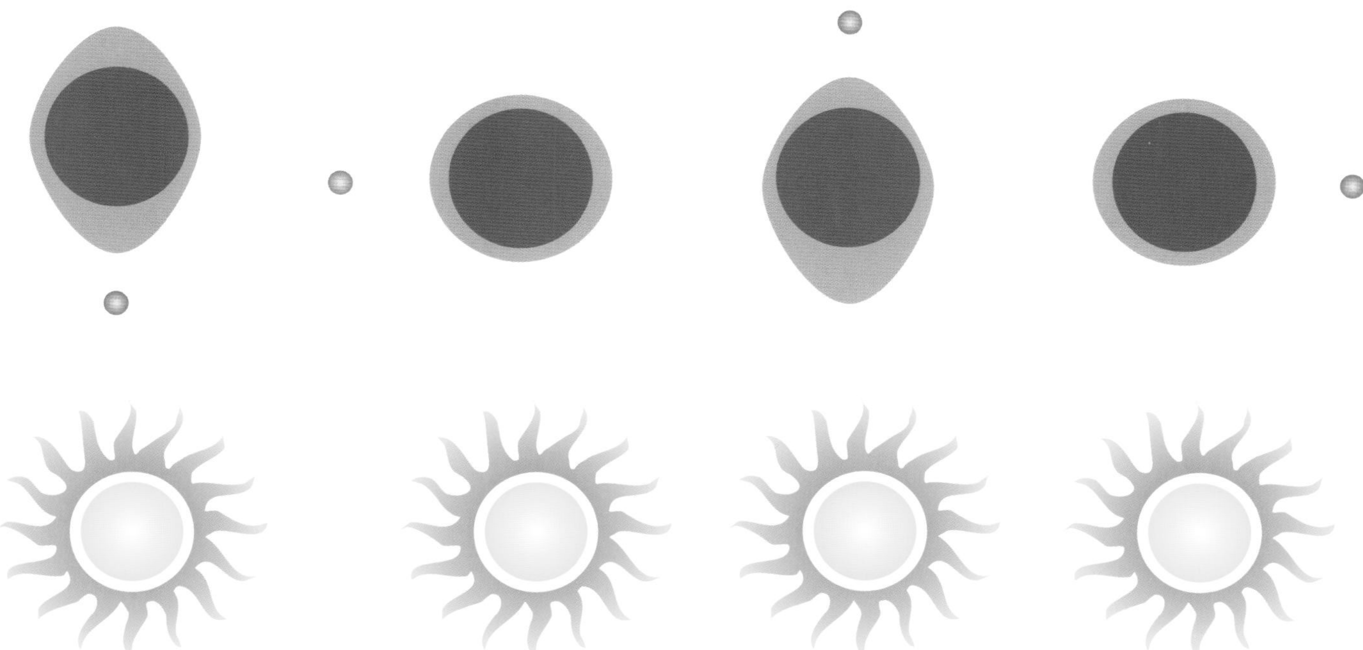

First: *During the new moon, the sun and moon align on the same side of the earth, resulting in the more extreme spring tides.*
Second: *At the moon's first quarter, when the sun and moon are at right angles to the earth, a weaker neap tide occurs.*
Third: *When the moon is full, the sun and moon are on exact opposite sides of the earth, and another spring tide occurs.*
Fourth: *During the moon's last quarter, the sun and moon are again at right angles, and a weaker neap tide results.*

between the crests (high tides). The progression of the waves around the earth means that even as one location may experience a high tide, a nearby location may be an hour delayed in experiencing that same high tide because the crest of the wave has not yet reached the second location. The practical importance of this to an angler is that it is not adequate to simply find out the tides at one location and assume the tides will be the same at other locations. Be sure to know the tides in your specific fishing area.

Because it takes slightly longer than a twenty-four hour day for the moon to complete a full revolution around the earth, a tidal "day" takes twenty-four hours and fifty minutes. This is why the timing of high and low tides changes daily—each tide approximately fifty minutes later than the day before—and follows a lunar cycle that takes about a month to complete.

The sun has about half as much influence on tides as does the moon. But the sun's influence is sufficient to enhance or dampen the moon's effect on tides. When the sun and moon are aligned (both are either on the same side or on exactly opposite sides of the earth), their combined gravitational pull makes the bulges of water higher than when the sun and moon are not aligned. And when the bulges of water are higher, the amount of water between the bulges is less, which translates to higher than normal high tides and lower than normal low tides. These extreme tides are called spring tides, and are associated with new and full moons. As if that wasn't complicated enough, the gravitational pulls of the moon and sun vary according to how close they are to the earth, meaning that the severity of spring tides can vary. Bonefish are tuned in to these phenomena.

When the moon and sun exert gravitational pulls that are at right angles to each another, they partially negate each other's influence, resulting in a more even distribution of water over the earth's surface and a less than normal tidal range. These less than normal tides occur during quarter moons and are called neap tides.

Within the monthly tidal cycle then, a flat will experience spring tides every two weeks. During the alternating weeks, the same flat will experience neap tides.

Because the earth is round, you might expect all locations to get two high and two low tides per day, but this is not the case. Differences occur due to the topography of the oceans and continents and the inclination of the moon's rotation relative to the earth. Some locations get two high and two low tides of approximately equal height per day (called semidiurnal tides), others get only a single high and low tide a day (diurnal tides), and some locations get two high and two low tides of unequal height per day (mixed tides).

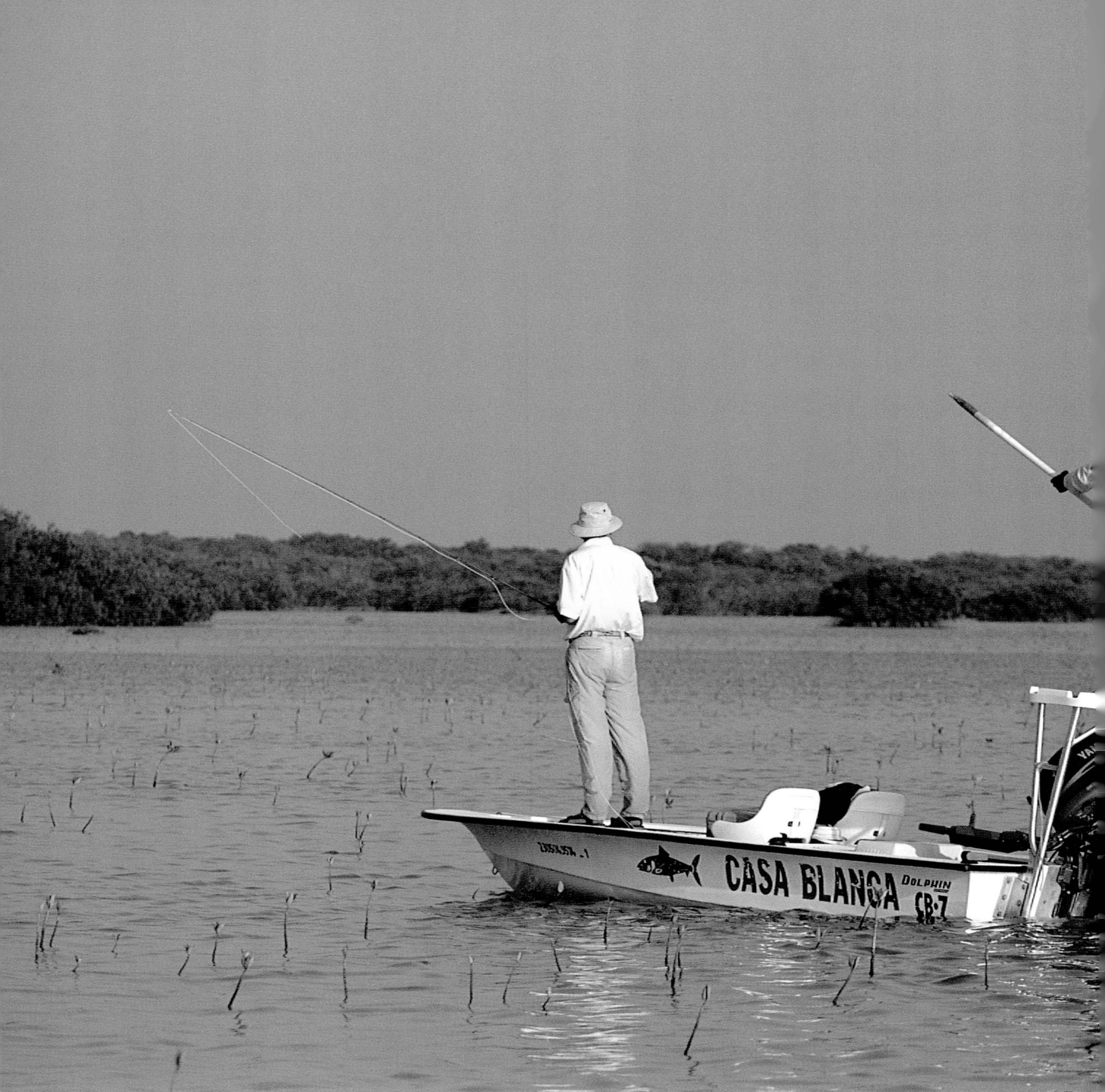

If you are going to pole for bones in water so shallow that the mangrove shoots are showing, you'd better know your tides, or you'll be part of the environment at low tide.

MARKUS HAUGG

In addition, the moon's inclination and ocean-basin topography influence tidal range, resulting in extreme tidal ranges in some areas (a 50-foot spring-tide range in the Bay of Fundy, for example) and minor tidal range in others (a 1.5- to 2-foot spring-tide range in most of the Caribbean). Fortunately for bonefish anglers, tidal range during spring tides in the part of the world inhabited by bonefish is typically 1.5 to 2 feet. But remember that spring tides are an area's maximum tidal range; the average tidal range experienced by bonefish is less.

As the height of the ocean changes with the tides, currents are created. Rising water travels around and over obstacles, filling coastal bays and flats. As the tidal bulge passes, the water level drops, and the ebbing tide drains the shallows. Since the amount of time between high and low tides in any given area is always the same, regardless of the tidal range, the strength of tidal currents varies between spring and neap tides. During spring tides, when tidal range is greatest, the greater volume of moving water creates stronger currents, whereas the weak neap tides cause the weakest tidal currents.

Since tides are caused by movements of such massive areas of high and low water, you might think tides are impervious to influence from any other force. Not so. Both barometric pressure and wind can greatly influence tides on a local scale, significantly changing tidal heights from the predictions of a tide chart. And while the wind- or pressure-induced differences in tide may sometimes seem minor to us, they can influence bonefish behavior.

Fishing literature contains a lot of material about the effects of barometric pressure on gamefish, but the apparent effects on marine gamefish might be due as much to the influence of pressure changes on tides as to changes in weather. During periods of low pressure, the atmosphere exerts less force on the ocean, and tides can rise higher. Since low barometric pressure is most often associated with either a warm or cold front, a region may experience a weather change in association with a change in barometric pressure. When barometric pressure is high, tides are suppressed by the atmosphere and might not rise as high as predicted. High pressure is usually associated with fair weather.

Wind can also have a dramatic effect on tides. Strong onshore winds can make high tides higher than predicted, and in extreme conditions can even prevent low tides from occurring—in effect creating a ghost tide. Offshore winds will have the opposite effect: both high and low tides will be lower than predicted.

In many cases, a strong wind won't prevent tides from occurring but will delay the onset of the ebb or flood. For example, a strong onshore wind may lengthen the duration of high slack tide, but eventually the force of the ebbing tide is too much and the water level drops quickly in the short amount of time remaining in the ebb.

The degree of influence from wind depends on water depth and the shape of the basin. Tides in an enclosed bay will be more affected than tides on a flat that has no surrounding land or shallows to restrict water flow. In enclosed basins, it may take a day or two for tides to return to normal once the wind subsides, depending on how long and strongly the wind blew and the size of the area affected. And when wind and tide travel in the same direction, stronger tidal currents can result, piling up water against flats. Often, the stronger currents from tide and wind along the edges of flats attract more bonefish.

A strong wind is one more variable that can help the tide empty a flat of water in a hurry.

HOW BONEFISH USE TIDES

Bonefish are experts at using tides to their advantage in the trade-off between feeding and avoiding predators. By riding the tides, bonefish are able to remain in the best habitats for avoiding predators, but still have access to prey. This is one reason bonefish specialize in prey that are also trying to avoid predation by living in shallow water. But because they live this life on the edge, bonefish must be keenly aware of tides and of all the things that influence tides.

Like many predators, bonefish try to get by with as little travel as possible in their search for a meal. There is no reason for them to expend energy swimming long distances if they can avoid it. When bonefish retreat from a flat during low tide, they usually do not stray far while waiting for the rising tide. The areas that give access to the most food and the most protection from predators throughout the tidal cycle will hold the most bonefish.

Like other species that live in shallow habitats, bonefish are especially sensitive to tides, even in areas with minor tidal range. Water depth in portions of the Caribbean, for example, may change only a few inches during a neap tide, but where and when bonefish feed are influenced by these small changes. The reasons bonefish react to even small tidal changes are numerous, and the factors that influence tides—such as wind and barometric pressure—will also influence bonefish.

In basic terms, a bonefish moves onto a flat with a rising tide and then reverses course and leaves the flat as the tide falls to avoid getting stuck high and dry. But while the standard behavior is for bonefish to follow a rising tide onto a flat and feed in shallow water before retreating to deep water with the dropping tide, the timing and extent of their movements are tempered by the factors influencing the tides. At low tide or in the early incoming tide, you can often find a bonefish or two feeding on a flat or along its edge. But these fish can be tough to cast to because they are often skittish in such skinny water. These early fish, while feeding, are often not very aggressive. Closer to high tide, however, you may find more and larger fish on the flat. These fish should be more comfortable in the deeper water, and should be feeding more aggressively. That bonefish often follow the same route onto a flooding flat—such as shallow depressions that cross a flat or channels that run between two flats—only underscores their ability to make the best use of their surroundings.

Of course, it's not always that simple. Although bonefish often follow established routes off a flat, the locations of these routes might vary according to the tide's height and the strength of the current. That is, bonefish will use certain routes during spring tides, and others during neap tides. To understand how bonefish use the often-subtle clues of tide and weather, we can start with the basic scenarios of spring and neap tides, and then add in factors such as currents, barometric pressure, wind, temperature, and time of day.

SPRING TIDES

When high spring tides flood the shallows, bonefish are quick to take advantage of the higher water to forage in areas they normally can't reach. Shallow sand and grass flats, shorelines, and shallow mangrove habitats hold many prey that are accessible for only a few days every couple of weeks. High spring tides are also good times to find bonefish feeding along the ridges of flats that don't have mangroves or shallow shorelines. Bonefish will move up the slope of the flats—from the deep edge to the ridge—with the rising tide, and return as the tide drops.

Spring tides are usually the best time to find bonefish feeding in the skinniest water, which makes for some great fishing. But the propensity of bonefish to head for the shallows during high spring tides can also work against you, because bonefish can be hard to find. For instance, bonefish will feed among the prop-roots of red mangroves in shallow water during these high tides.

While you're wading the flats, the bonefish are feeding to their hearts' content deep within the impenetrable labyrinth of mangrove roots.

You might argue that the bonefish must cross the flats as they travel to and from the mangroves, and you can fish for them during this transit. Yes, but this will give you shots at these fish only while they are in transit. They will do most of their feeding around high tide in a place where you can't reach them. And even if bonefish are not feeding among the mangroves during a high spring tide, they have access to a large expanse of shallow habitats and may be more spread out than usual. This is more than an academic concern for anglers planning a trip to a bonefishing destination, particularly one that has expansive flats fringed with shallow mangrove forests.

A big log at the edge of a bonefish flat is the only place for these cormorants to rest during an extra-high tide.

From the bonefish's point of view, however, there is a catch. While bonefish do enjoy a feast in the shallows during high spring tides, these shallow areas tend to be farther from the deep-water edge of the flats. And since the amount of time between high and low tide is always the same—regardless of whether it is a spring or neap tide—bonefish must be mindful of how rapidly the tide will drop during spring tides. Even though the shallows provide protection from many predators, bonefish must also be concerned with becoming stranded too far from their deep-water refuge during low tide.

A flat that is too expansive can result in bonefish behavior that seems contrary to what you would expect. Where the mangroves and shallows are too far from the safety of deep-water edges, bonefish might move onto the flat only a certain distance, and then retreat to hide in the shadows of the drop-off at high tide. The opportunities afforded by high spring tides tend to concentrate feeding by bonefish from the middle of the rising tide through the early falling tide. Even though bonefish might seem ready to eat at any time on many occasions, they may actually rest rather than actively feed at low spring tide as they wait for the next shallow-water bonanza brought on by an incoming tide. This doesn't mean that you should stop fishing, but you might have to change your strategy to entice bonefish during low spring tides.

Since they know that a high spring tide will let them feed in areas they usually can't reach, and since they also know that this opportunity will pass pretty quickly, bonefish often group along the edges of flats in anticipation of the incoming tide. As soon as the flooding tide allows, the bonefish make haste to the shallows to maximize their feeding time. As they rest, waiting for the next flooding tide, the bonefish often remain along the edges of flats. Why expend energy unnecessarily?

An angler can use this information to his advantage. Early in the rising tide and late in the outgoing tide, find the bonefish's travel avenues and you should have brief, but intense periods of casting to cruising fish. On either side of high tide, search the shallows for bonefish intent on feeding in skinny water.

Coupled with the extreme tides are the full and new moons. During full-moon spring tides, bonefish sometimes venture into the shallows at night to feed. It's not known if they do this on a regular basis or only when the higher of the two daily high tides occurs at night. Regardless, the conventional wisdom is that when bonefish feed at night, they feed less aggressively during the day. One way to combat this problem is to fish at dawn and dusk, when night-feeding bonefish may be ending or beginning their hunt.

NEAP TIDES

During neap tides (which coincide with the quarter moons), tidal range is at its minimum for the monthly tidal cycle. The skinny water where you found schools of tailing fish at high tide just the week before might not even be deep enough to hold fish during a high neap tide. The shallow mangrove flats that attracted so many fish into their shadows may still hold water but are probably empty of bonefish. Even if some areas seem deep enough, the lackluster tidal currents may put these areas outside of the bonefish's comfort zone.

Bonefish are still keyed to the tides, but not to the same extent as during spring tides, and they won't venture as shallow. They still move from the edges of flats onto a flat as the tide rises, but they won't travel as far onto the flat, and the concentration of fish along edges will likely be smaller. And because bonefish aren't keyed into water movement to such a high degree during neap tides, they are more likely to feed throughout the tidal cycle.

But the apparently subdued nature of neap tides can work to an angler's advantage. Bonefish resting during a low spring tide might be harder to catch than bonefish that are feeding throughout the tidal cycle during neap tides. In addition, at high neap tide, fish may be more accessible because they aren't as spread out on the flats and aren't as far into the mangroves as they are during high spring tides. Edges of flats are good places to search for cruising bonefish during the weak neap tides. And bonefish may be actively feeding in deeper areas, such as over grass beds, along channel edges, and in depressions and troughs between flats, providing fishing opportunities throughout the tidal cycle.

BAROMETRIC PRESSURE AND WIND

As mentioned earlier, barometric pressure and wind can either dampen or enhance tides. High pressure and strong offshore winds will tend to dampen a high tide and enhance the corresponding low tide, while low pressure and onshore winds will enhance the high tide and dampen the corresponding low tide. In areas with a small tidal range, the changes in barometric pressure and wind can have a greater effect than a normal tide does, and can influence the behavior of bonefish much as spring and neap tides do.

Let's take a look at the potential effects of wind and changes in barometric pressure on bonefish. First, a strong offshore wind (or strong high pressure) might completely offset the high water expected from a spring tide, which will prevent bonefish from accessing the shallows as they normally would. The low spring tide will then be even lower than expected, perhaps forcing bonefish off the flats altogether. If the same wind blows during a neap tide, the minor high tide that was predicted might not happen, and the tide will seem low throughout the entire cycle. During spring or neap tides, strong offshore winds can make the edges of flats, deeper holes and troughs between flats, deeper grass beds and sand basins, and the deeper water on the back sides of fringing coral reefs the best feeding spots for bonefish.

In contrast, a strong onshore wind (and approaching strong low pressure) may give bonefish an extended stay at the shallow-water buffet. A strong onshore wind can push a spring high tide even farther into the shallows and mangrove flats, can delay the onset of the ebbing tide, and can keep the water level from dropping as far as predicted at low tide. In a sense, the predicted tide heights shift up a notch. The extra water gives bonefish a wider selection of locations and, potentially, a longer time to forage. In general, when the wind and tide are working in concert to push more water onto the flat, the result is more bonefish.

In addition to affecting tide heights, wind can have a dramatic influence on tidal currents. A strong wind pushing against the tide can slow the current and dampen the effect of the tide. In contrast, a wind blowing with the tide can increase the current's speed and may help to pile up water in the shallows. Given the importance of currents to bonefish behavior, it pays to note the interaction of wind and tide and their joint effects on currents.

CURRENTS

Currents, whether completely tidal or caused by a combination of tide and wind, constantly refresh the water on bonefish flats. Portions of flats closer to deeper water have stronger currents than backwaters far removed from deep edges, and are more thoroughly flushed by the tides. The new water delivered by currents supplies food to filter-feeding organisms such as clams and some worms, which in turn feed crabs, shrimps, and other small carnivores. Bonefish feed on all of these, and by being in tune with the tides they are also in tune with many of their prey.

A basic tenet in fishing for bonefish—that if you find tidal current you will find bonefish, all things being equal—is largely true. But even though many anglers believe that bonefish always swim into the current, this is not always the case. Bonefish will use currents in the way that benefits them most—for example, to remain in their preferred temperature range. During the hot season, when water in the shallows warms above the bonefish's comfort level, tidal currents carry cooler water from adjacent deeper areas onto the flats with the rising tide. As the tide rises, the cooler water flows first along the edge; if the incoming tide is strong enough, the cooler water will flood the flat. Under these conditions, bonefish will initially remain along the edge of the flat, moving onto the flat only with the cool water of the rising tide.

STEPHEN FERNANDEZ

A strong current is flattening the turtle grass on this flat.

During cold seasons, sunny days may warm the water in the shallows, or water flooding onto a flat may absorb the warmth of the sun-baked bottom. In either case, bonefish that find warm currents moving across a flat will use those currents to feed in their comfort zone.

But don't expect bonefish simply to come onto or leave a flat as water floods or drains the shallows, because the conditions on a flat will influence how bonefish use the currents. An early rising tide bringing cool water onto a flat on a warm summer day might collide with sun-warmed water that is still draining the upper reaches of the flat. In this instance, rather than swim onto the flat and continue into the warm current, bonefish might move laterally along the flat, staying along the line where the two currents meet, in order to remain in the best water temperature.

Even if water temperature on a flat is not an issue, bonefish sometimes prefer to stay at a particular depth, moving across rather than into a current. Where bonefish find the right depth and current depends on the strength and height of the tide. Not only do spring tides let bonefish access hard-to-reach shallows, but the spring tides may also move the best currents farther onto the flat. During neap tides, the appropriate depth and current may never be far from the edge of the flat. Thus, the strength of the tides can alter the locations of the avenues that bonefish use to enter a flat.

Currents during spring tides are also stronger. Areas that are not inviting to bonefish because they experience only minor tidal currents during neap tides may receive currents strong enough to attract bonefish during spring tides. In some instances, the effect of tidal currents is so great that some flats are only productive during spring tides and others only on neap tides. This has to do not only with depth of the tides, but also with the amount of water exchange a flat will experience.

Research of bonefish movements using sonic tags corroborates the conventional wisdom that bonefish tend to follow the tides onto and off the flats. Researchers in the Bahamas tagged bonefish with a sonic tag and tracked the fish through tidal cycles. The tagged fish followed a repeated pattern of foraging on a flat from mid-rising tide to mid-falling tide and resting in deep holes on the flat during low tide. Although recent research in the Florida Keys showed variation among the eleven bonefish tagged, in general the tagged fish used the flats at high tide and retreated to deeper water at low tide. This is the kind of behavior pattern that fly anglers like to hear about.

BIG FISH AND SMALL FISH

The extent to which bonefish use shallow water, and the extent to which fish are keyed into tidal changes in the shallows, may differ among bonefish of different sizes. Larger bonefish are generally not found in skinny water like small fish. This might be because the older fish are too large to get into such shallow water, or it may be they aren't as comfortable as they are in slightly deeper water. This may be one reason large fish are more likely to be on shallow flats near high tide, particularly during spring tides. Another explanation may be that larger fish are less worried about being eaten than are smaller fish. Since they can remain in deeper water, the bigger fish aren't as closely keyed to riding the tides into the shallowest water. But in addition to depth and worries of predation, behavioral differences between large and small bonefish may also be related to food: larger bonefish generally feed on larger prey items, and larger prey are more common in deeper water. That leads us to chapter 4, "Bonefish Foods."

Chapter 4

Bonefish Foods

Now that we've covered the principal features of the bonefish's world, examined how bonefish are adapted to this world, and reviewed how bonefish take advantage of tides, it's time to think about what bonefish eat. You need to know what they eat to choose the right fly and fish it properly.

As he steps onto a flat, an angler often asks, "What are they eating?" A better question might be, "What aren't they eating?" Bonefish are opportunistic feeders, able to take advantage of the great diversity of prey they encounter. Bonefish eat many species of crabs, shrimps, fishes, worms, clams, snails, brittle stars, and other unlucky animals they encounter in their travels. In a recent study in the Florida Keys, well over 127 species of prey were recorded in the stomachs of 385 bonefish.

With their subterminal mouths, bonefish are best adapted to feed on benthic organisms such as crabs, shrimps, worms, and clams. However, they are also adept at catching mid-water prey such as baitfishes. A bonefish's diet has two sides: most of their food consists of bottom-dwelling organisms, but bonefish will grab other meals when given the opportunity.

But a huge list of prey is useless to most fly anglers—there are just too many choices. And if bonefish eat so many things, why do some flies work better than others at different locations at different times of year? The short answer is that bonefish do have a varied diet, but they seem to have preferences for particular prey, and the types of prey they encounter (and prefer) vary with the habitat and time of year.

What we know about bonefish prey comes from only a few scientific studies, and some of the prey species found in those studies are not found everywhere. But since species of similar behavior, size, shape, and even color may be found in other locations, we can use this information as a guideline to the bonefish's diet.

The first order of business is to simplify things by addressing the differences in diet among locations. For example, the diets of bonefish studied in the Bahamas and Puerto Rico were dominated by small clams. In contrast, clams and their relatives were second to crustaceans (crabs and shrimps) in bonefish stomachs in the Florida Keys. Upon reading this, some anglers will throw up their arms in frustration at the thought of creating an entirely different fly selection for each location. Fortunately, these differences really don't matter to fly anglers, regardless of how common clams are in bonefish diets. Clams that live buried in the sediments do not lend themselves to imitation with a fly, so they shouldn't be of concern to fly fishers. Many other types of prey eaten by bonefish are appropriate for imitating with a fly, and the rest of this chapter will attempt to answer the question, "Of all the things that bonefish eat, which ones are worth imitating with a fly?"

Historically, scientific literature has listed, described, and reported the percentages (by weight, number of prey, or number of stomachs containing a particular food) of different prey in the stomachs of bonefish. More recently, research has examined the seasonality of bonefish diets and how diet varies with location and habitat. By combining past and recent studies of bonefish diets, other research that has described communities of prey in different habitats, and what we know about bonefish behavior, we should be able to infer the types of prey a bonefish will encounter and where. This information will give us a better chance of tying on the right fly.

What's more, combining these varied sources of information with our knowledge of bonefish behavior will get us closer to evaluating prey from a bonefish's point of view. If a bonefish could think, it wouldn't say to itself, "I'd like to have snapping shrimp today" and go off in search of snapping shrimp. Instead, a bonefish takes advantage of the habitats that tides, temperature, weather, predators, and boat traffic allow it to access, and it feeds on whatever prey it finds, albeit somewhat selectively.

Scientific studies of bonefish diets break the prey into small, explicit groups—different species of shrimp, for example. While important for studies of bonefish ecology, the differences among many of these prey species are often small enough that a couple of flies can imitate many of them in most situations. Although there are differences among half a dozen species of grass shrimp, their overall shape and coloration are similar enough that a couple of fly patterns will suffice. For that matter, juvenile shrimp up to 2 inches long in the family Penaeidae (these are the shrimp we eat) living in grass beds are tough for all but the experts to distinguish from one another, and they, too, can be imitated with one or two fly patterns.

In addition, many organisms found in bonefish stomachs are hardly abundant. In a research project in the Florida Keys, only eight of the sixty-one families of prey organisms recorded in bonefish stomachs occurred in more than 10 percent of the stomachs. In other words, a small group of prey dominated the diet, but a lot of different types of prey were eaten. As you can see, a long, exhaustive, detailed list is not really necessary for most situations. Rather than provide a detailed list of all possible prey species a bonefish might encounter, I'll focus on the major groups, list the most common species in these groups, describe the habitats where these species live, and address some of the seasonality of these prey.

BONEFISH PREY

The major groups of prey eaten by bonefish are crustaceans (crabs and shrimps are the main members of this group), teleosts (bony fishes, including toadfish, gobies, and worm eels), polychaetes (numerous species of segmented worms), echinoderms (brittle stars, sea stars, and sea cucumbers), bivalves (bonefish eat numerous species of clams), and gastropods (snails are also frequent prey items).

Bivalves and related gastropods don't lend themselves to imitation with a fly, so I will not mention them again. All of the remaining groups have species that are eaten by bonefish in reasonable numbers and can be imitated with a fly. The group that makes up the bulk of the bonefish's diet is the crustaceans. In two Florida Keys studies,

MARKUS HAUGG

A mix of grasses is a good place for bones to find food.

crustaceans occurred in more bonefish stomachs than any other group. And discounting bivalves, crustaceans were also the most common prey in the stomachs of bonefish in the Bahamas and Puerto Rico.

Just to give you an idea of the relative importance of the most common groups of prey in the bonefish diet, here are some results of recent research. Excluding clams, in the Florida Keys the most common items (as measured by weight) were mud crabs (29.9 percent), Gulf toadfish (17.2 percent), swimming crabs (10.9 percent), snapping shrimp (9.2 percent), and common shrimp (7.7 percent). Although measured by volume, the numbers in Puerto Rico were similar—crabs (31 percent) and shrimp (11 percent) dominated the diet when clams and other bivalves were removed from consideration. In the Bahamas, swimming crabs (20.1 percent), mud and spider crabs (15 percent), and small fishes (4.9 percent) were important in the diet of bonefish. Many other groups of prey come in at 1 to 5 percent in each location. The differences in bonefish diets among locations may be due, in part, to the habitats that researchers studied and differences in the availability of prey.

Differences among locations are evident in the apparent preferences for certain prey, and these differences can even occur within a location. Preferences are calculated by comparing the numbers of different prey items in bonefish stomachs to the numbers of prey items collected by scientists in the areas where the bonefish were captured. In the Florida Keys, bonefish caught on the Atlantic Ocean side of the Keys preferred snapping shrimp, mud crabs, common shrimp, and Gulf toadfish. On the Florida Bay side of the Keys, mud crabs, snapping shrimp, Gulf toadfish, common shrimp, and swimming crabs topped the selection. The bonefish selected these prey over other, more abundant species. In the Bahamas, common shrimp and mantis shrimp were preferred by bonefish.

Because bonefish might use different habitats at different times of year, their diets may be dominated by different prey in different seasons. The abundance of different prey species, and even whether some are present at all, may change among locations. Although the general list of available prey may be similar in two locations, the specific favored prey items of bonefish will likely vary. This, in part, explains why some flies are pounced upon by bonefish on one sea-grass flat but completely ignored by fish in other locations. In the Bahamas, for example, bonefish in sea-grass beds eat a lot of common shrimp (19.5 percent), snapping shrimp (14 percent), and swimming crabs (8.5 percent), as calculated by percent of number of prey eaten. Bahamas bonefish in sandy areas also eat a lot of common shrimp (10.5 percent), but they eat more mud and spider crabs (14 percent). Again, we are discounting the high numbers of clams and other bivalves in the diets of Bahamas bonefish because it's tough to imitate a clam with a fly.

Factors such as water temperature and their own life cycles cause seasonal changes in the abundance of prey species. Most species preyed upon by bonefish undergo a life cycle similar to that of bonefish, which results in seasonal changes in the size and abundance of these prey. Although the list of potential prey depends on where you fish and even on the time of year, you can use your knowledge of the general makeup of prey communities found in bonefish habitats to generate a list of prey items most likely to be present when and where you are fishing.

Again, research in the Bahamas provides clues. In sea-grass beds, common shrimp make up a larger part of bonefish diets in the winter (28 percent of prey eaten by bonefish) than in summer (11 percent), while more swimming crabs are eaten in the summer (12 percent) than in winter (5 percent). Since common shrimp and swimming crabs grow rather large, perhaps these seasonal differences occur because bonefish focus on these species during the season when juveniles are most common. Snapping shrimp were more common in bonefish stomachs in winter (19 percent) than in summer (9 percent), but mud and spider crabs were eaten in similar numbers (6 percent in summer, 4 percent in winter). On sand flats during the winter, mud and spider crabs (17 percent), snapping shrimp (16 percent), and mantis shrimp (7 percent) were at the top of the bonefish's diet (excluding clams). During the summer, bonefish on sand flats ate more common shrimp (20 percent), mud and spider crabs (11 percent), and polychaetes (6 percent). In the Keys, bonefish tend to be abundant in Florida Bay in the summer and on the Atlantic Ocean side during the winter, so it is difficult to separate season and habitat in trying to decipher their diets.

Don't get too distracted by these seasonal changes in diet. The differences are mostly changes in ranking among the top few groups, and crustaceans (crabs and shrimps) are always high on the list. Bonefish feeding among mangrove prop-roots probably eat fiddler crabs and marsh crabs throughout the year.

With differences among locations, habitats, and seasons taken care of, we can now focus on the major prey items. As you will see, there are common themes within the major prey groups that fly anglers can use to their advantage.

CRUSTACEANS

Crabs

Although the number of species may vary among locations, crabs are present in all habitats used by bonefish. However, since each species is best adapted to one or a

STEPHEN FERNÁNDEZ

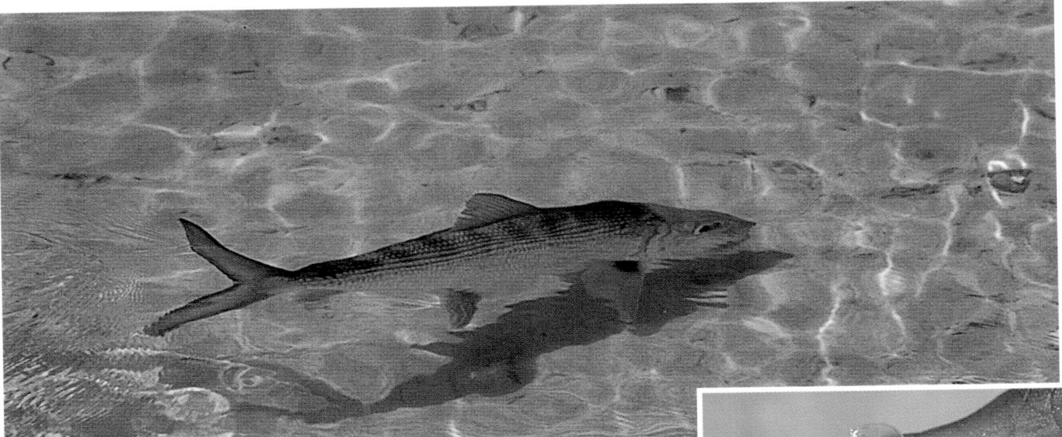

This bonefish took a tan crab pattern that matched the color of the bottom.

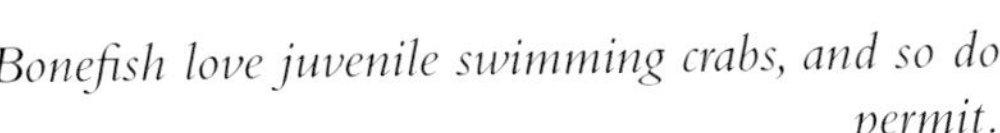

Bonefish love juvenile swimming crabs, and so do permit.

few habitats, we can narrow the list of crabs we might find in a particular habitat. More important, we can focus on similarities among species to minimize the number of flies we need. For instance, although the species of crabs may vary from place to place, the general colorations and behaviors remain strikingly similar within any given type of habitat.

Swimming crabs (family Portunidae), mud crabs (family Xanthidae), and spider crabs (family Majidae) are the most common small crabs in shallow tropical habitats such as sea-grass beds and open bottom near sea grass or rubble. Some species of swimming crabs are also common along sandy shorelines.

Crabs from all three families are well camouflaged. They are green in areas of thick turtle grass or mixed tan and green where coral rubble is mixed with sea grass. Although the maximum sizes of these crabs vary among species, the sizes most often eaten by bonefish tend to be similar. This means that we can use a few fly patterns to imitate many species of crabs. An olive green crab fly cast into a grass bed or a tan crab fly cast on a sand flat will match the color of either swimming or mud crabs in these habitats.

The greatest difference among these families of crabs is their behavior when being pursued by a bonefish. While species from all three groups will scurry for cover rather than try to outrun a bonefish, the behaviors of these crabs are sufficiently different to influence the action you impart to a fly.

Species of swimming crabs are all similar in shape (think of a blue crab) and are probably the most active crabs in grass beds. They can be voracious predators and scavengers, and always seem to be on the move. Their color varies from the olive green of blue crabs, to tan with eye spots for some tropical species, to light tan on sand flats. Swimming crabs can be found crawling along the bottoms of grass beds, clinging onto grass blades, swimming near the surface, digging small holes in patches of open bottom as they excavate a clam dinner, and even wandering along shallow, sandy beaches.

Once you've chosen your fly pattern and color, the action you give the fly will have to convince a bonefish that it is an easy meal. When chased, swimming crabs may initially make a quick dash to escape—either by scurrying along the bottom or swimming quickly—before burying themselves in the bottom or hiding under shells, rubble, or rocks. Swimming crabs usually swim sideways as they flee. When cornered and unable to bury themselves, swimming crabs will attempt to ward off a bonefish by waving and slashing with their claws, regardless of the relative sizes of crab and bonefish. You can impart the same behavior to your fly. First, strip your line so the fly swims through the water or scurries over the bottom until seen by the gamefish. Then let the fly sink quickly to the bottom as if to hide.

A main consideration when choosing a fly pattern to imitate a swimming crab is its orientation and shape. You'll need a fly that, when stripped, will appear to swim sideways. And the fly must be weighted so it sinks to the bottom where natural crabs seek shelter when chased by bonefish.

Bonefish like blue crabs and their relatives, but sometimes do not eat the crabs whole. This is especially true of smaller fish. Instead, bonefish will pick at the crab to dismember it, and then eat the mortally wounded creature. This cautious approach by bonefish may be due to the crab's slashing claws. Although you might think that larger bonefish would be better equipped to tackle the feisty swimming crabs, research findings are inconclusive: studies in the Florida Keys indicated that only bonefish larger than 17 inches ate swimming crabs, while data from the Bahamas indicated that bonefish less than 16 inches long ate more swimming crabs than did larger fish.

So, what is the right size for a swimming-crab fly? Although swimming crabs can grow rather large, research in the Florida Keys found that bonefish ate swimming crabs whose carapace measured between about 1/3 of an inch and 2 1/3 inches across, with the most common size about 1 inch. Species found in bonefish stomachs include blue crabs (*Callinectes sapidus*), ornate blue crabs (*Callinectes ornatus*), and swimming crabs (*Portunus depressifrons*). Although one or more species can be present in bonefish habitats year-round, the juveniles tend to be most abundant in the summer.

Mud crabs and spider crabs are walking crabs. They lack the rear paddlelike legs that allow swimming crabs to move through the water. Therefore, mud and spider crabs maintain a close association with hiding places on the bottom. In addition to living in sea grass, species in this group can be found among rubble and shells lying on open bottom or among grass blades, on rubble flats, and along mangrove shorelines throughout the year.

Mud crabs are most at home feeding along the bottom, and hide at the base of grass blades, burrow into the mud, or scurry under a rock or shell when chased. As their name implies, they are most often associated with soft bottoms, including sea grass, mangrove swamps, and open muddy bottoms near sea grass. Mud crabs usually try to hide rather than defend themselves with a showy slashing of claws. The species of mud crabs found in bonefish stomachs in Florida include the common mud crab (*Panopeus herbstii*), Florida mud crab (*Cataleptodius floridanus*), Say's mud crab (*Neopanope sayi*), and Packard's mud crab (*Neopanope packardii*). Depending on the habitat, though, bonefish have many species of mud crab to choose from. While sizes of mud crabs range from 1/2 inch to 1 3/4 inches across, the best size for a fly is about 1 inch across. Data from the Florida Keys indicates a range from about 1/4 inch to 1 1/4 inches across, with most measuring between 1/2 and 3/4 of an inch. Most mud crabs have claws tipped with black or another dark color.

The spider crabs eaten by bonefish generally live in the shallows. They are especially abundant among rocks and shells on sea-grass beds and sand flats, and on rubble flats. These species feed along the bottom and scurry for the underside of shells and rocks when chased. The species of spider crabs identified during research of bonefish diets include the Pitho crab (*Pitho mirabilis*), gray Pitho crab (*Pitho aculeata*), green reef crab (*Mithrax sculptus*), and tan reef crab (*Mithrax coryphe*).

As with the swimming crabs and mud crabs, there are additional species of spider crabs for bonefish to choose from. Fortunately, they are similar in shape and size within each group. The species of Pitho crabs listed here are teardrop shaped, with their heads at the narrow end of the teardrop. Reef crabs are more triangular, with rounded edges. All four species listed here grow to 1 inch, but are often smaller. The green reef crab is one of the most common crabs (and an important bonefish prey) on shallow flats of mixed sea grass, finger coral, and rubble.

When fishing a fly that imitates mud or spider crabs, give the fly very little action. All species of walking crabs remain close to shelter (whether under a rock, among sea-grass blades or algae, or burrowing into the bottom), and they don't scurry over long stretches of open bottom when chased.

When choosing a fly to imitate mud and spider crabs, you can reduce color to the basics—dark green, brown, or tan, depending upon the species. The Florida mud crab has a yellowish to tan carapace and brown legs, and often red or brown spots. In contrast, the common mud crab is brownish green, while Say's mud crab ranges from medium green to brown. The Pitho crabs mentioned above are tan to gray, the green reef crab is dark green, and the tan reef crab is, not surprisingly, tan.

Fiddler crabs (family Ocypodidae) are not often listed in studies of bonefish stomachs, but fiddler crabs are certainly eaten by bonefish. Perhaps scientists rarely find fiddler crabs in bonefish stomachs because the researchers collect fish on open flats or other places where fiddlers don't live, and because bonefish have limited access to fiddler crabs. Along with marsh crabs and mangrove crabs (family Grapsidae) and a few species of

Polychaetes are segmented worms that have various body shapes, but we can divide the many species into two general categories: tube dwellers and free-moving. Among the most recognizable tube dwellers are the numerous filter-feeding species with large, bushy crowns that extend from the worm's tube or burrow (Christmas Tree worms are typical of this group). The colorful crown quickly retracts into the tube if the worm senses danger. Free-moving polychaetes search for food along the bottom, and can live in tubes, burrow into the sediment when seeking shelter, or simply crawl along the bottom. In shape, they are variations on the earthworm theme. The species of polychaetes of most interest to bonefish grow up to 3 or 4 inches long.

BONEFISH SIZE AND PREY SIZE

Like many species of gamefish, bonefish undergo diet changes as they grow. Diets of small bonefish are usually dominated by smaller, less mobile prey, such as small shrimps, worms, and clams. As bonefish grow larger, their diets expand, become more varied, and include larger prey. Their diets continue to include many of the items they ate as smaller fish, but larger shrimps, crabs, and fish are added. For example, bonefish longer than 23 inches (fork length) eat more fish, including gobies, toadfish, snake eels, and juvenile snappers. In a Florida Keys study, small fishes, such as toadfish, made up 17.8 percent of the diet of bonefish larger than 17 inches, while smaller bonefish (less than 17 inches) ate more common shrimp than larger bonefish did. Larger bonefish also ate more snapping shrimp and mud crabs than smaller individuals consumed, and blue crabs (genus *Callinectes*) were only eaten by bonefish larger than 17 inches.

Now that you're aware of the environmental requirements of bonefish, the habitats where they can be found, how they use tides to their advantage, and their menu, it's time to take the next step and fit this information into strategies for fly fishing. You've learned their general habitat patterns, so you now know where to look for bonefish when exploring new areas. You also know that their diet varies depending on where they are feeding, so you can narrow your selection of flies. And you know the importance of tides to bonefish movements and feeding, so you know which locations to start your search. Now it will all come together in learning the best approaches to fly fishing for these elusive fish.

Acknowledgments

My thanks to Craig Dahlgren and Bob Miller for helpful comments on chapters 1 through 4.

Bibliography

Adams, A. J. *Fisherman's Coast: An Angler's Guide to Marine Warm-Water Gamefish and Their Habitats.* Mechanicsburg, PA: Stackpole Books, 2004.

Bruger, G. E. *Age, Growth, Food Habits, and Reproduction of Bonefish,* Albula vulpes, *in South Florida Waters.* Florida Department of Natural Resources, Marine Research Laboratory. Research Publication no. 3, 1974.

Colborn, J. R. E. Crabtree, J. B. Shaklee, E. Pfeiler, B. W. Bowen. "The Evolutionary Enigma of Bonefishes (*Albula* spp.): Cryptic Species and Ancient Separations in a Globally Distributed Shorefish." *Evolution* 55 (2001): 807–20.

Colton, D. E. and W. S. Alevizon. "Feeding Ecology of Bonefish in Bahamian Waters." *Transactions of the American Fisheries Society* 112 (1983): 178–84.

Crabtree, R. E., C. W. Harnden, D. Snodgrass, and C. Stevens. "Age, Growth, and Mortality of Bonefish, *Albula vulpes*, from the Waters of the Florida Keys." *Fishery Bulletin* 94 (1996): 442–51.

Crabtree, R. E., D. Snodgrass, and C. W. Harnden. "Maturation and Reproductive Seasonality in Bonefish, *Albula vulpes*, from the Waters of the Florida Keys." *Fishery Bulletin* 95 (1997): 456–65.

Crabtree, R. E., C. Stevens, D. Snodgrass, and F. J. Stengard. "Feeding Habitats of Bonefish, *Albula vulpes*, from the Waters of the Florida Keys." *Fishery Bulletin* 96 (1998): 754–66.

Hildebrand, S. F. "Family Albulidae." In *Fishes of the Western North Atlantic*, edited by H.B. Bigelow, 132–47. Memoir Sears Foundation for Marine Research, volume 1, number 3, 1963.

Humstan, R., J. S. Ault, and M. F. Larkin. "Habitat Selection and Movement of Bonefish (*Albula vulpes*) in Biscayne Bay, Florida, Determined by Ultrasonic Telemetry." Tarpon Bonefish International Symposium. Dania Beach, FL, 2003.

Kaplan, E. H. *A Field Guide to Southeastern and Caribbean Seashores: Cape Hatteras to the Gulf Coast, Florida, and the Caribbean.* Boston: Houghton Mifflin Company, 1988.

Mojica, R. Jr., J. M. Shenker, C. W. Harnden, and D. E. Wagner. "Recruitment of Bonefish, *Albula vulpes*, around Lee Stocking Island, Bahamas." 1995.

Ross, David A. *The Fisherman's Ocean.* Mechanicsburg, PA: Stackpole Books, 2000.

Valiela, I. *Marine Ecological Processes.* 2d ed. New York: Springer-Verlag New York, Inc, 1995.

Warmke, G. F. L. and D. S. Erdman. "Records of Marine Molluscs Eaten by Bonefish in Puerto Rican Waters." *The Nautilus* 76 (no. 4, 1963): 115–20.

PART II

Tackle and Equipment

Chapter 5

Bonefish Flies

I'm all about throwing quality food toward 'em, but in the end, presentation is still the key.
—Tim Borski, artist and fly tier

As bonefish travel from flat to flat, the type and amount of food that they find keep changing. But bonefish don't always eat everything that is available. They often become selective and eat only certain types of foods.

I guess we do the same at a party. If only potato chips are served, we eat potato chips. But if the host puts out a big spread of foods, we may choose the cold shrimp or the stone-crab claws. We leave the chips. I think bones act in much the same way.

As the availability and choices of the bonefish's food change, we can find it very hard to pinpoint what the fish are eating at a particular time. Fortunately, while bonefish can be choosy, they usually still eat a great variety of foods on the flats. As you saw in chapter 4, we have a pretty good idea of which foods they prefer and what those foods look like.

Tim Borski, one of the great saltwater tiers, has influenced many of us with his bonefish patterns. Top: *Three Bonefish Critters.* Bottom: *Chernobyl Crab and Bonefish Slider.*

To me, though, selecting a bonefish fly is still more about presentation than imitation. Sure, you want to cast a fly that either looks like whatever they're eating or at least resembles something they'd like to eat. But it might be more important to select a fly that will help you make a good presentation. This is perhaps a good time to redefine presentation, because it is not merely casting in front of a fish.

In my view, presentation to a fish consists of *showing him the fly in a natural manner*—that is, making a cast in front of the fish and letting the fly sink to the proper level so that eventually it enters the fish's area of awareness. At the same time, the fly should swim perpendicular to or, better yet, away from the predator, but never toward the bonefish. This is a presentation.

If you cast too far in front of a bone, the fly probably will not get a response. If you do not let the fly sink to the right depth, the bonefish still won't see it, even if it's only a few inches too high. And if the fly is moving toward him during the retrieve, as when you cast to a fish that is going away from you, the bonefish will probably spook when he sees the fly "attacking" him. It is just not natural.

So, part of selecting a fly is trying to choose one that will let you make a presentation that appears like natural prey to the bonefish. Although it happened more than thirty years ago, I still remember an old bonefish guide in the Bahamas telling me, "Show it to him, show it to him!" I was casting to a single tailing bonefish, and this was the guide's way of telling me to make a good presentation. Very eloquent of him. And I've never forgotten it.

To make sure that a bonefish sees the fly and that it looks good for him to eat, we have a great variety of patterns, both imitators and attractors, that can sink to the right depth and look pretty real in the water when properly manipulated. With time on the flats and a bit of trial and error, which is always fun, you'll develop a list of

MARKUS HAUGG

A good bonefish guide can help you select the right fly for his area.

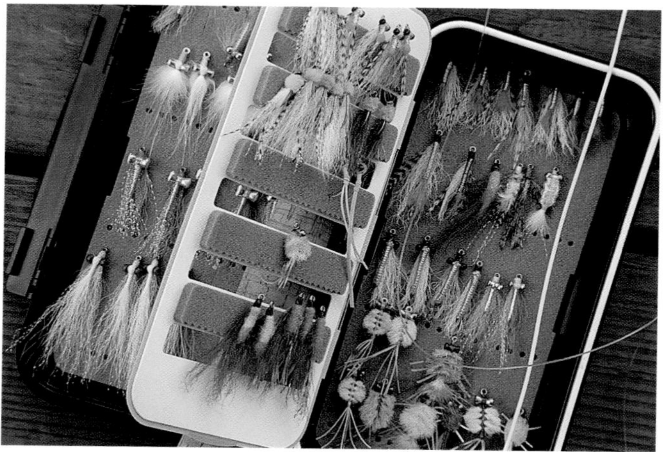

Make sure that you have an ample variety of bonefish flies during your trip. Conditions can change within minutes, often dictating a completely different pattern.

favorite bonefish flies that work for you. Another way to learn about flies is to fish with a good bonefish guide. For sure, this will save some time in the learning process, because a really good guide knows the flies that work in his area. You'll often find that when you face similar conditions in other parts of the world, the same flies will probably work there, too.

Little by little, we keep gaining knowledge and catching more bones, until we start to think we are experts. And then we hit days when we can't seem to get a fish even to look at our flies. It can be a humbling experience, but that's fly fishing. Frankly, I am glad it's that way. I am very curious, mind you, but deep down, I really don't want to know it all.

The suggestions I am going to give you are only guidelines, rules of thumb about where to start. Please remember that there are times when nothing works. When that happens, I advise you to break every rule and do something like cast a big size 2 orange fly over a dark turtle-grass bottom. Yes, it's unlikely that anything that color lives there, and if it does, it probably only comes out at night to feed. But many are the times when breaking the rules has worked for me.

SELECTING A FLY

I don't know how other people do it, but here is my usual thought process in selecting a fly. My tendency is to select pattern, then color, and then size and weight.

First I would select a pattern, such as a Merkin crab or a Clouser fish imitation. Then I would select the color. Usually, I try to match the surrounding habitat, though I might pick a bright color if I decide to use an attractor. Then, to make sure that the bonefish will see the fly but will not be spooked by it, I will choose the size and weight.

There are exceptions, of course. If I am going to cast to a school of mudding bonefish in four feet of water, where they usually keep moving, a fly that quickly sinks to their level is essential. In this case, I look first for a heavily weighted fly that will sink fast. Then I worry about pattern and color.

PATTERNS

Before looking at different types of bonefish patterns, let's tackle a basic decision: to invert or to guard? That is, do we want the fly to ride with the hook up or to ride with the hook down and have a weed guard? In the shallow water of the flats, a bonefish fly often touches or drags on the bottom. In doing so, it comes in contact with rubble, coral, long blades of turtle grass, and other hazards. But it must avoid getting snagged, and it must also travel through the water without picking up grass. If a fly does either of those, it will almost always spook the fish.

Personally, I don't have a preference between inverted bonefish flies or those equipped with weed guards. What matters is that a fly can usually swim in the bonefish's world without snagging or picking up loose grass. I say "usually" because no fly is completely snag- and grass-proof.

I feel that the method that makes the fly weedless should follow the pattern's design, and not the other way around. Some flies are best tied inverted (such as a Clouser Minnow or Bonefish Special) and some are best tied with weed guards (such as many shrimp imitations).

There are at least five major different kinds of bonefish flies today, with some patterns falling between the major kinds. As you might expect, they all have their times and places. As I see it, we have conventional or

Conventional flies. Top, left to right: *Chico's Bonefish Special and Bob Stearns's Snapping Shrimp (tied by Stephen Fernández).* Bottom, left to right: *The Horror designed by Pete Perinchief was the first inverted fly for bonefish (tied by Stephen Fernández); Chico's Honey Shrimp (tied by Capt. Chris Dean).*

classic flies, patterns with bead-chain or lead eyes, epoxy flies, shrimp flies, and crab flies.

Conventional Flies

Bonefish were caught with fly rods in the 1930s and probably earlier. There is an old photo of Capt. Bill Smith with a bonefish taken on a fly rod in 1939. But these catches were mostly accidental. Then, in 1948 or so, Joe Brooks went to the Florida Keys to catch a bonefish on a fly rod on purpose. And he landed two in one day.

Still, anglers were using regular streamers to take a bonefish here and there while they fished for other species. Then, in the early 1950s, Pete Perinchief tied the first inverted bonefish fly. This was a big step. The fly worked great and still does. Pete called the fly the Horror, after his then-young daughter, who was probably not behaving quite up to par.

In its original colors, the Horror was tied with brown bucktail and a yellow chenille head. We mostly used red thread, though it probably didn't matter. I have landed hundreds of bonefish with this fly over the years, and it is still one of the best patterns for extremely shallow water. It doesn't seem to hit the water; it just enters it.

The conventional category usually encompasses the older designs such as the Frankie Belle, Chico's Bonefish Special, Bob Stearns's Snapping Shrimp, and Chico's Honey Shrimp. In the old days, we did not weight our flies, or at least not very often. If we had only known!

After Pete began tying inverted flies that were relatively weedless, the rest of the fly-fishing world started to do the same. Most of the flies of the late 1950s and '60s are of the conventional inverted design. These flies usually have sparse to medium dressings and are usually unweighted. They remain some of the best flies to cast to tailing fish in very shallow water or to fish running around feeding with their backs partly out of even shallower water. This is super-exciting fishing for which one often needs a very light fly that enters rather than plops onto the water. If you are a light-rod fan—a 5- or 6-weight, say—the conventional designs are light and aerodynamic, making casting much easier on the windy flats.

When the classic patterns are tied weighted, it is usually done by wrapping lead wire around the front of the hook shank before applying the body of the fly. Tied this way, they can still make a very quiet presentation.

From time to time I see someone put bead-chain eyes on these flies, but I don't think they work as well. The bulk in the head that comes from tying the body and wings does not lend itself to the addition of bead chain. Besides, there are better designs to get down fast.

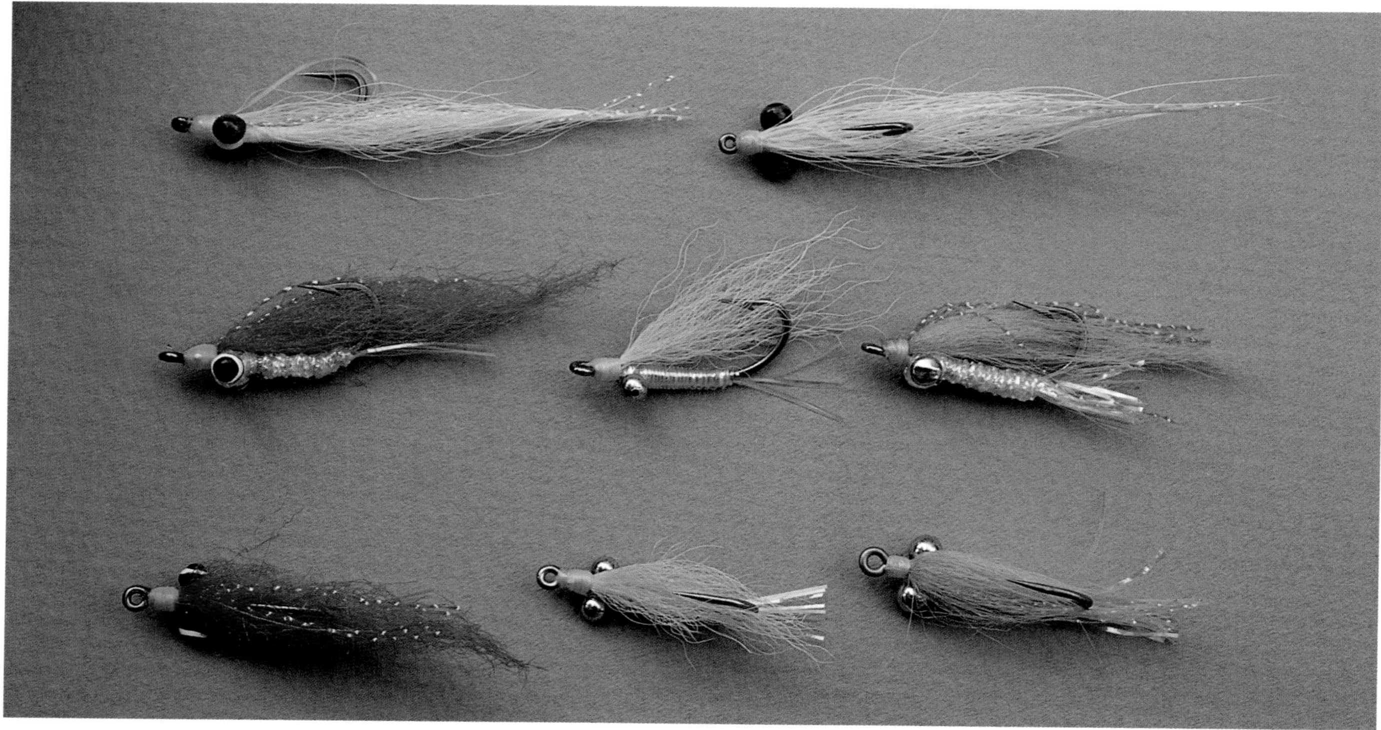

Lead or chain eyes. Top: *Clouser Minnow, side and top view.* Middle and bottom, left to right: *Orange Gotcha, side and top view; Pink Charlie, side and top view; and another Gotcha, side and top view. (All tied by Capt. Chris Dean).*

If you are wading in very shallow water and want to imitate a small fish such as a baby snapper or one of the many shad that inhabit this environment, my Bonefish Special is made to order. To imitate a shrimp or a darker fry, Bob Stearns's Snapping Shrimp or the original Horror will do nicely.

If you look at records from some of the early fly-fishing tournaments in the Florida Keys, back in the late '70s, you will see that Sandy Moret won many tournaments. He used mostly Bonefish Specials and Snapping Shrimp. I know: I tied the flies for him.

A few years back, during one of the early Redbone Tournaments, I landed the largest bonefish while fishing with Capt. Mike Ehlers. When we got back to the dock, everyone wanted to know which fly I had used. When I told them it was a size 4 Bonefish Special, they were surprised. "A Bonefish Special?" said one of the anglers, with some hesitation. "I guess I'm not too impressed. That's kind of an old pattern, isn't it?"

"Well," I said, "the bonefish was impressed."

Many conventional designs are out of vogue these days. But I haven't stopped using my Bonefish Specials, Horrors, and Snapping Shrimp, and I still catch fish with them in the right situations.

In 2003, I went to Casa Blanca on the Yucatan Peninsula with my son, Stephen, looking for more photos for this book. It was very windy the first two days, and we ended up in some protected lagoons full of small mangrove shoots and barely six inches of water. Even the tiny *plop* of the smallest crab fly would send entire schools of bonefish out of the lagoons. But we switched to Horrors and Snapping Shrimp and landed enough bonefish to take some of the photos in this book. The difference was amazing. And it was just a matter of casting the right fly for those super-shallow waters.

So carry some of the old-fashioned flies in your box, and when you face extremely shallow water, pull one out. You'll remember me.

Eyes of Chain, Eyes of Lead

Conventional inverted flies work beautifully in extra-shallow water. Day in and day out, though, a bonefish fly that is weighed up front so that it dives for the bottom like it's trying to reach cover is deadly. Eyes can be added to nearly any pattern, but we're talking about flies designed with eyes in mind. This group includes such great flies as the Crazy Charlie, Gotcha, and Clouser Minnow.

These flies can have bead-chain or lead eyes. Please do not underestimate the difference in weight and rate of descent between a fly tied with bead chain and one tied with a medium-size lead dumbbell. The former will sink

Epoxy flies. Top, left to right: *Harry Spear's Mother of Epoxy fly and John Emery's Orange Epoxy Fly. I saw John hook a huge mutton snapper with that fly in Key West in the 1960s, but we lost him in the sea fans.* Bottom row, left to right: *Capt. Chris Dean's Epoxy Bone and Bob Branham's Inverted Epoxy.*

much faster than a conventional fly and still land fairly lightly. The latter will hit the water with an audible plop and sink even faster than a bead-chain pattern. Believe me when I tell you that there is room in your fly box for both. That's right—you want the same pattern and size in both weights to deal with different water depths.

There is a great difference between fishing a flat with eight inches of water and one with a foot of water. It may not look like much of a difference, but the second flat is 50 percent deeper. That can be enough to make you change from a bead-chain pattern to a lead-eye fly.

On sandy flats that have little in the way of obstructions, you can use these weighted flies to great advantage. You can let the fly hit bottom and then bounce it along as you retrieve, creating puffs of sand or mud as it hops. This is sometimes very effective.

When casting to a school of spooky bones on a sandy bottom, I sometimes drop one of these weighted flies, say a Gotcha, well in front of the school and let it lie on the bottom. Then I wait until the school is almost on top of the fly before starting the retrieve. This almost always produces a hookup.

If a school seems very spooky—and it is almost always the first few fish in a school that dictate the degree of fear—let a few fish pass the fly and then, carefully, start the retrieve so that a fish inside the school sees the fly. This, too, usually leads to a hookup.

But when using a weighted fly over turtle grass, try to retrieve so that the fly rides just over the tips of the grass blades. You do this by feel and by trial and error with the fly you are using at the moment, but it works well. One of my favorite weighted-eye flies for turtle grass is a white and chartreuse Clouser Minnow. It just works.

On deeper flats, whether you're sight-casting or casting to mudding fish, these weighted flies are great. Here, the main thing is to use a fly that sinks quickly enough. On a deep flat, you might need a lead dumbbell rather than bead chain.

Besides the normal Clouser pattern, my son, Stephen, likes to tie a very sparse Clouser on a size 4 or even size 6 hook. It's deadly on bones, especially on calm days. I used to tell him that his fly was much too sparse, and that the original pattern calls for twice as much hair. But since he kept hooking bonefish with it, I finally borrowed a few and stopped telling him that it was tied wrong.

Epoxy Flies

As far as I know, Capt. Harry Spear came up with the first epoxy fly. He called it MOE for Mother of Epoxy.

The head was made of hot glue. At the time, in the pre-crab-fly era, it was the most effective fly for permit. Since then, epoxy heads or bodies have appeared on a variety of bonefish flies. A small MOE is a great bonefish fly.

Epoxy flies don't need to be very heavy to get down to the right level on the bonefish flats. An epoxy head or body also has a translucent look, much like many shrimps and other bonefish foods. Indeed, the grass shrimp is completely transparent regardless of the bottom color, and it strikes me that a clear epoxy design would be a good imitation of one of these crustaceans.

These flies can be very durable. I have taken bonefish after bonefish without putting so much as a dent in an epoxy pattern. About the only time I have to replace an epoxy fly is when a small barracuda cuts me off.

Epoxy flies can be made very light so that they do not drop to the water too loudly or sink too quickly. Tied without any weight, they make a very good alternative for tailing bonefish. But the majority of my epoxy flies, which are mostly shrimp imitations, are used over turtle grass, where a great variety of shrimps are found. I have also had excellent results using them on mudding bonefish or bonefish working around a mudding stingray. Just remember that unless they are tied extra light, epoxy flies are usually not the choice for an ultralight fly rod, such as a 5- or 6-weight outfit.

The epoxy that forms the body or head lends itself to installing a good and permanent monofilament weed guard. This feature means that epoxy flies can be fished almost anywhere.

Shrimp flies. Top to bottom: *Chris Dean's Woolly-Worm Bonefish Fly, Steve Huff's Joe-to-Go, Tim Klein's TK Special (tied by Capt. Chris Dean).*

Shrimp Flies

Studies tell us that shrimp can be anywhere on the flats but that they are more likely to be in grass than on sand, often by a ratio of more than three to one. The juvenile shrimp that bonefish look for seem to be most abundant during the summer and fall, though there are many around all year long.

Using a shrimp fly for bonefish that are feeding in grass, particularly turtle grass, is an excellent choice. If the fly is lightly weighted and has a good weed guard, you may be able to work it just under the tips of the grass, but still not deep enough to get snagged. You should do well.

Among the shrimp patterns I use are Steve Huff's Joe-to-Go, Tim Klein's TK Special, and Tim Borski's Epoxy Shrimp. But there are hundreds of good patterns out there.

The really small shrimp flies are some of the best patterns for choosy bonefish tailing or cruising in very shallow water. Because these flies are often very light, you can go down to a 7-weight or lighter. When bonefish get selective in shallow water, a shrimp pattern will often do the job.

Crab Flies

The crab flies we use today for bonefish are mostly spin-offs from the successful permit patterns. Not long after we discovered that crab flies would catch permit with great regularity, some anglers started to use smaller specimens of the same patterns for bonefish. And boy, did they work! Now that anglers know how well they work, more and more fly tiers are creating crab patterns for bonefish.

Slowly, I started to add a few crab flies to my bonefish fly box. Then, little by little, they started to take over the fly box. Soon I had two bonefish fly boxes: one for crab flies and the other for everything else.

I admit that there have been weeks in the Bahamas when the crabs did not do as well as other flies, but day in and day out, they have become my favorite flies. I use them for bonefish at least 50 percent of the time.

Crab flies. Top: *Rag head, small Merkin, Lenny Moffo's Fleeing Crab.* Bottom: *Dean's Hopper, Tim Borski's Crab Critter (tied by Capt. Chris Dean), Merkin, Harry Spear's Tasty Toad (tied by Chris Dean).*

In 2003, during my stays at the North Riding Point Club in the Bahamas and Casa Blanca on the Yucatan Peninsula, 80 percent of the bonefish that I landed were caught on small crabs, such as size 4 Merkins, size 4 Ragheads, and the like. I have done so well with them in the past two years that I sometimes have trouble using other flies. And I am certainly never going bonefishing again without a few crab flies of different colors and weights.

Crab flies have also taken other fish for me on the bonefish flats. Permit, mutton snappers, big mangrove snappers, yellow bar jacks, and other species all fall for crab patterns.

A couple of years ago, I went fishing with Capt. Dale Perez, one of the truly great guides of the Lower Keys and Key West. After a good day's fishing in which I hooked three permit and landed one, we were poling off the flat, searching for a bit deeper water where we could crank up and go home. But I was still on the bow looking, just in case. I spotted a sunken boat at the edge of the flat in three feet of water or less. The low tide had revealed part of the hull. When we got within casting distance, we could see lots of small mangrove snappers and a few schoolmaster snappers swimming around, partly under the shadow of the boat.

Just for kicks, I cast the crab fly, a green Merkin, by the edge of the sunken boat and let it sink a couple of feet. I was expecting a 6-inch snapper. But to my surprise, the strike was extra hard. Even with a 12-pound tippet, I could barely force the fish away from the protection of the boat. A few minutes later we had ourselves a big mangrove snapper, maybe a couple of pounds. He was beautiful.

Now, a big mangrove snapper is a smart fish. Al McClane used to call them the Aristotle of the mangroves. But Aristotle was fooled by the green Merkin. So are many bonefish.

And then there is the permit factor. One of the pleasant problems that an angler often faces when fly fishing for bonefish is that a big permit may come into the picture. The angler is usually armed with a bonefish fly, which is rarely the best choice for permit. If the angler is ready, a fast switch to a heavier outfit with a permit crab fly will result in a hookup. Often, though, the angler doesn't have time to make such a switch, or he is wading and doesn't have a second outfit handy. But if he is fishing with a bonefish-size crab fly, our friend has an excellent chance to hook the permit (well, as excellent as one can expect with a permit).

If you don't go to the extreme of carrying a fly box full of only crabs, at least make sure that you have several crab flies of different weights and colors in your bonefish fly box. Trust me: you will be glad to have them.

MINNOW PATTERNS FOR BONEFISH

In a conversation with famous saltwater fly tier and artist Tim Borski, the subject of minnow patterns for bonefish came up. Tim mentioned that in his estimation, not enough has been done by fly tiers and anglers in this area. That's an interesting observation, because we know that big bones love to eat juvenile snappers, toadfish, pinfish, parrotfish, and many other small fishes.

I know that we have the Clouser Minnow and Chico's Bonefish Special and a few other generic patterns that imitate baitfish, but we probably need more. I didn't have enough time to research and add more minnow patterns to this book, but I intend to start experimenting with some snapper and silverside patterns very soon. Just some food for thought for all you fly tiers and bonefish fanatics.

Small barracudas will attack nearly any fly, and even the smallest one can clip the leader. I was lucky with this one—I got to keep my crab fly.

COLOR

As you read in chapter 4, most creatures eaten by bonefish on the flats—shrimps, crabs, fishes, worms, and so forth—change color constantly to match their surroundings. A shrimp's likelihood of becoming lunch increases greatly if it's not well camouflaged. In thick turtle grass, many prey creatures take on a greenish color. In areas of coral rubble or mixed sand and grass, the food has a mottled pattern of tan and green. Light tan or gray are camouflage colors on a sandy bottom.

When you select a fly for a particular flat, it's not a bad idea to follow the rule of "light bottom, light flies; dark bottom, dark flies." From there, you can always change, but it's a good start.

Besides the changes in color mentioned above, many mud crabs also appear dark green and brown on darker bottoms. Most have a black or very dark color at the tips of their claws.

The colors of shrimps range from green to gray (a color that most fly tiers rarely use, but probably should) to light brown to medium brown. All of these colors, of course, are more or less translucent. Grass shrimp, a common bonefish prey, are transparent on any bottom.

Some mantis shrimp on certain bottoms can get very dark green and practically black, but I have never had good results with black flies for bones. Maybe I have not tried them enough, but I can take only so many refusals before I have to change flies and go back to a pattern that works or something that I have confidence in (which is probably why it works).

The bony-fish diet is, in my opinion, very important. Although small fishes do not make up a big percentage of the average bonefish's diet, they are very important to the bigger bonefish, and we are all interested in catching those guys. To a scientist, a bigger bonefish is one with a fork length of more than 23 inches. That means a measurement from the tip of the nose to the fork of the tail. And while the weight will vary with the girth of the fish, a bonefish with a 23-inch fork length is well over 6 pounds, maybe 7 pounds. The bonefish's fish diet is important.

A lot of toadfish and killifish have colors that match their surroundings, ranging from light to dark brown. Mojarras tend to be silver with a light gray top and often a bit of yellow in the fin.

White and chartreuse Clouser Minnows, Bonefish Specials, and other flies are good fish imitations. I have done well throughout the years using the Bonefish Special on sandy flats where so many different species of mojarras live, including the yellowfin mojarra.

But I often find that it pays to cast a bright attractor pattern that doesn't match the natural colors of the environment. Bright pink Charlie-type flies have done well for me in many different countries. Patterns that are all orange or all chartreuse, with a couple of grizzly feathers to show some segmentation, work well for bonefish. Though I can't call them attractor patterns, I often have great results with other light, pastel colors on sandy flats, such as light pink, light yellow, chartreuse and white, and so on.

You might want to change the color of a fly while fishing. Any of a variety of felt-tipped markers with permanent or waterproof ink can do the job. Many anglers know about this, but few put it to use. A marker can add bars to create segmentation or darken the top of a fly to make it resemble a baitfish. Even a little bit of marking can often change the appearance of a fly and improve its effectiveness.

Sometimes a little extra color can make a big difference in a fly. Capt. Tim Klein, one of the best bonefish guides in the Florida Keys, has a rule about the flies he ties for his home waters around Islamorada. All his patterns, including his TK Special, have a little bit of chartreuse. It just works great, he tells me. And Tim's clients land lots of big bones throughout the year.

SIZE

As you saw in the food chapter, most of the crustaceans consumed by bonefish on the flats run from 1 inch to about 2½ inches. Most of the bony fishes range from over 1 inch to 4 inches or so. However, because bonefish can be incredibly nervous about being in such shallow water, the size of the fly is often dictated by the size of the fish, water depth, and wind conditions.

In the Miami area and the Florida Keys, where fish run much larger on average than in any other bonefish destination, hooks average about one size larger. In most areas, a size 4 hook is pretty much the average, but in the Miami area and the Keys, size 2 is the norm. You will find that many fly shops that cater to bonefishermen offer a box of bonefish flies for the Bahamas, Belize, and other Caribbean destination, and another collection for the Florida Keys and Miami area. The difference, besides some favorite local patterns, is size. And rightly so. If you plan to fish both bonefish worlds, and I hope you do, you need to get both boxes of flies.

When I have found big bonefish in the Bahamas and the Yucatan, the big Keys flies worked great on them. So do bring all your bonefish flies on your trip; you never know.

I am talking in hook sizes because bonefish flies have to be balanced to the sizes of their hooks, which makes hook size a good indicator of fly size. The most common sizes used for bonefish are 6, 4, and 2, and the most practical range is probably from 8 to 1. I have not found that I need flies below or above those sizes. The sizes I use most often are 4 for most bonefishing and 2 for big bones and most Florida Keys fishing.

If you use a size 4 fly and a heavy tippet—say, 10-pound test or higher—for big fish, you will probably experience a few open hooks. So, if you must use a small fly but still feel that you need a heavier tippet than you would normally use with that size fly, go a little easier during the fight.

While writing this book, I opened a couple of size 4 hooks on good-size bonefish, simply because a 10-pound tippet let me put a little too much pressure on the hook as I tried to keep each bone from wrapping the line around mangroves. I got in a situation where I felt it was too calm to cast a bigger fly, but the area had many small mangrove shoots. So I fished a size 4 hook on a 10-pound tippet. I got the hit, I had the tippet strength to handle the fish, but the tippet was a little too strong for the small hook. Just be a little careful with size 4 or smaller hooks.

Probably the most important factors in bonefish-fly size are water depth and wind conditions. A good angler learns to compute these factors to select a fly that's big enough for the bonefish to find, but not so large that it will spook him while landing on the surface or when he sees it.

Here are the basics. The shallower the water, the smaller the fly. In shallow water, a bonefish will often spook when he encounters a big fly, even if the fly did not spook him when it landed. The deeper the water, the larger the fly. A bonefish in a couple of feet of water or more will not spook from a larger fly, and he can find it easier.

On calm, clear days, use smaller flies. On a calm and sunny day when a bonefish can see well, you do not need a big fly. A smaller fly will probably not spook him, and chances are he will find the small fly easily.

On windy days, go with larger flies. With the surface of the water broken by the wind, a bonefish will not spook as quickly, so this is a good time to use a bigger fly. You might want a heavier outfit, even a 9-weight, to fight the wind and cast the larger fly with less difficulty. And sometimes a bigger fly, especially in deeper water or on a windy day, will excite a really big bonefish.

While talking about using bigger flies for bigger bones, Tim Borski told me a story about bonefishing on one of the outside flats below Islamorada in the Florida Keys. He sight-cast to a big bonefish that promptly took his fly. When Tim finally landed him, the fish spit out a fresh, 6-inch yellowtail snapper that he had eaten just before taking Tim's fly. As far as Tim can remember, the fish was under 10 pounds. Talk about big bones wanting a mouthful. We know that big bones eat all types of juvenile snappers—but a 6-inch yellowtail? That's a meal and a half.

WEIGHT

I have sight-fished for bonefish in water so shallow that the edges of their eyeballs were almost out of the water. And I have sight-fished for them in almost five feet of water. You may think that the super-shallow fishing is the

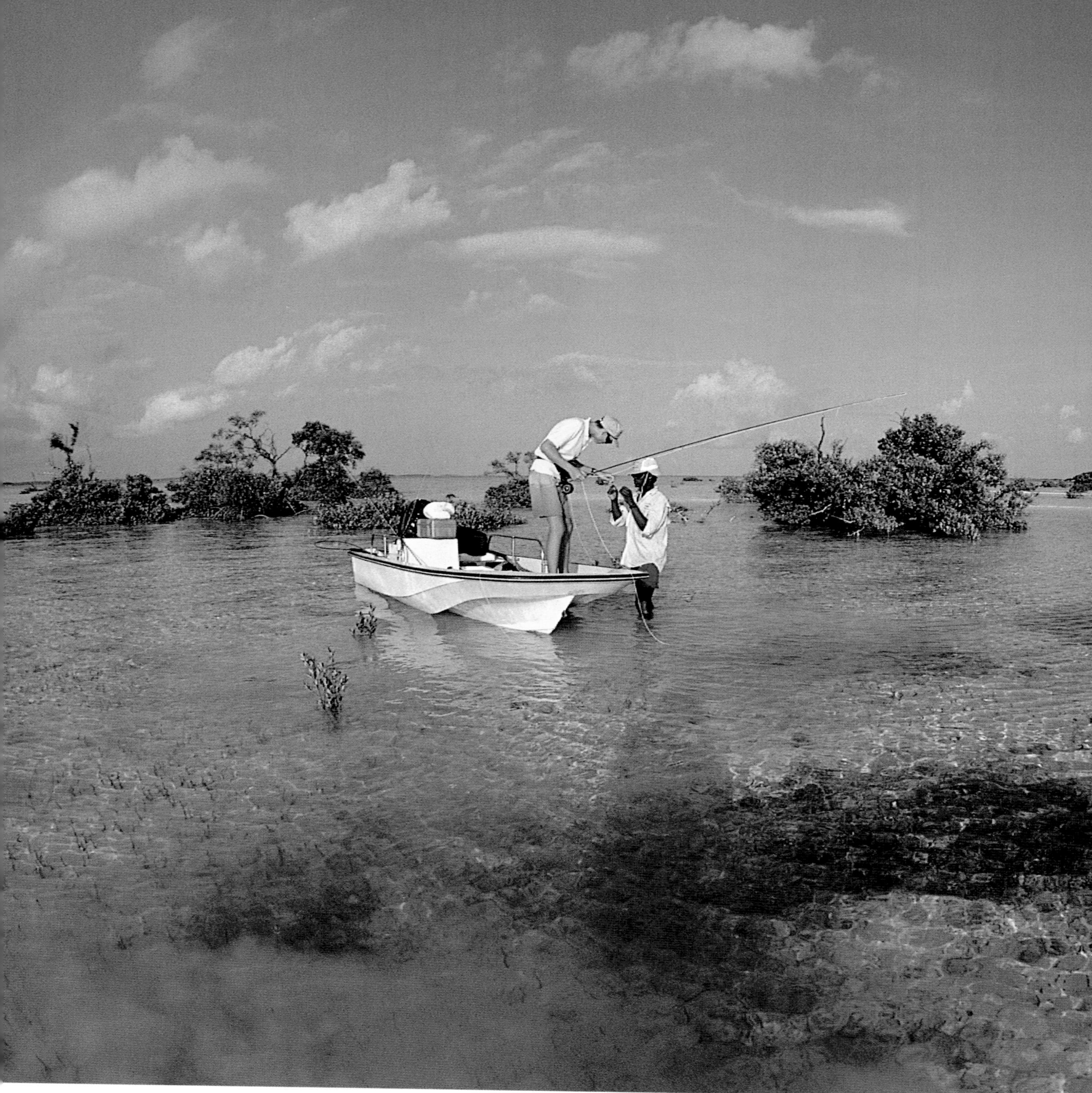

A classic moment in fly fishing: a guide and his client discuss the selection of a new fly. I decided not to give my opinion, but just to take the photo.

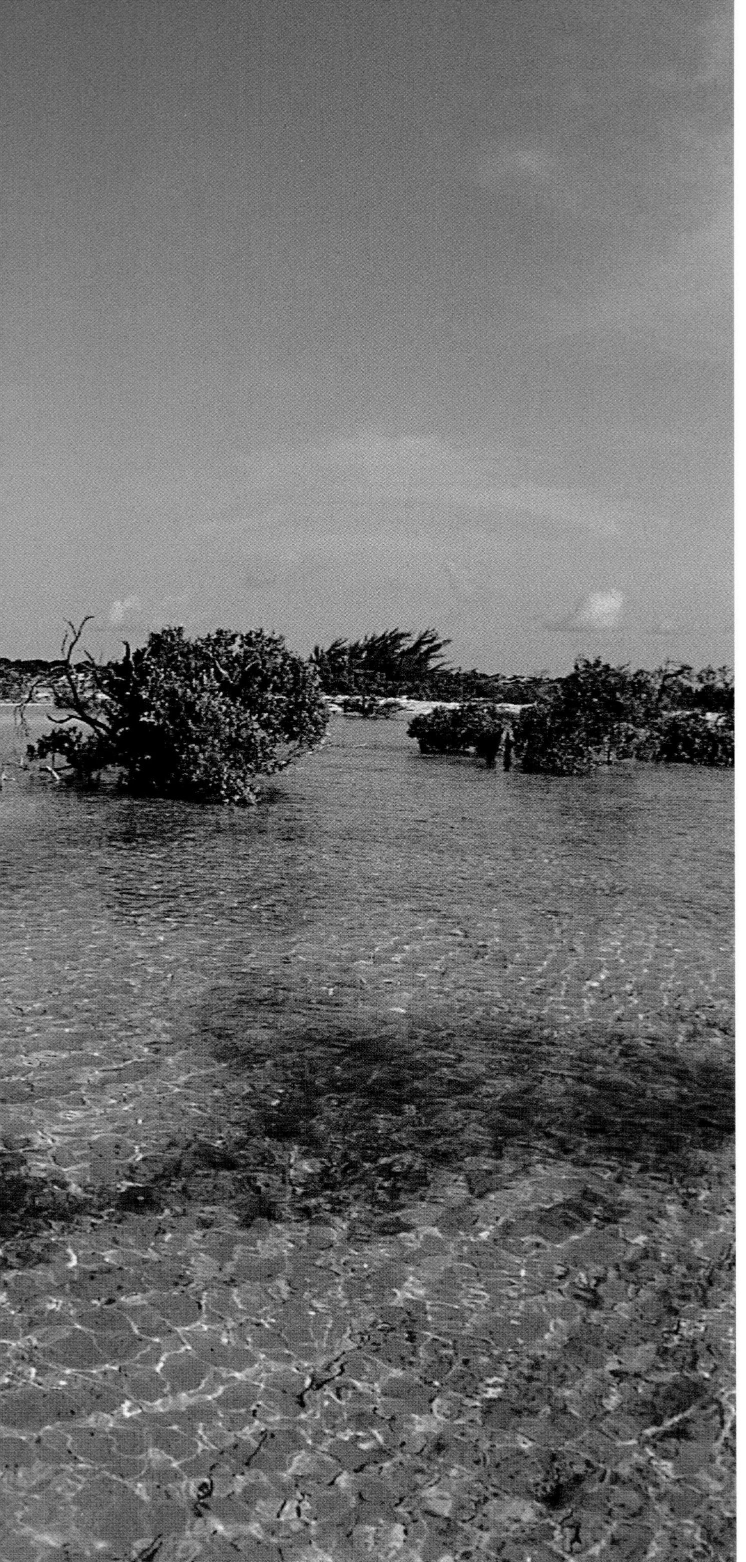

most exciting, and it often is, but some of the deep-water sight-casting involves very big bonefish, and it, too, can be very challenging and exciting.

To present flies to bonefish at all these different depths (remember that presentation consists of showing the fish the fly in a natural manner), you need not only the right pattern, color, and size, but also the right weight. The fly needs to quickly reach a depth where the bonefish can see it and be comfortable reaching for it. Remember that most bonefish do not like to rise to a fly; they want their food at their level or below.

In a day's fishing, it is not unusual to sight-cast to tailing bones early in the morning, cast to mudding fish in three feet of water in late morning, and, after a midday thunderstorm, to go back to nine inches of water, now with the flat-calm conditions that often follow a storm, and cast to super-spooky bonefish. The angler who fished that day did a lot of fly changing, constantly trying to figure out which fly would work best every time conditions changed.

The shallower the water, the lighter the fly you must use to avoid spooking the fish. The deeper the water, the heavier the fly, in order to get down to their level. In deeper water, a heavier fly rarely spooks bonefish when it plops down; on some days, the plop will attract their attention and they will rush to take the fly. But don't get too confident; on other days with the same conditions and in water of the same depth, your heavy fly will terrify the fish as it hits the water. That's bonefishing.

If you have a favorite shrimp or crab pattern, you should carry it in at least two different weights. Crab flies are almost always weighted; you should have them with both bead chain and dumbbells. You want unweighted, bead-chain, and lead-dumbbell versions of shrimp patterns. You'll thank me for this one.

If they are well kept and rinsed in fresh water after being used, flies will last many years. I have some that are almost twenty years old, and they still work. So don't feel bad about spending more than $100 on a fly box and an assortment of bonefish flies. You need the variety. I bring two fly boxes to the game: one with crabs and one with everything else. Those boxes contain over 100 flies.

Imagine going to a bonefish camp. During your week there, high tide occurs mostly during the middle of the day. The area the camp fishes is mostly sandy flats. You will probably need a light-colored fly (to match the bottom) that is weighted (to get down to the proper level). You open your fly box, which has thirty flies of different colors and different weights, and you have about ten light-colored flies. Half of them, five, are weighted. You have five flies to fish most of the week. Granted, very early or very late in the day the water will be lower and you'll be able to use unweighted flies on other flats for tailing fish. Maybe. But this is only a small part of each day.

See how quickly thirty flies became five? It is really good to have a wide selection.

Other times, of course, you will fish both shallow and deep flats or over light and dark bottoms, and then you will change flies as you need to and probably try half the flies in your arsenal. Again, it pays to have a lot of flies.

Have a few very heavy flies, too, patterns that will plunge to the bottom in three to six feet of water for those situations when fish are mudding deep and you need to drag bottom. A Crazy Charlie style is a good one to have as an extra-heavy fly because it is so sparsely tied that the lead eyes carry it to the bottom very quickly.

I have often taken twenty bonefish out of a school of mudding fish in deeper water. The casting is easy and the fish don't often spook when you hook a few. It is not nearly as challenging as sight-casting in shallow water, but it's fun. And then you go back to sight-casting. So bring a couple of bomb flies, just for fun.

Because the fishing often moves from shallow to deep, or at least deep enough to require a heavier fly, I often fish with two outfits in the skiff. One is a light rig, say a 7-weight, with an unweighted or lightly weighted fly. The other is a bit heavier, say an 8- or 9-weight, with a weighted fly. This works very well for me. If a quick change is required, I am ready, and I have a spare if one rod breaks. The heavier rod can also double as my barracuda or permit outfit.

CHANGING FLIES

Because bonefish are constantly changing their preferences while they feed on a flat, and we don't know for sure what those preferences are, the thing to do once you have had a few refusals is to change to another pattern. Makes sense, right?

But how do you know that you got a refusal? Maybe the fish just didn't see the fly.

I've hosted many fly-fishing groups in different places around the world. One such trip was to Peace and Plenty in the Bahamas. On the very first day we encountered a large school of fish very actively mudding in a couple of feet of water. We all spread out to work the school.

One angler had bought most of his flies at a fly shop, but had also tied a few. His pride and joy was a thing he called the Purple People Eater. It was dark purple and shocking pink, and it had some green in it somewhere. I didn't like the fly. Actually, I hated it.

He waded to within casting range of the school and proceeded to try a white and green fly. After a couple of casts, he changed to a brown fly. He didn't get a hit and changed to a pink fly. And so on.

After he had gone through half his fly box, I tried to explain to him that he was not getting deep enough. He was not getting refusals; it was just that the bonefish had not seen any of his flies. The fish were so numerous and feeding so hard that they probably would have taken anything. But he did not pay attention to my advice and shrugged it off with a "Yeah, yeah, yeah."

Finally, he came to the Purple People Eater, which was a heavily weighted fly, and which I hated. And of course the PPE went down to the bottom like a rock, and he had a fish on.

As the fish started to run, he turned around and yelled to me, "They're taking purple." He wanted to help me with my fly selection, I guess. Never mind that the rest of the anglers fishing this large school had been hooked up for an hour. The names in the story have been omitted or changed to protect the innocent, but the colors of that fly are accurate.

So, before you change flies, you have to be fairly sure that the fish saw the fly but did not like it. That is, make sure that you made a good presentation and still got a refusal.

Your cast may be pretty good and the fly may have landed very close to the fish, but if he is busy tailing or if the fly landed out of his area of awareness and he is not working in that direction, the fact that you made a very close cast means nothing. You did not get a refusal; he just did not see the fly.

You have to try to read the fish. See if he starts for the fly (which probably means that he has seen it) and then turns and goes looking for something better. Or did he follow it and then turn away? You need some acknowledgment, however slight, that the fish saw the fly. Then you know.

Time and good communication with your guide will help you learn this subtlety. And that means that Dr. Chico advises more time on the water, preferably with a good guide. Tell your spouse I said so. Doctor's orders.

Usually, I change flies after I get about three refusals, if I am confident in the fly. If I am not confident in a pattern, I will probably change flies too quickly. I know this, but I can't help it.

Depending on the situation, I might just change colors if I feel that I have the right pattern, say a crab fly, and it is reaching the right depth. If the problem is that the fly is just not getting down fast enough, I change weights. For a big change, I switch to an entirely different style, say from a crab fly to a Bonefish Special that imitates a shad or juvenile snapper.

MY FAVORITE BONEFISH FLIES: THE MAGNIFICENT SEVEN

Like most people who have fly fished for bonefish for many years, I have developed a group of favorite flies in which I have lots of confidence. Sometimes I have too much confidence in them and refuse to change flies after being turned down half a dozen times, but that's loyalty for you. Maybe I'm not always smart, but at least I'm loyal.

On the other hand, some flies fall out of favor as better ones, or ones that we perceive as better, come along. The bonefish crab patterns are a case in point. These days, I can't go on a bonefish trip without them. But ten years ago, they were not in my bonefish box; my only crab flies were large ones in my permit box.

Here are the Magnificent Seven.

1. Crab patterns (Merkins and the like) in sizes 4 and 6.
2. Gotchas in size 4 (a must-have in the Bahamas).
3. Clouser Minnows in sizes 2, 4, and 6 (mostly size 4 flies tied the way my son likes, very sparse).
4. Borski's Bonefish Critter and Borski Fur Shrimp.
5. Bonefish Specials (an old favorite that I designed in 1968 and still prefer for super-shallow fishing).
6. TK Special (Tim Klein's great fly for big bonefish).
7. Crazy Charlies, heavily weighted (for small and medium-size bones mudding in deep water).

I reserve the right to change any of the above at any time, and probably will. For now, though, that's my must-have list.

This bonefish fell for a small crab pattern.

FLY-TO-TIPPET KNOTS

I attach most bonefish flies with a loop knot because a free-swinging loop lets them sink faster with less weight, while also allowing the fly more action during the retrieve. But when fishing super-shallow water where I am fearful of hanging on the bottom no matter how light the fly is, I use a seven- or even eight-turn clinch knot (the standard knot, not the "improved" version) to keep the fly from sinking too fast. We look at these matters in more detail in chapter 11.

IS YOUR HOOK SHARP?

Once you have selected a fly and tied it to your tippet, you should always check that the hook is sharp by testing it against your thumbnail. If the point sticks in your nail, it's fine; if it slides, it needs to be sharpened. Generally, I sharpen a hook so that the point has a diamond-shaped cross section, but a triangular cross section is also fine.

Even after you have sharpened your hook, you still have to check the point every so often, because during the day the point will touch bottom a few times, perhaps hit the side of the boat while you cast, or bounce off a bony part of a fish's mouth during a hookup attempt. Check the hook frequently to see if it's still sharp. The best way to make sure that you do this is not to keep the hook file in your tackle box under one of the boat's hatches, but to keep the file with you at all times. That way, if you suspect that the hook may not be sharp enough, the file is right there; you take it out and touch up the point, and you are ready again.

IS YOUR BARB CRIMPED?

The purpose of a barb is to help keep the hook in the fish during the fight. In order to work, the barb has to penetrate some part of the fish's mouth. But the higher the barb, the harder it is to bury in the fish. A high barb also makes it harder for you to remove the hook from the fish's mouth. And it makes the whole experience very hard on the fish, too.

On the other hand, a hook that had no barb at all would penetrate very easily, but it would not hold nearly as well. So, a compromise is needed.

Some hooks have too much barb, and flies tied on them work better when you file down the barb as you sharpen the hook to no more than 50 percent of its original size. This helps a lot.

Better yet, crimp the barb down with a pair of strong pliers, turning it into a hump rather than a sharp prong. This makes hooking a fish infinitely easier, yet this hump will hold fish almost as well as the original barb would have. And because it can penetrate much easier and deeper, you often end up landing more fish with the crimped hook than the fully barbed hook.

How much to crimp? You can crimp all the way; this is easy and works great. I do this all the time and have landed everything from bones to billfish with fully crimped hooks. Or you can flatten the barb most of the way but leave a gap between the barb and the hook wire, creating a tiny barb, if you will. This also works great.

Fly fisher Bob Stearns, who has done lots of experimenting with barbless hooks throughout the years, wants more control in the crimping process. Bob takes strong pliers, and then, depending on how barbless he wants the hook to be, he mashes the barb down to whatever gap he desires. He controls the gap very carefully. If Bob is hooking lots of fish, he may crimp the barb all the way to the metal. But if he is looking for that one huge bonefish in the Upper Keys, maybe he will allow a bigger gap between the barb and the hook. Makes sense.

Most importantly, the fish benefits when you use a hook with a lowered barb. The hook causes less damage when being removed and comes out more quickly, letting you get the fish back in the water in no time. This is especially true when releasing a bone after a long fight on a hot summer day. The hot weather leaves the fish exhausted and raises the mortality rate after release. In the summer, it's very important that a bonefish go back in the water as soon as possible. Should a fish break off during the fight, a debarbed hook will be that much easier for him to get rid of so that he can return to his normal life.

So remember, a sharp hook and a low barb are the perfect combination for better penetration and faster release.

Chapter 6

Fly Lines for Bonefish

No other piece of fly-fishing gear has a bigger potential of making or breaking your day than your fly line.

—Bruce Richards, Scientific Anglers line designer

One of the most pleasant byproducts of my work as an outdoor writer and lecturer is taking groups of fly fishers to exotic destinations. These days, that often means a bonefish destination such as Belize, the Bahamas, Venezuela, or Islamorada in the Florida Keys.

During each of these trips, I fish with about a dozen anglers and get to see the selection and rigging of many outfits. If an angler has done a fair amount of bonefishing, bought his equipment from a good fly shop, or has previously fished on one of my trips, chances are good that his equipment is properly selected and rigged. But many anglers show up with outfits that are . . . well, let's just say that the bonefish need not fear the confrontation.

Poor rod and fly-line selection, inadequate backing capacity (what looks like a lot for fresh water is too little for the salt), short or soft leaders, and weak knots are among the problems I see. It's really a shame, after going to some exotic bonefish paradise and finding a big fish, not to be able to cast or present a fly properly, or to lose a big bone because of weak knots. The right outfit, properly rigged, is essential for meeting the high demands of today's bonefishing.

Most fly fishers start out by surveying fly rods first. "Which rod do I need for bonefish?" is the typical question. But you should start looking for an outfit by thinking about the size and weight of the fly you need to cast and the distance and accuracy needed for the presentation. Then you select the fly line you need. Once you have selected the fly line, and only then, you can start looking for a fly rod that will load well with it. Later, much later, after you have selected leader length, which will also govern rod length to some extent, you can think about reels.

These are the questions: What kinds of flies will I need to cast? Which fly line can carry these flies to the fish and provide the distance and presentation that I need? Which fly rod will cast this fly line? Then worry about reels. I've seen anglers buy the reel first! But until you select the flies, line, rod, and leaders, the reel is only a paperweight. So, let's select a bonefish fly line.

WEIGHT

In fly casting, the mass of the fly line in the air loads the rod and then drags the fly to its destination. In bonefish angling, you need a fly line heavy enough to carry the bonefish fly to a target in an environment that's often windy.

Since a typical bonefish fly is tied on a size 6, 4, or 2 hook, a 7-, 8-, or 9-weight fly line is usually ideal. If these lines seem a little too heavy for the size and weight of most bonefish flies, remember that most bonefishing is done on wide-open and often windy flats. A lighter fly line that would work fine on a flat-calm day will not work on most days. That's why bonefish angling usually calls for a heavier line than the size and weight of the fly might seem to indicate.

Where the average bonefish is smaller and most flies are sizes 4 and 6 (such as in the Bahamas, Belize, and Mexico), a 7-weight line is a great choice. In areas such as Miami and the Florida Keys, where heavily weighted, size 2 flies are more or less standard, an 8- or 9-weight is perfect.

If you had to have one outfit, and I refuse to have just one outfit, an 8-weight is surely the best all-around bonefish rig. It can handle both the big flies of the Keys and the smaller flies of the Bahamas or Belize. Personally, though, I prefer to have 7- and 9-weight outfits in the boat. On calm days and with small flies, the 7-weight does a better job than the 8, landing softly on the water. For casting large flies on typically windy ways, the 9 works better than the 8. Besides, having more toys is usually better.

If you want to use lighter rods for casting size 6 or 8 flies, a saltwater 6-weight outfit can be great fun. On a

These days, anglers have many choices in fly lines. For bonefishing, I prefer one with a stiff core that will not wilt in the heat, a mid-length head about 45 feet long for a controlled presentation, and a light, pastel color I can see while casting.

calm day when bones are tailing in very shallow water, it will often outfish the heavier outfits because the 6-weight line lands so softly. Just don't confuse this outfit with the slower-action 6-weight rods used in fresh water to cast Woolly Buggers and heavy nymphs. To fish the salt, you really need the faster, stiffer saltwater action.

I often find that an angler who has an 8-weight outfit wants a lighter rod to bonefish on very calm days, but a 7-weight is too close to an 8 to make a difference. In this case, a saltwater 6-weight may be the right choice, but you have to be a good caster to bonefish with a 6.

A few manufacturers are now producing 5-weight saltwater rods, and some fly-line manufactures are making bonefish lines to match, trying to extract more fun out of smaller bonefish. I'm all for fun, but it is my opinion that a 5-weight line (which weighs only 140 grains in the first 30 feet, compared to 210 grains for an 8-weight) is reaching the point of diminishing returns. Only on perfectly calm days, with sparsely tied small flies, and in the hands of a *very* good caster will such an outfit produce consistent results.

Anything lighter than a 5 is simply too light to cast the fly and battle even the slightest wind. While I have landed bones with 4- and even 3-weight rods, these light lines have no realistic application in bonefishing. It is more of a game or stunt that we all like to play sometimes. And it can be very frustrating because these lines are simply too light to carry even a size 8 fly. Once casting ceases to be fun, I don't feel that I am really fly fishing.

On the heavier side, a 10-weight line is simply too heavy and bulky for most quiet presentations to bonefish. A few anglers in the Florida Keys and south Florida area are still using them with some success, mainly for cruising or mudding fish on deeper flats. But a tailing bone usually spooks from such a heavy line hitting the water, no matter how long the leader. On a calm day, a 10-weight line puts you out of the game. However, 10-weights are great permit and barracuda fly lines because they have enough weight to carry and turn over the awkward permit crab flies or the extra weight of a wire shock tippet on a barracuda fly. You might want to have one in the boat, but it's not for bonefish.

Fly-line weights do not increase in a perfectly even progression. Here are the American Fishing Tackle Manufacturers Association (AFTMA) fly-line standards that have been in use for many years. The weight refers to the first 30 feet of line, exclusive of any short, level tip section past the front taper (usually only a few inches).

Fly Line	AFTMA Standard (in grains)
5	140
6	160
7	185
8	210
9	240
10	280

The difference between a 5-weight and a 6 is 20 grains, whereas the difference between a 9 and a 10 is 40 grains. Twenty grains constitutes a roughly 14 percent increase over the weight of a 5-weight line, while 40 grains is a 16 percent increase over the weight of a 9 weight. As you look at the numbers, you will understand why the difference between an 8-weight line and a 9 might feel greater than the difference between a 7 and an 8, or why a 10-weight rig feels a *lot* heavier than a 9. The differences are real.

TAPER

Once you have settled on a line weight, you select taper. The only type of taper to consider is the weight-forward design, because of its ability to sustain plenty of line in the air while you false-cast and still shoot long distances when needed.

But nothing is simple, and there are many different sizes, stiffnesses, and shapes of weight-forward lines. A good weight-forward line for bonefish angling needs to have several qualities. It needs to cast quickly in the wind, with a good degree of accuracy, and then present the fly delicately. This is a tough order. To cast fast, you need a line with a short head so that you can get enough weight out of the rod tip very quickly, but to cast accurately you want a longer head that provides more control. For casting into the wind, you need more weight up front to turn over the fly, but for delicacy you need a longer front taper. You need a line that does contradictory things. Still, today's manufacturers have fly lines for bonefishing (and any other tropical fish) that do a wonderful job compared to the lines we had only ten years ago. And they seem to be constantly improving them.

Your fly line also needs to stay stiff in the typically hot weather and be very visible while you cast. We'll look at these qualities in detail a little later.

A delicate presentation is mainly a product of a line's front taper design. One purpose of the front taper on a fly line is to transfer energy smoothly from the fly line to the leader and help turn the fly over. The constantly decreasing diameter of the front taper also makes for a nice, quiet presentation.

Everything else being equal, a longer front taper makes for a more delicate presentation, but it also makes the line more susceptible to the wind. The shorter the taper, the easier it is to turn over the leader into the wind, but a short front taper can make the fly land too hard on calm days or when you cast downwind.

You would think that in an environment that's so frequently windy, the shorter front taper would win. But thanks to their materials and construction, today's weight-forward lines cast into the wind very well, and most good bonefish lines have medium to long front tapers. Don't make the mistake of shortening the front taper too much just to gain turnover power. You may find yourself spooking more bones than you hook.

Ideally, to increase loop control and accuracy, you want a head long enough that the fattest part of the line, the belly, is still in the rod tip while you are false-casting. Having the belly of the line inside the rod tip while false-casting gives you greater control and therefore accuracy. But a weight-forward fly line with a head long enough to still be inside the rod when you are false-casting will reduce your shooting distance because of the resistance of the fat belly against the guides and tip-top. On the other hand, if the head is really short, and you are false-casting with ten or more feet of running line out of the tip-top of your fly rod, you are going to lose control and accuracy. The windier it gets, the less control you will have.

For accuracy and control, the ideal head length (the sum of the front taper, the belly, and the rear taper) is one that puts most or all of the head out of the rod tip on the great majority of your casts. You still have excellent control, but you can shoot line freely.

Since a beginner carries less line in the air than an advanced caster does, the ideal head length for one may not work for the other. Casting ability plays a part in selecting the ideal line for bones. If you are a beginner who can hold only 30 feet of line in the air before shooting, you are better off buying a fly line that has a shorter head. An advanced caster who can easily false-cast more than 50 feet on a windy day will want a line with a longer head. One of my favorite bonefish fly lines has a

40-foot (or longer) head, and with a 10- or 12-foot leader, it can help me make very good presentations in a great variety of conditions.

A bonefish line, like most premium fly lines today, is made by applying a coating over a core material. You can think of it as 30-pound-test braided line covered with plastic that adds weight and creates the desired shape. The type of core, the coating, and additives used in the fly line directly influence qualities such as flotation, stiffness, and memory.

The most often-used core materials are braided nylon, braided monofilament, and single-strand monofilament (this last is often called a mono-core line). In most saltwater fly lines, the core strength is 30 to 40 pounds, so you don't need to worry about breaking them on fish.

Braided nylon is very limp, but a line with this core can be made a bit stiffer with the proper coating. Braided monofilament, when combined with the right coating, can be made very stiff. Single-strand monofilament cores can also be made stiff, and they have the unique quality of producing a crystal-clear, slow-sinking fly line.

The coatings are mostly PVC or polyurethane—plastics or polymers—with a variety of additives that help achieve the desired properties. Among the additives are microballons or hollow glass air bubbles to make the line float, powdered metals, such as tungsten, to make it sink, lubricants for less friction, and stiffening or softening agents.

HOT-WEATHER LINES

You will generally fish for bonefish in a tropical setting with temperatures between the 70s and the low 90s. The sun is far more powerful than it is in temperate areas. Humidity ranges from high to very high. In these conditions, a regular freshwater fly line will sag like wet linguini between the guides of your fly rod, refusing to shoot through the guides or to slide back and forth as you try to double-haul. It's a frustrating experience to watch a bonefish tailing well within your casting range and then find that you simply cannot reach him because your fly line has become soft and sticky. The line may have felt fine early that morning when you tried a few casts. But by mid-morning, as the temperature rises, you may find that you can't shoot more than a couple of yards. It's maddening.

Fly lines for this environment need to be much harder and stiffer than their freshwater counterparts or saltwater lines made for cooler places. Most have a combination of a stiff core and a hard coating. And what a pleasure they are to cast in hot, sticky weather!

You can select from several types of cores and coatings from different manufacturers. Each company has its own solution to the hard-and-stiff requirement.

Using a single-strand mono-core is a good way to produce the stiffness required. Some very good bonefish lines, both floating and sinking, are made this way. Monofilament cores make possible the production of perfectly clear, slow-sinking lines that don't spook bonefish as much as opaque lines do. When you need a slow-sinking line, a clear one is a big advantage.

Another way to make a stiff line is to use a soft nylon core with a very hard coating. I find these lines good and stiff in hot weather, but not stiff enough. They typically float higher than other lines, but they're still too soft and often a bit sticky in very hot, humid weather. I like them for fishing from mid-Florida north for redfish and other species, but not as much for bonefish angling, though they work well enough from late fall to early spring.

My favorite solutions are lines made with braided-monofilament cores. These lines tend to be extra hard and stiff, and they stay slippery even in the hottest and most humid conditions. The coarse, almost pebble-grain texture of the running line (which is produced by the braided-mono-core beneath the coating) exhibits considerably less friction in the guides when you double-haul or shoot line. In the tropics, these lines shoot like no other weight-forward line I have tried so far.

But more stiffness means more memory. You must take the time to really stretch the line. If you have to crank the line onto the reel to try another spot a half-hour away, you may find that the line needs another stretching when you reach your new destination. Do it. It will pay off in great casting performance. A perfectly straight line always casts better. Once on the water, it will lie flatter than a line that still has some memory. And with practically no slack, you will be able to impart better action to the fly and set the hook faster.

North of the bonefish's world, the water becomes too cold for fly lines designed for the tropics. Once water temperatures fall below about 65 degrees, bonefish lines with braided-mono-cores require constant straightening. Switch to a more conventional fly line, such as one with a limp, braided-nylon core, which will work fine and not have the memory of the braided-mono-core.

As I was preparing to go to Alaska some years ago, I had all my tackle ready when I decided that I needed one more 7-weight floating line. Not wanting to rig another line the night before the trip, I just grabbed an already rigged Bonefish Taper. No problem, I thought. At camp two days later, with the thermometer at 40 degrees, the fly line did not want to come off the reel. When I finally stripped 50 feet out, the coils were so tight that they looked like a spring. No amount of stretching would help. The line wasn't the same until it got back to Miami a week later. So remember, these lines were not designed to be fished above bonefish territory. If you must take one to Alaska, wrap a nice wool blanket around it to keep it warm until you get back to the tropics.

DENSITY

Your first fly line, and maybe your only one for bonefish, should be a floating line. The essence of sight-casting to bonefish can be summed up as accuracy and control: accuracy to place the fly in front of a moving bonefish, and enough control to pick up the line quietly after a bad cast, change directions, and try again. A floating line meets these needs best.

A floating line moves through the air slowly and smoothly compared to sinking lines. This quality gives you plenty of time to decide whether it's headed in the right direction or not. It gives you time for corrections. And when you finally let a cast land on the water and it stills need redirection, a high-floating line will let you pick the whole line off the water and change directions.

Flotation has a price: air resistance. A fly line designed to float very high has lots of microballon air bubbles, and that means a larger diameter and more wind resistance than a sinking line the same weight. But since bonefish live in salt water, which is much more buoyant than fresh water, we can use floating lines that have fewer air bubbles and smaller diameters than their freshwater counterparts. The result is a line that casts into the wind much better and still floats high enough to provide the control you need. An added bonus is that these denser floating lines are much more durable than freshwater lines, which makes a difference in tough saltwater environment. Most contemporary bonefish lines are made this way.

Why go into all this detail about the construction of floating fly lines? One reason is so that you can understand why the tip end of a floating fly line or the running line sometimes sinks. A floating line has the most buoyancy where the coating is thickest, which is the belly of the line. Where the coating is thinnest—the tip and the running line—the line is least buoyant.

Not only does the line's tip have a very thin coating with relatively few microballoons or air bubbles, but it is also attached to a leader that is denser than water. By itself, the tip of the line barely has positive buoyancy; with a monofilament leader attached to it, the tip sometimes cannot remain afloat. But don't despair; there are things we can do here.

First, tie the leader to the fly line with the lightest possible knot. In salt water, this is probably a seven-turn nail knot. Put the minimum amount of protective coating on the knot. Since most glues are much heavier than water, a thick layer of Pliobond or whatever you use for coating knots will pull the knot under the surface, bringing the tip of the fly line with it. Apply line dressing to the tip of the fly line, the leader knot, and the butt of the leader to improve their buoyancy. Every time you dress the fly line, remember to dress it all the way into the leader's butt section. This will help a lot. Before casting, stretch the leader so it will lie flat on the water; the surface tension of the water will help it stay afloat a little longer.

Because the running line also has a very thin coating with relatively few air bubbles, it, too, barely floats, and sometimes it sinks a few inches. A thicker coating would make the running line more buoyant, but it would also make it too fat to shoot well. When you wade for bonefish, you will sometimes notice that some of the running line trailing in the water has sunk. There are things we can do here, too.

First, most anglers wading for bonefish drag more running line than they need, which only impairs their casting. The trick is to strip out only as much running line as you think you will need, considering the present situation of wind, visibility, and your own casting ability. The less line you have dragging behind you, the fewer problems you will have. If you do see a fish too far away for the line you have out, just strip out a little more and cast. The truth is that you seldom need to cast far and fast while wading. If you do need to cast far, you have time.

Be extra picky about keeping the fly line, especially the running line, well stretched. The less coiled the line is, the higher it will float. Finally, make sure that the whole line, but mainly the running line, is well dressed to help it float as high as possible.

These suggestions will help you a lot, but not all of the problems will disappear. That's part of the trade-off for great casting performance on the flats. It's worth it, believe me. If you don't want to put up with a line that needs some attention to stay afloat, you can always go back to a regular line. There are quite a few good saltwater-taper fly lines that work quite well in hot climates (and particularly in subtropical Florida) from late fall through early spring. But if you use them in extremely hot and humid summer weather, be prepared to put up with a soft and sticky line.

A great bonefish line is not an all-around line. It is a line made for a very specific and difficult environment. It will not float very well in fresh water. Its memory and stiffness increase in lower temperatures to the point of making it unfishable. But for sight-casting on the bonefish flats, these specialty lines are magnificent.

COLOR

In sight-casting, a fly line that you can easily see will give you better control and accuracy. A visible line also helps

STEPHEN FERNÁNDEZ

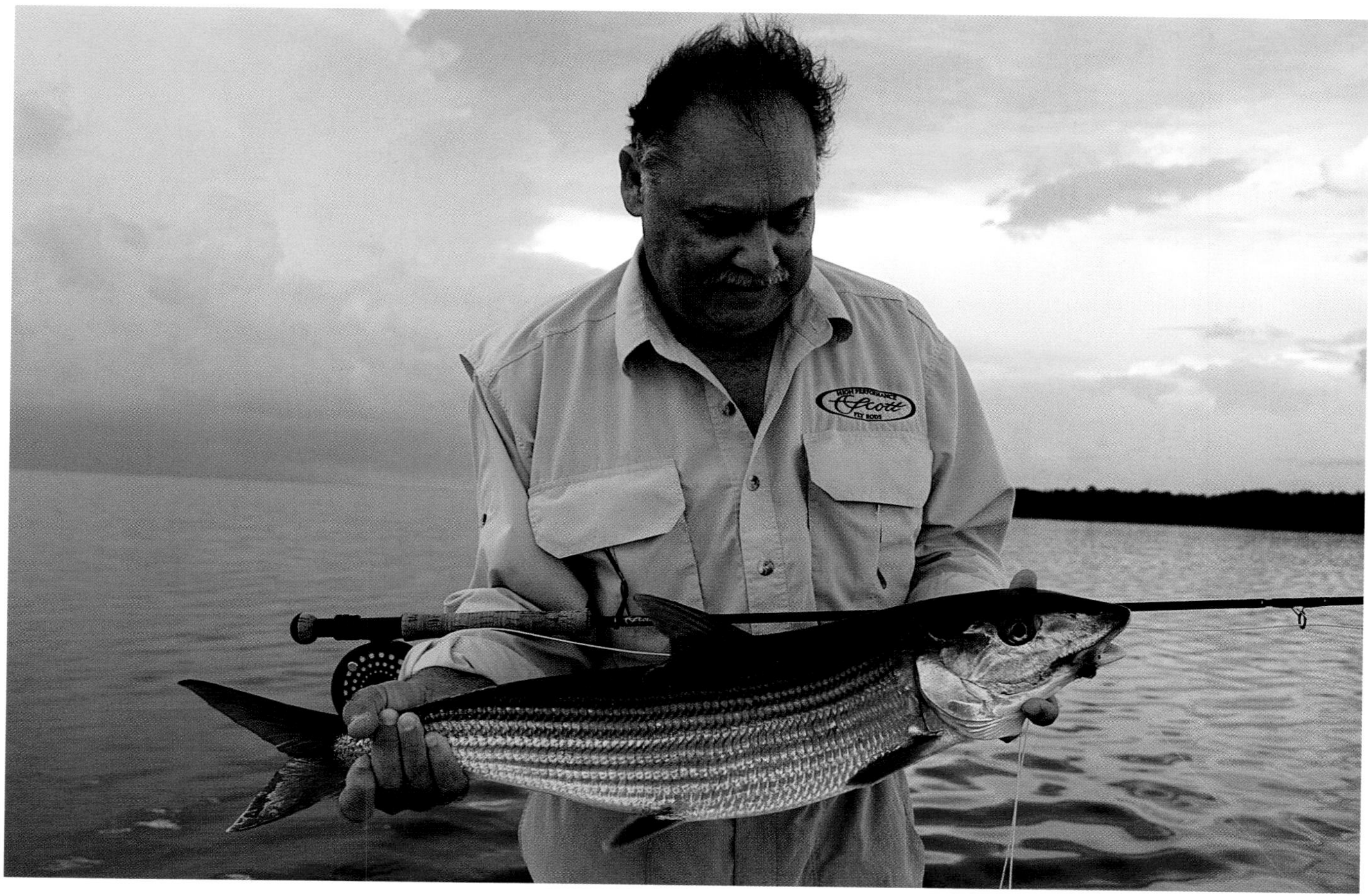

Early in the morning, when light and visibility are poor, a light-colored fly line is easier to see as you make that last false cast and get ready for an accurate presentation. Seeing the fly line in the air at this time is very important if you want to be accurate.

you determine whether your presentation is good or not, and can help you track the fly's movement.

Imagine you are casting to a big bonefish. Your eyes are locked on the bonefish, but your peripheral vision still sees the fly line moving through the air. As you false-cast, you constantly make corrections in timing, distance, and direction. Finally, you drop the fly, ideally in the right place. My point is that all these corrections and judgments were greatly helped by casting a fly line that was easily visible from the corner of your eye.

If you are not convinced, try casting a gray floating line, especially on an overcast day, and watch your timing and accuracy deteriorate. I tried such lines in the early 1970s and stopped using them after a few weeks.

When you make a good cast, a more visible fly line will help you determine where your fly is in relation to the fish. Suppose you made a 50-foot cast to a bonefish and the small, weighted fly disappeared as soon as it plopped into the water. You can still see the bonefish, but you can't see the fly. You don't know where the fly is in relation to the fish. You know it's close, but is it a good presentation, or should you pick up and cast again?

With a very visible fly line, you can easily see the end of the line out there. You know that you are fishing about a 10-foot leader, so you can make a good guess where your fly is and whether you should continue the presentation or try another cast. Bonefish guides use the end of the fly line all the time to judge a presentation and advise the angler. A visible fly line can be a big advantage in sight-casting.

Many anglers fear that a high-visibility line, such as a fluorescent orange one, will also be visible to the fish as you false-cast. What to do? There are so many theories around that one could fill several books.

I have my theory, too, which may or may not be 100-percent accurate, but it's based on a few facts that I feel are solid. Remember that we are talking about floating fly lines. If a bonefish sees a fly line during a cast, it is usually against the sky. I have looked at many different fly lines against the sky while sitting underwater in a swimming pool, and backlit against the sky, they looked remarkably similar to one another—sort of a dark gray, I remember. Besides, with a proper leader and a good presentation, you will never let the fish see the fly line. When you make the mistake of lining a bonefish (and we all do), he is going to leave the area in a rush—whether the line is pale, dark, or very bright.

Still, I must admit to a little apprehension about super-bright fly lines, even though I have caught many bonefish, permit, snook, and tarpon sight-casting with bright, fluorescent orange lines. Today, my favorite line colors for sight-casting to any saltwater fish are pastel colors (such as pale yellow, pale blue, or tan) and white. I can see these colors well enough to cast and fish the line, but I feel comfortable that they are not too bright.

SLOW-SINKING CLEAR LINES

You will probably never need any fly line but a floater for bonefish. Still, a case can be made for a slow-sinking, crystal-clear line on the bonefish flats. These lines, having no air bubbles in their coatings, sink slowly because they are more dense than water. That also means that they have a smaller diameter for the same weight and therefore cast much better into the wind.

If conditions are right, bonefish will still come onto the flats to feed on a very windy day, but the wind will play all kinds of games with a fat floating line. All but your best loops get blown off target as the wind pushes against the thick line. The fly line on deck also gets pushed around and often blows overboard. Accuracy is almost nonexistent.

A slow-sinking, clear line puts a new face on the situation. Its thinner diameter makes a sinking line much easier to cast in the wind, even into a stiff wind. The loose line on deck is less likely to be blown out of the boat. Since it's clear, the line is less likely to spook a bonefish. It sinks as soon as it touches the water, and waves have no effect on it. With a straight line between you and the fly, the slightest stripping movement will make the fly move.

On trips to the Bahamas and the Yucatan, I have fished with 6- and 7-weight slow-sinking lines in winds that would have forced me to use a 9-weight floater. The lighter outfit made every bonefish, even the little guys, fun to catch.

But like everything else in fishing, using one of these lines is a compromise. You feel some resistance when you try to pick up 40 feet of floating line from the water, but a long, slow stroke will break the surface tension and lift the line into the air for a backcast. But a slow-sinking line is *under* the water. The resistance is so much greater that you simply may not be able to pick up the line for a conventional backcast stroke, particularly if you have allowed the line to sink for a few seconds or you are trying to lift a fair amount of line. In both cases, you must retrieve the line to within about 30 feet before you can make a backcast. That costs time.

When you cast to a bonefish, a clear line completely disappears when it hits the water. You have no way to tell where your fly is in relation to the fish. Often, you can only guess about the accuracy of the presentation.

Still, while a floating line is the best bonefish line in most situations, these slow-sinking lines have a place on the flats. They're just not your everyday, workhorse lines.

CLEAR SINKING TIPS

A sinking-tip line is a weight-forward floating fly line with 10 to 13 feet of sinking line at the front end. Sinking-tip lines come in a great variety of densities, but we bonefishermen are concerned with only the slowest-sinking kind, which is a clear tip. Obviously, such a line has a single-strand monofilament core.

In bonefishing, the main advantage of a clear tip is that its greater density helps turn over a fly in the wind. But that's not the only advantage. By acting as the butt section of your leader, the clear tip lets you use a shorter leader that simplifies casting into the wind. Although it sinks slowly, the tip also helps you get a fly a little bit deeper while fishing for mudding bonefish in deeper water. But since most of the line floats, you can easily pick it up for another cast, something you can't often do with a full-sinking line.

Unfortunately, the clear sinking tips I have used to date seemed like they were made for fresh water. I found the lines, particularly the running portions, too soft for the high heat and humidity of the bonefish flats. It's only a matter of time, though, until at least one manufacturer comes out with a line that has a perfectly clear, slow-sinking tip and a belly and running line stiff enough for the environment of the bonefish flat. Perhaps it will have happened by the time you read this.

FASTER-SINKING LINES

Lines any denser than the clear, slow-sinking models have no place on the bonefish flats. They land too hard and sink too fast. I've taken hundreds of bonefish with fast-sinking lines—just not on the flats.

At many bonefish destinations, large schools of fish will mud in relatively deep water—five to more than ten feet—near the same flats that you came to fish. Once you start looking for them, these large muds become very conspicuous. Some are 100 or more feet wide by several hundred feet long.

I know that this is not real bonefishing, and many anglers frown on it, but if you approach it with the right attitude, you will enjoy a few hours of this fishing. Besides, sometimes the choice is fishing deep or going home. A few years back, I took a group to Los Roques, Venezuela. This area can produce great fishing, but not on the day we arrived. Strong winds and an outgoing tide had taken all the water off the flats, and as the winds continued they did not let the water back onto the flats—for several days! The flats were literally several inches out of the water. No bonefish on those flats, for sure.

But just a few minutes away by panga skiff, in about eight feet of water, there were acres of mudding bonefish. All you needed was a medium- or fast-sinking line.

In the three days that passed before the water finally returned to the flats, most boats with two anglers took dozens of bonefish on flies. I think the highest score was eighty-nine bones. We could have taken more than a hundred, but no one wanted to put in a full day of deep-water fishing with sinking lines. Still, it was great fun for a few hours a day.

If you care to do this, you will have to get the fly close to the bottom to get strikes consistently. In less than three feet of water, a floating line and a weighted fly will work, and in three to five feet of water, a Monocore (clear sinking) line will do fine. However, in deeper water than this, where one sometimes finds large schools of bonefish, a fast-sinking line is needed to get the fly down quickly and keep it close to the bottom where the bones are feeding and creating the mud. A six-foot leader and any weighted fly will do.

I have also taken yellowtail snappers, mutton snappers, jacks, and other species while fishing for bones in these muds. Great fun.

Of course, you may have to keep those fast-sinking lines hidden from your more purist fishing buddies, or word will get around at the club.

CLEANING AND DRESSING FLY LINES

Take good care of your fly lines and they will cast better, float higher, shoot farther, and last much longer. If you let your fly line stay dirty, it will not shoot or float as well. Because a clean line has less friction, it will develop higher speed through the guides while you false-cast or double-haul, and it will shoot farther. Dirt adds weight to a line, making it sit lower in the water or even causing parts of the line to sink.

How frequently you need to clean a fly line depends on how often you fish and where you fish. But you can easily see when your line is dirty, and you can easily tell by its performance, too.

If you are in the habit of applying dressing when the line does not perform at its best, first check to see whether it's dirty. A dirty line needs to be cleaned before it is dressed; otherwise, you just trap the dirt under a fresh coat of fly-line dressing. The line might feel slick again, but it still has all the dirt on it, and it will still float lower in the water, which makes it harder to pick up.

I like to use hand soap, a cloth, and warm water. Wet the cloth, soap it up, and gently scrub the line with the soapy cloth. Then rinse the line. Be sure not to use any strong detergents or solvents that may cause the line to crack.

Now that the line is clean, you may or may not want to apply dressing. Some lines are made with materials that constantly ooze some type of water-repellent lubricant, and they're not supposed to need dressing. Others need to be cleaned and then dressed. As long as a line looks clean, I generally apply dressing if I feel that the line is a bit dry and not shooting as it should.

One day in the early 1960s, I stood at the bar of the Rod & Reel Club in Miami Beach, almost at attention. The legendary Joe Brooks, that great pioneer of saltwater fly fishing, was leaning over the bar and explaining to a few of us the correct way to apply dressing to a fly line. If memory serves me correctly, this is what he said: "It will sound like a paradox. Put the dressing all over the fly line, and then take it all off. You won't be able to take it all off, of course. And what little dressing is left will be the ideal amount."

More than forty years have gone by since that day, and fly-line dressings and fly lines have come a long way. Even today, though, if you put the dressing on and then wipe it off, you can't go wrong.

I use the dressing recommended by the manufacturer of the fly line I am using, and I've never had a problem. Just apply the dressing by pouring a bit onto a cloth or an applicator and running the line through it so that it gets lubricated.

The little boxlike applicators are handy because you can keep one in your pocket to use at any time. Keeping the line dressing in your pocket is a big help when sight-casting from a skiff. Any time you feel that the line is not performing as it should, you can instantly dress your line. Experience has taught me that if I have to put the rod down, get off the front casting platform, get to the back of the boat and get my tackle bag, search for the dressing, go back up front to dress the line, go back astern to put the dressing in the tackle bag, and then come to the bow to start fishing again, I simply won't bother to do it. I will fish with a sticky line until I can't stand it. Believe me, dressing in your pocket is good.

As Joe Brooks advised us many years ago, don't leave excessive amounts of dressing on your fly line. If you do, the line may feel slippery in your hand, but in reality it does not have a lower coefficient of friction. With the excess dressing, it will pick up debris with superb efficiency, and that will only increase friction. So, put the dressing on and take it all off.

I never go fishing without my dressing kit, which consists of a small container of dressing, an applicator or a cloth to apply it, and a clean rag to wipe or buff the line clean. Everything fits in a heavy-duty Ziploc bag.

PROTECTING AND STORING LINES

Besides keeping fly lines away from certain detergents and solvents, you need to watch out for damaging substances while fishing. Fly fishing in the tropics means exposure to the sun and a variety of bugs. Almost always, you will apply sunscreen, and you will often need bug repellent. Insect repellents, particularly those containing DEET, are very harmful to fly lines. Many sunscreens can also hurt lines. I always clean the palms of my hands with water and a rag or towel to make sure that I do not transfer any repellent or sunscreen to the fly line. It really makes a big difference.

The secret to storing your lines has not changed over the years: keep them in a cool, dark place. Do the same with leaders and leader materials. The cooler the better. In fact, you could store your fly lines in the freezer or refrigerator, though this practice may not be permitted in some households. Get permission first. Or look for an out-of-the-way cool place in the house.

The glove compartment of your black station wagon is not the right storage facility. If a line stays inside a car through a series of very hot days, it will age very quickly and ultimately start to crack.

Keep lines in the dark. The number-one enemy of lines is ultraviolet light, which will bleach the color out of them and deteriorate the PVC coating. It is also hard on leader materials.

Besides these measures, I also wipe each line clean with a cloth before putting it away for a long time. This removes any harmful substances that might otherwise be on the line for several weeks or months.

Don't put a line away wet (by sealing it in a bag, for example). If you do, you may find that the line develops mildew, which you will have to wipe off. Not a fun chore.

Storing a line on your reel or a spare reel spool is fine. While the line may take a set after being stored a long time, all you have to do is give it a good stretch before you start fishing again.

Chapter 7

Fly Rods for Bonefish

It's Saturday morning, and our hero is headed to the local fly shop to purchase the ideal bonefish rod. And he is bringing reinforcements: with him are a couple of his buddies, one of them the club's expert. Expectations are high.

After wiggling most of the rods in the store (the owner and staff are used to excessive wiggling), they select three rods to test and take them outside. Using a fly line with about a yard of leader on a reel borrowed from the store, they take turns casting the three rods—as far as they can, ripping their shirts and popping off buttons as they double-haul with all their might. They quickly determine that one rod can cast the whole line for them easier than the other two can. That's the rod, they decide. After all, if it can cast 95 feet, it should easily cast 40 feet on the flats. Forty-five minutes after entering the store, our friend is headed home with his new rod.

The next weekend he goes fishing on the flats and tries the new rod. His first shot is at a tailing fish about 35 feet away. This should be easy, he thinks. But to his surprise, it takes forever to get enough fly line out to shoot some, and when he finally does, the line doesn't shoot very well.

The fish is still tailing, unaware of the angler. Our hero tries another cast, picking up about 30 feet of line, but the rod barely bends and he has no feel for what the line is doing, so he has no accuracy and drops the fly far to one side of the fish, which is still unaware of him. On his third try, holding more line in the air, he feels the rod load. He hauls and shoots. The fly lands well past the fish, and the fly line drops on top of him. The water explodes and the fish practically leaves some of his scales behind on his way off the flat.

A bit disappointed, our friend dresses the fly line for good measure (always a good idea) and strips all of it on deck. After a few false casts, he gets the rod working and shoots nearly the entire line. Well, it's working again, he thinks to himself.

The next fish is about 70 feet away. Instead of tailing, it's swimming at a fair speed toward the boat. Our friend cannot get the rod working in time, no matter how many false casts he makes. By the time he has 40 feet of line out, the fish is 30 feet away. You know the rest.

Later, over adult drinks, he has a conference with his buddies about the results. Many different opinions are voiced at such conferences, depending on the quantity and type of adult drinks consumed (for serious fly-fishing or jazz talk, I'm partial to single-malt Scotch at least twelve years old). But none of the opinions leads to a solution.

What really happened? Well, the tests our hero and his buddies performed determined the best rod for casting very far (the stiffest one, most likely) without a fly and without worrying about turning over a long leader. That's great, if they planned always to fish at 90 feet with a short leader and no fly and to cast only to fish that waited for them to throw that much line. But to make the typical 25- to 65-foot bonefish cast with the added weight and wind resistance of a fly, they needed a different rod, probably a softer one.

The rod they got may have been a good rod, but it was too stiff for the purpose. Once the angler had enough line in the air, say 50 feet or more, and therefore more weight pulling on the rod tip, the rod started to bend, the caster could feel it working, and he could shoot lots of running line. It is probably a fine rod for making long casts in the surf. Let's hope that our friend likes the surf, because he owns the right rod.

Select a fly rod for bonefish (or any other fish) by line weight first. Then by length. Next, decide how many sections you need. Finally, select the action, which, roughly speaking, is the rod's stiffness and the shape in which it bends.

LINE WEIGHT

As we noted in the last chapter, you select line weight, and therefore rod weight, according to the size, bulk, and weight of the fly. The best all-around line for bonefish angling is probably still the 8-weight. It can do almost everything. If I could have only one rod for the Bahamas and the Florida Keys, it would probably be an 8-weight. But I'm not limited to one rod. Furthermore, it doesn't make sense to travel to some bonefish destination for a few days or a week with just one rod. Let's see what other line weights can do for you, since sooner or later you will carry more than one rod to take advantage of all the opportunities—not only with bonefish, but with permit, mutton snappers, barracudas, and many other species, too.

Some areas tend to produce lots of small to midsize bonefish. The Bahamas, Belize, Christmas Island, Los Roques in Venezuela, and Mexico are among these places. This doesn't mean that you will never face a big bonefish at one of these destinations; you probably will. But because the average fish is small, the flies are usually tied on size 4 or 6 hooks. In these areas, I prefer to drop down to a 7-weight rod or even a 6-weight. The lighter rods, with their lighter fly reels, are fun to cast and can handle smaller flies easily. When you do hook up, any bonefish is a great adventure on a light-line rod. On a calm day, a light line lands softly and spooks fewer fish than a heavier line does. I bet that you'll land more fish on a flat-calm day with your 7-weight than your buddy with a 9-weight will.

At the very extreme of the light bonefish outfits is the 5-weight. With ultra-small flies and on a calm day, a 5-weight rig can work. There are even a few 5-weight bonefish fly lines and 5-weight saltwater fly rods. To me, though, this is going too far. A 5-weight outfit is just not practical. I have landed small bonefish with 3- and 4-weight fly rods, but it was stunt fishing and I did not enjoy it. The lightest rod that I recommend for bonefish is a 6-weight, and even it will work only under ideal conditions. And I don't mean a soft 6-weight trout rod, but a true saltwater-action rod.

Now let's go to a place like the Florida Keys, where the average bonefish is huge and the flies are also huge, at least by bonefish-fly standards. Here, a typical fly can be size 2, heavily weighted, and bulky. The crab flies for bones in the Keys are the size of the permit flies used in most other places. To cast these flies accurately in the wind, you need a heavier line.

In places like the Keys, my preference is an 8- or 9-weight outfit. Since the flies I use in southern Florida and the Keys keep getting a little bit bigger every few years, I am starting to use a 9-weight more and more. If I decide to try a small fly on a flat-calm day (and occasionally a small fly works very well with these big fish), I may go to a 7-weight. Maybe. But my workhorse rods in the Keys are 8- and, increasingly, 9-weight rigs.

A few old-timers still use 10-weight outfits for the big bones in the Keys. These heavy rigs can work well in deeper water, especially for mudding fish. But a tailing fish or a cruiser in shallow water usually spooks from such a heavy line, no matter how long a leader you use. A 9-weight can cast any bonefish fly I have seen so far, though 10-weight outfits can be great barracuda and permit rods, and also serve as light tarpon rods.

Here's what I usually have in the skiff these days. In the Bahamas, Belize, and similar places, I may carry a 7-weight for bones and a 9 for permit and barracudas. In the Keys, maybe an 8-weight for bones in shallow water and a 9 for windy flats, permit, and bonefish in deeper water. I might also have an 11-weight rigged for tarpon or sharks.

LENGTH

By now, you know the requirements. The rod needs to make fast casts, usually between 25 and 65 feet, with the greatest possible accuracy. The day might be calm, windy, or very windy. The target is usually moving, often erratically. Casting distance, the fish's speed, wind force and direction, and other factors change constantly. Fun, isn't it?

After reading these requirements, one might conclude that bonefish angling calls for a very specialized rod. It doesn't. Day in and day out, a 9-foot rod is king on the flats. It is simply a very good all-around rod.

There are, however, reasons to deviate a little from the 9-foot length. A slightly shorter rod feels lighter in the hand and lighter while casting. Although the rod might actually weigh a fraction of an ounce less than a 9-footer, that's not why it feels different; after all, the reel alone may weigh over 10 ounces with the backing and fly line. The shorter rod feels lighter because it has less leverage against you when you hold it and when you cast.

A good short rod can be great fun to fish with. You will also find a shorter-than-average rod more accurate, partly because the line is a little closer to your eyes, but mostly because the rod magnifies side-to-side movements of your wrist less than a 9-footer does. Many tournament casters use shorter rods in accuracy competitions. And a good short rod will help you produce a tighter loop easier than the longer rods. On windy or overcast days, when low visibility forces you to make plenty of quick, short casts into the wind, short rods are at their best.

The biggest bonefish I have ever landed, a 14-pound fish, was taken on a very windy day with poor visibility. I used an 8-weight rod measuring 8 feet, 8 inches long. Worked like a charm. That rod is also a great choice for casting accurately against a shoreline all day without tiring.

On the other hand, a short rod cannot pick up quite as much line (to correct a cast, for example) as a 9-footer can. In theory, the shorter rod cannot cast as far, though a good caster can still throw the whole line with a short saltwater rod, and casting 65 feet is no problem.

A long rod, such as a 9½-footer, also has advantages. For starters, a longer rod with the proper action will cast a bit farther. But remember that you still have to learn to cast well to make a long cast. A longer rod will not help a poor caster. You need to have the stroke before you can reap the benefits.

A longer rod will pick up a bit more line from the water for a quick second cast. If your fly lands a few feet off the mark, you can pick up the whole 50-plus feet of line and drop it back again with one false cast. The extra length also allows the rod to easily handle a longer leader.

On a calm day when fish are spooky and hard to approach, the long rod can help a lot. It can make a longer cast with a longer leader, dropping the fly softly on the water. And if you miss, you will find it easy to pick up and cast again.

On the other hand, the extra length makes the rod a bit less accurate. If you're casting all day, a long rod is more tiring. But since bonefishing doesn't involve lots of casting all day, this is not a big factor.

My favorite use for longer rods is while wading, because my casting hand is closer to the water and the long rod lets me more easily keep the backcast high. This is no substitute for learning how to cast properly; until you do, all these different rod lengths will make no difference.

If I were selecting a long rod for bonefish, I'd probably choose either a 7- or an 8-weight model, depending on the types of flies I anticipated casting with it. Most 9½-foot 6-weights are a bit too soft, and most long 9-weights feel too heavy for bonefishing. These are just my opinions, of course.

There is such a thing as too long. For me, 10- and 10½-footers are too heavy and clumsy for the fast, accurate casting that is the norm in bonefishing. These rods are, by their very length, much heavier in actual weight. They feel tip-heavy, too, which makes them very tiring to cast. The extra few feet of line they may be capable of casting is totally immaterial in bonefishing. They are much less accurate, and that most definitely is material.

In theory, give me a short rod in the wind and a long rod on calm days. One can never have too many fly rods.

MULTIPIECE RODS

It used to be, not many years ago, that unless an angler needed a four-piece rod for a special reason (backpacking, for instance), he automatically bought a two-piece rod. And he was right to do so. Not that long ago, most multipiece rods cast like department-store rejects. But that is not true today. Most top-of-the-line multipiece fly rods today are excellent and in some cases surpass their two-piece counterparts. Most of the rods I get these days are multipiece models. The main reason, of course, is travel.

With more and more fishing pressure on our local waters and the ease of traveling to a remote fishing camp, a great number of us are traveling more and making it a way of life. Besides, bonefish camps, by their very nature, are much less expensive than most other camps.

When I started fishing at bonefish camps abroad, almost all airlines would accommodate the awkward two-piece rods that most anglers used. In the closet, under the seat—there was always a way. But, as you know, today it's different. You often have to be ready to check your rods. And if you do get a chance to carry them on the airplane, they'd better be multipiece rods.

Reaching a remote fishing camp generally requires a short flight in a small plane. Chances are that if you have two-piece rods, eventually you'll have to get on a plane that has too little space inside to accommodate your rods. Unless you know that you are not going to travel, ever, you are much better off getting a multipiece rod.

All the better manufacturers make their saltwater rods in three-piece or four-piece designs. Some make them in both. Believe me, you have choices. A case that holds three-piece rods is about 39 inches long, and one for four-piece rods is only 30 inches. I often travel with the 39-inch case because it can hold both the four- and three-piece models. There are also some fine five-piece rods on the market, and they are a bit smaller to pack. But for my tastes, this is getting beyond the point of diminishing returns.

Get one of the many PVC cases on the market, put your rods in their cloth sacks, and make sure they are nice and snug inside the case—no loose rods rattling around. They should travel fine that way. I have heard of a few rod cases being broken by baggage handlers, but I have never witnessed any. It happens, of course.

Your rod's ferrules should not need much care, other than keeping them clean. Should the ferrules start to get squeaky when you join or separate the rod sections, try wax or paraffin. Take the wax and paint one or two lines on the male ferrule. *That is all.* The wax should stop the noise, and it will help keep the ferrules from loosening too quickly and thus coming apart during repeated casting.

ACTION

"Action" is the common word in the industry for the way a rod bends. It's not a very precise term, at least as it's commonly used. Actually, there are two parts to a rod's action: the shape of the bend, and how much effort it takes to bend the rod (in other words, the degree of stiffness).

If the upper third or so bends during the cast, the rod is said to be a fast-tip rod or fast-action rod. If the rod bends into the middle (more or less), it is said to be a medium action. And if it bends deep into the bottom of the blank, almost to the cork, it is said to be a slow rod. In terms of stiffness, a rod can be stiff, medium, or soft.

But what I want you to understand is that a rod can be slow and stiff. In other words, the rod may be hard to bend, but when it does bend, it bends all the way into the butt. The tip is probably straight and stiff all the time. Or it can be a fast-action rod with a soft tip. There are many combinations.

I like a rod stiff enough to support a long cast when needed or to drive a tight loop into the wind. But I also want a tip section sensitive enough that I can feel the rod load when I need to make a quick, short cast. This, in my opinion, is the rod you need for bonefish, and there are many good ones on the market today.

The bend of this rod would probably fall somewhere between medium and fast, depending on your tastes and casting style. I find that Type A personalities select faster rods than Type B personalities. Better casters tend to select faster rods.

There are some very good slow and/or soft rods on the market, but I just don't feel that a soft or slow rod is the right tool for casting accurately and quickly in a windy environment. It can be done and done well, if you carry the stroke a little longer so that the tip does not collapse. But I just don't care to do it.

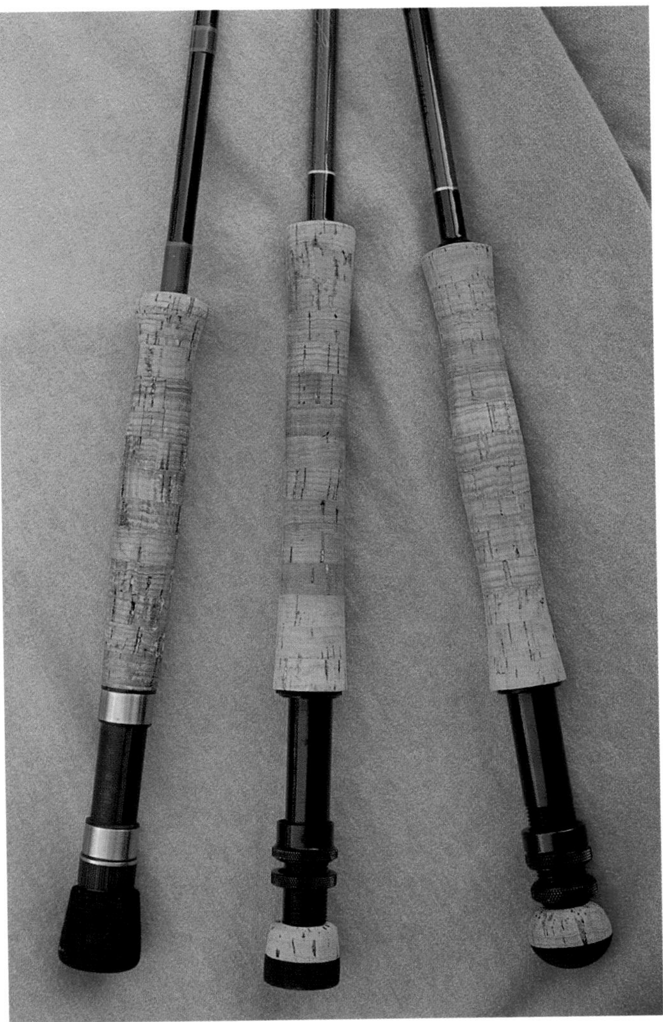

Whether it's a half Wells, Ritz, or full Wells design, the grip of a saltwater fly rod should flare at the top and offer a place where your thumb can apply power.

MISCELLANEOUS CONSIDERATIONS

I like a full Wells grip on saltwater rods. The flare of the cork at the top of the grip fits my thumb just right for control and power, and the flare on the bottom lets the hood of the reel seat fit inside the grip so that the reel sits just a tad closer to my hand, which helps a bit in casting all day. It's a subtle thing, but it matters (to me, anyway).

I also like an uplocking reel seat that keeps the reel closer to my hand. This makes for more comfort while casting. Expensive rods all have uplocking reel seats, but many lower-priced rods do not.

On bonefish rods, I like a fighting butt just long enough to keep the palming rim of my reel off my belt when I fight a fish or crank line. If the fighting butt is too long, your fly line will often wrap around it, usually as a big bonefish starts his first run.

WHAT TO BRING TO THE STORE (BESIDES YOUR BUDDIES)

Let's go back to the store and find a great bonefish rod. You are trying to find a rod with an action that, in your hands, will perform as close to ideal as possible on the bonefish flats. But you're going to the fly shop, not the flats, and will probably test the rods on a strip of grass. That's fine. To reproduce as closely as possible the conditions of the flats, you should bring a few things with you.

First, of course, bring your favorite fishing hat and glasses. It is safer and more realistic to cast while wearing them. Bring the reel and line that you are going to use with the new rod. If you are also going to buy the fly line, then borrow from the store exactly the same type of line that you intend to purchase. Have the line rigged with a 10- or 11-foot leader that has a long, stiff butt

A medium-action rod loads into the midsection of the blank under the load of a weight-forward line. This rod will give the caster good distance and very good accuracy.

section. Bring a tape to measure your casting distances. I don't want you to estimate casting distance; this time, you really need to know.

I also want you to bring a couple of flies. Yes, I know that you can cast much better without a fly. But you need to know how the different rods cast while towing a fly and how well they will turn over the fly at the end of the cast. This is very important. You can't evaluate a rod until you cast a fly with it. A soft-tip rod may have just enough power to move the fly line really well, but faced with the extra weight and wind resistance of a fly, it may slow down too much. You need to know this on the lawn, while the store owns the rod, and not on the water, when you own the rod.

Finally, if you want to carry this test a bit further, you could bring an extra identical reel, line, leader, and fly. This will facilitate comparisons, especially when you are down to two rods.

For testing accuracy, bring something to simulate a fish. I have a pillow in the shape of a 10-pound bonefish. But a two- or three-foot stick will do. Do not bring a ring. You have to get used to casting in front of your target, not *on* your target, or you are going to spook lots of fish. Keep your test drives as realistic as possible, and you will avoid surprises when you get to the flats with your new rod.

TEST-CASTING

You decided that you need a 9-footer for an 8-weight line, and now you are shaking and wiggling every 8-weight in the store, looking to select a few rods to test on the lawn. As you do this, remember what you are looking for. A knowledgeable salesperson may be able to help you here—but not with the final decision.

Lawn and water are both fine for test-casting. Do not cast your fly line in a parking lot; you could ruin it pretty quickly. Drive to a park or sports field if necessary.

Resist the temptation to cast without a fly. It proves nothing.

Rig the first rod with a fly and get ready to cast.

The rod should bend enough during short casts for you to get a feel for the weight of the fly line, leader, and fly. You should see and feel the rod bend, regardless of action.

At this point, resist the temptation to strip out the whole line to try casting as far as you can. And keep in mind that the most important thing on every type of cast you make is whether the fly is turning over. A 70-foot, tight-loop cast in which the fly landed behind the fly line is a bad cast. The fly's position on the lawn will show you that.

If it's windy, start by casting sideways to the wind. For now, I don't want the wind to either help you or hurt you.

Start with a 30-foot cast. Cast normally, and then try making a delivery with your backcast. Is the line easy to cast, or are you making an effort to flick the rod to load it at that short distance? Is the loop just as nice or almost as nice on the backhand cast? Is the fly turning over and landing ahead of the leader? Walk over and check for yourself that the leader straightened; don't guess.

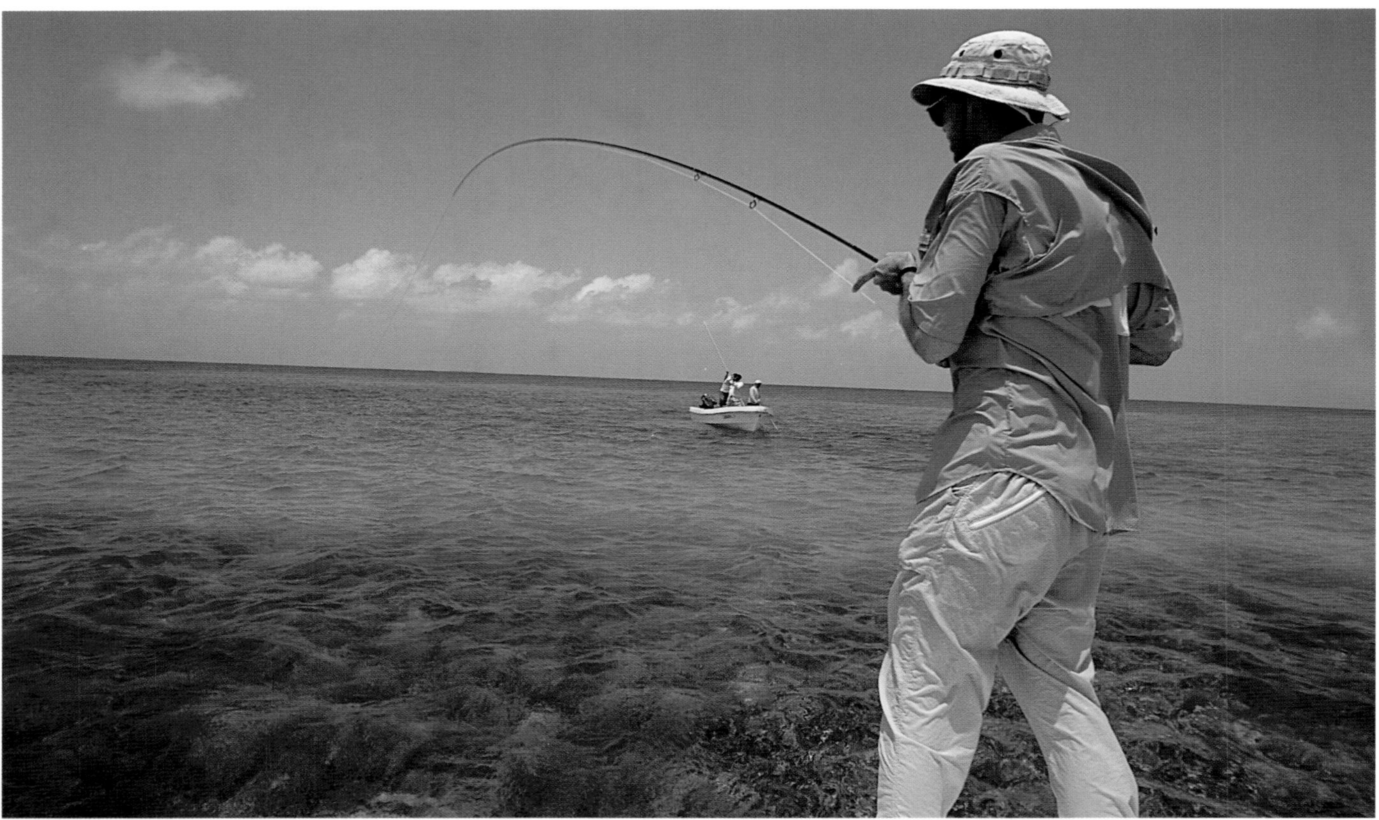

When you hook a bonefish, the rod acts as a shock absorber to keep you from breaking the tippet. The angle of the rod changes constantly during the fight, but a good all-around angle, one that lets you apply pressure while still having some cushion, is around 45 degrees.

Now check loop control. Are all the loops more or less the same on all of your casts? As you and your friends take turns, watch one another and pay attention to the line in the air.

Try the next rod and then the next, all with short casts. See how they stack up against one another in *your* hands.

Now try casting at medium range, say 50 feet or so, Measure the distance, don't estimate it (but do estimate fish; they'll be bigger). Take turns and try every rod.

Next, try making the "fast draw." Starting with the fly in your hand, see how many false casts it takes you to present the fly at, say, 40 feet. A good fast-draw rod feels smooth through the whole process.

If it's windy, and I hope it is, try casting against the wind. Is the fly turning over? This exercise is not about which rod casts the farthest, but which one turns the fly over at a variety of distances and with good accuracy.

A word about the importance of casting from your backhand. When you're standing in a skiff, half the opportunities come from the wrong side. Generally, the only way to present the fly to a fish approaching from your right side (if you're a right-handed caster) or behind you is to make a backhand cast. You can't simply turn around and cast normally, because you might hook the person on the poling platform or some part of the boat. In saltwater angling, presenting a fly on the backcast is an everyday skill. I tend to make a better backhand cast with a slightly softer rod than I need for regular casting. It's all a compromise, isn't it?

It's also a good idea to have your friends watch your backcast and make sure that it stays high, not touching the grass or, worse yet, dragging on it.

You may also find that one of the "8-weight" rods casts better with a 9-weight line. To me, that's a 9-weight rod that has been mislabeled, at least for you. Let that one go.

Finally, go ahead and make the longest cast you can. It is not important in this test, but I know, and you know, that you are going to do it. Just don't count the length unless the fly turns over. Getting rid of all the line and having the leader and fly land in a pile does not count. It doesn't count while fishing, either.

At the end of these tests, the best rod should stand out. Buy the rod and go home. The next time you get together with your friends, you will be showing photographs of a big fish instead of telling hard-luck stories.

Don't worry about the colors and appearances of rods. When you find a rod that is just right for you, it is going to look beautiful. Love is blind, you know.

Chapter 8

Fly Reels for Bonefish

If you don't enjoy just cranking your fly reel in the living room, you've got the wrong reel. —*Bob MacChristian, designer of the Seamaster fly reel*

Bonefish are fast, powerful for their size, and, on rare occasions, capable of making a first run of well over 100 yards. That's more than the length of a football field. Since most bonefish fly reels are 4 inches in diameter or less, the reel feels as if it's turning at 6,000 rpm during that first run. It is pushed to the limits of its design and materials. I have experienced thousands of those first runs over the past forty-plus years, yet the next one will still thrill me as much as the first. And I've learned that having the right reel matters very much.

I started bonefishing in the mid-1950s, when most reels had clicker drags (like my Hardy Zenith and St. George) or very light drag systems (like my Pflueger Medalist 1496 and 1498). The old reels would vibrate like crazy during a bonefish's run. After a day's fishing, they needed extra care to prevent corrosion, but there was always rust somewhere on a reel; it was inevitable in the saltwater environment. Many reels did not survive more than a few years, and others did not survive a single season. Today, we have reels with great drags and nearly total resistance to the salt.

Here I am in the late 1960s with a Hardy St. George clicker reel, a Scientific Anglers fiberglass rod, and a Miami bonefish.

When you fish on the flats, nearly anything that you hook—bonefish, permit, barracudas, mutton snappers—will fight hard, and most fights last some time before one of you wins. If you fish the bonefish flats often enough, sooner or later you will face a really big fish such as a large permit or tarpon when you don't have another rod available. I have taken several tarpon to 70 pounds on 8-weight rods and one 100-pound fish on a 9-weight rod. Two of my friends, Capts. Steve Huff and Flip Pallot, have taken tarpon over 100 pounds on 8-weight outfits. A permit over 40 pounds is always a possibility.

Now, I'm not saying that you should deliberately fish for 100-pound tarpon with an 8-weight rod. Eventually, though, you are going to face a really big fish with only your bonefish outfit, and I know that you are going to make the cast. I would, and I have. So be ready with a good fly reel.

Select a fly reel by these criteria: capacity, proportions, simplicity, weight, drag, and then a few miscellaneous features. And finally, by looks. Yes, looks.

Before we examine reels, we should spend a moment on backing. Because the fly line is only 90 to 100 feet long, you need quite a bit of extra line—backing—to cope with a fish that makes a long run. On the flats, you want a couple of hundred yards of backing.

In my opinion, Dacron is still the best material for backing. It doesn't stretch very much and it's thin enough so that a lot of it will fit on a bonefish-size reel. In the past, some anglers have tried monofilament for backing. Don't do it. Because mono stretches so much (30 percent in many cases), it can produce extreme pressure on the reel's spool when wound on under tension, such as during a long fight with a strong fish. Sooner or later, the tightly stretched mono will create enough pressure to bend or break the spool. I have seen that happen a few times. Furthermore, when you fight a fish that has made a long run, Dacron's low stretch will help you apply pressure to bring him back. You don't want the rubber-band effect of mono.

In recent years, GSP (gel-spun polyethylene) line has become all the rage in some circles for backing. Its advantage is that it is much thinner for its strength than Dacron, effectively increasing a reel's capacity by a big margin. In theory, this is good. These days, though, a typical bonefish reel carries more than 200 yards of Dacron backing and the fly line. That's more than enough. Being able to carry, say, 400 yards of gel-spun line does not help at all. At the same time, gel-spun backing is so thin and abrasive that it can easily cut you to the bone if it touches your hand while a fish runs.

I should note that Scientific Anglers has a highly lubricated gel-spun backing that seems much less abrasive than other kinds as of this writing. Still, I normally don't need the extra capacity. The one situation in which an angler may want gel-spun backing for bonefish is if he is using a small fly reel with limited capacity, either because it's part of a light outfit or because it's the only reel he has. In this case, gel-spun polyethylene line might let the little reel hold enough backing. But that's a rare situation. If you have a proper bonefish reel, stick to Dacron.

CAPACITY

The first consideration in selecting a reel is capacity. A reel has to accommodate the whole fly line and enough backing. One that holds the fly line and 200 yards of 20-pound-test backing has more than enough capacity for any bonefish's run. Although anglers use outfits as light as 5-weight to as heavy as 10-weight, the amount of backing required is about the same on all these rigs.

Common sense may tell you that 200 yards is too much. The average small bonefish runs less than 40 yards, and the average big bone does not run much over 100 yards, and even that's unusual. But there are reasons for the excess capacity. For one, you are fishing tropical flats at the edge of the ocean, and you could hook a giant bonefish, a 40-pound permit, or some other large fish. If that happens, you would gladly trade your favorite rod for an extra 100 yards of backing. An extra-long run can happen anytime in the salt.

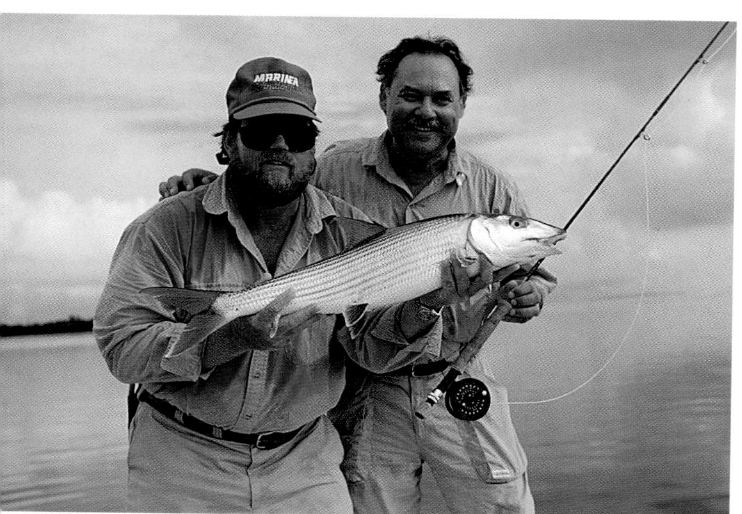

Capt. Mike Ehlers and I with a very strong ocean-side bonefish that made a long run against a light tippet. You remember these moments.

Even if you never hook a monster fish with your bonefish outfit, the extra backing still helps you. If you use a small reel with little capacity, many bonefish will take out most of the backing on their first runs. When you fight a fish close to the end of your backing, the circumference of line remaining on the spool becomes very small. When the fish finally stops and you begin to regain line, each turn of the handle brings in only a few inches of backing. It is exhausting to fight a fish with such a slow retrieve. Look for a reel that holds 200 yards.

The color of the backing also makes a difference. Highly visible backing is often a great help during the fight because the person following the fish, either by poling the boat or idling the engine, can easily track the fish by looking at the backing. This is especially true in low light levels like those early and late in the day or on heavily overcast or rainy days.

You might be wondering how I am so sure that bonefish do not run 200 yards. After all, the first run always looks so far into the horizon. Well, many years ago I got into an argument with some older fly fishers in the Keys who told me that bones run 200 yards all the time, often 300 yards. No one won the argument. But I went home and did an experiment.

My backing in those days was light-colored or white. I stripped 100 yards of backing off my reel, measured it carefully, and then dyed the next 10 yards bright red. If a fish ran over 100 yards, the 10 yards of highly visible red backing would come out and I would notice it.

In the next year and a half, I landed several big bones that ran very far, a 20-pound-plus dolphin, midsize tarpon, and other nice fish with that reel. I forgot all about the red backing until one summer day while fishing the flats in the Everglades for sharks. Most of the sharks we were casting to weighed from 40 to 60 pounds, but eventually I hooked one that went well over 100 pounds, and, boy, did he make a run! We could see him way out on the flat, still running. It really did look like a 200-yard run. We just couldn't catch up with him. And then the red backing came out. I had forgotten all about it, but instantly I knew that the shark's run was just over 100 yards. A long run, but not a 200-yard run. Not even close.

I ran into the old-timers after hooking that shark but thought it wise not to mention the incident to them. They seemed happy with their 200-yard runs, and I was happy with my newly gained knowledge. Diplomacy, you know.

PROPORTIONS

Once you have found several reels that have the capacity you need, think about the proportions or shape of the reel. The relationship of width to diameter plays a big part in the performance of a reel. Two reels can have the same capacity but have very different proportions—one has a small diameter but is very wide from side to side, while the other is bigger in diameter but narrower. Faced with that choice, go for the big, narrow reel.

The bigger reel will retrieve faster, even after is has yielded 80 yards of backing. That's very important because you will be able to keep the line tight during the fight. When a big bone runs at its usual high speed, the bigger spool will turn slower to yield the same amount of line, and therefore will be easier to control and easier to feather with your hand to apply extra drag. Between trips, the fly line will rest in a larger circle and develop less memory. It's a win-win situation.

One way to get the fast retrieve is to use a large-arbor reel. This is a reel that's both large in diameter and wide. The arbor—that is, the center of the spool—is very big, so that all the line lies on a large-circumference, wide, fairly shallow area. When a fish makes a long run, the diameter of the line remaining on the spool barely diminishes; the circle simply doesn't get much smaller. That does two things: the spool turns at the same speed during the entire run (as opposed to spinning faster and faster as a fish takes line), and you can recover line quickly (thanks to the spool's large circumference) when a big bonefish stops after 80 or 90 yards. To keep these larger reels light enough, most manufacturers use slightly thinner walls or put more or larger perforations in the spool and frame.

Most of the reels I use in salt water these days are large-arbor models. Once you get spoiled by the super-fast retrieve, it's hard to go back to a conventional reel. I recommend this design over most others. But a big and narrow reel, even without a large arbor, can still work very well.

Back in the 1960s, I fished mostly with small, wide fly reels. I liked their looks and did not want to change. But my old friend Lee Wulff tried many times to convince me to change. "Go for the narrow drum, Chico," he would say (we called spools "drums" then). I did not pay attention to that advice for a few years, but eventually I came around. Lee was right again.

SIMPLICITY

Open up a top-quality fly reel and look inside it, and you might think that you got taken. There are almost no parts in it, especially when compared to your spinning or bait-casting reels. But that is as it should be. If the reel does all that it needs to do, then the only improvement would be to make it even more simple so that it's more reliable.

Every year a few new reels come onto the market promising even smoother drags or greater ease of retrieve. Some of these reels have many parts that complicate taking them apart. With some, changing spools is tricky. Don't buy such a reel. You want a simple one. You will find that most of the well-respected fly reels today are simple inside. That's part of what makes them great.

While looking to buy a new fly reel, have the store owner take the spool off and show you the inside of the frame. It should be a fairly fast and simple operation.

You should know how to take your reels apart. Sooner or later you'll have to take a reel apart in the field or at a remote fishing camp, if only because a little sand found its way inside. You should be able to open it (that is, take the spool off), clean and lubricate the parts, and put the reel back together with no problems. If your reels require any tools for disassembly, bring them with you on a trip.

WEIGHT

If a large-arbor reel provides a much faster retrieve, and if the fast retrieve is important, then why not just get a bigger reel? Why not put a tarpon-size reel on a bonefish rod? It would certainly retrieve faster than a smaller reel—and carry 600 yards of backing that you don't need, too.

The reason is weight. A tarpon reel on an 8-weight rod will throw the outfit out of balance and make it feel like a 10-weight. What you really want is a reel light enough to make an 8-weight rod feel like a 7-weight rig.

Weight is a big thing with me. When several reels meet all the other criteria, I look for the lightest one. I like my outfit to feel light. It's less tiring to cast and helps my accuracy because I have more feel while casting.

Reels are constantly getting a bit lighter, so it is hard to give you any guidelines here. But while you're at the store, try putting a heavy reel and then a light reel on a particular rod, and you'll see what I mean about how a reel's weight changes the feel of an outfit.

In the 1960s and early '70s, when we were still using fiberglass fly rods for saltwater fishing, heavy reels were fine because they balanced with the heavier rods. Then came first-generation graphite, and it made those reels a bit too heavy. Now, we have third- and fourth-generation graphite rods, and my reels from the 1960s are much too heavy for them. As rods get lighter, you will start leaning toward lighter fly reels.

Keep in mind that your reel is going to gain a lot of weight after you buy it. The fly line and backing have weight. Most bonefish fly lines weigh about 1¼ ounces, and 200-plus yards of Dacron backing weighs over 1½ ounces. You will add about 3 ounces to your reel.

An empty marlin-size reel, which is an immense fly reel, always feels so light for its size. But then add a 13- or 14-weight fly line and 700 yards of 30-pound backing, and the reel feels like a brick. Keep this in mind when selecting your reel.

I have never owned a fly reel that, having the right capacity and retrieve, was too light. Some people say that there is such a thing as a fly reel that's too light, but I've never seen one.

DRAG

The proliferation of fly reels on the market has produced many types of mechanical drags (cork-to-spool, caliper, compression disk, clicker, and many others) and just as many types of drag surfaces (composite, Teflon, cork, metals, leather, and more). This isn't the place for a lengthy dissertation on drag designs or the benefits of different drag materials. Many different designs and materials work very well.

More than anything else, you want a smooth, consistent drag. A drag that chatters or fades will cause trouble on the flats. The drag should start smoothly; that is, it should not exhibit extra resistance until the spool "breaks loose" and begins to turn. As a bonefish makes a long run, the drag pressure should neither increase nor decrease.

The larger the drag surface, the better off you are because you won't have to tighten the drag as much to get the few pounds of resistance you need. A larger friction surface usually means a smoother, longer lasting, and more reliable drag, too.

I used to think that cork was the best drag material, and it was years ago, but today there are many fine reels with all kinds of drags that work very well for bonefish. About half my fly reels (and I have dozens of them) have cork drags, and the other half have something else.

The main thing is to have a smooth drag. Given a choice, take a larger drag surface over a smaller one.

OTHER FEATURES TO CONSIDER

Anodized Finish

These days, all good fly reels are anodized. Anodizing comes in many colors, letting you indulge your tastes. Unless you're on a budget, don't get a painted reel for saltwater fishing; it won't last nearly as long as an anodized reel, even with constant maintenance.

Rim Control

Nearly every modern fly reel has a spool with an exposed rim that lets you "feather" the spool as a fish runs. This gives you the option of adding any degree of drag you want and, more importantly, letting go instantly. I would not get a modern reel without rim control, but sometimes I do enjoy fishing an old reel, which does not have rim control.

Clicker Direction

Some reels are silent and some make noise by means of a clicker. On some reels, the clicker operates in both directions; other reels have clickers that make noise in only the line-out or the line-in direction. In theory, you won't land more fish with one type than with another.

Given a choice, I prefer a reel that makes noise when a fish takes line and remains silent when I recover line. Many guides like their clients to have reels with line-out clickers so that they can hear if a fish is taking line. Remember that your guide is behind you, up on a platform and a skiff length away. He can help you better if he can hear what's going on during a fight. My second choice is having a clicker that operates both ways, though I still like the reel to make less noise with line coming in and more with line going out.

The sound of a clicker when a bonefish runs is music—great music, to my ears.

DIRECT DRIVE OR ANTIREVERSE?

A direct-drive reel is the standard type of fly reel with the handle fastened to the spool. You turn the handle and the spool turns. When a fish takes line, you must let go of the handle and keep your fingers away from it as the spool spins at high speed.

On an antireverse reel (the old-timers called them slip-clutch reels), the handle does not turn as line goes out. That is, the spool revolves, but the handle remains in the same place. This means that you can hold on to the handle as a fish runs. But with a light tippet and correspondingly light drag setting, you can have trouble retrieving line unless you pump the rod to create slack. If the drag is set light, the reel's clutch will slip as you crank, and you won't recover much line.

An antireverse reel is not my choice for bonefishing. These reels tend to work better with 11-weight and heavier outfits, heavier tippets, and tighter drag settings. Although I used a Seamaster antireverse in the 1960s, I use only direct-drive reels today.

There are a few dual-mode reels around, which are direct drive when you retrieve, but antireverse when the fish pulls line. They can work fine for big fish and long fights, but they tend to be very heavy. They are not for bonefishing, at least in my book.

Besides, part of the fun is seeing the handle spin during a run. This kind of simple, basic equipment is what fly fishing is all about. No push buttons, please. Get a direct-drive reel.

LOOKS

After you have gone through all the technical criteria, you should hold the reel and consider its looks and feel. Bonefishing is all about having fun, you know. I've always believed that you've got to like a reel to take it home.

Most good reels are guaranteed for many years or for life, and a really fine one can last for generations. My

While I appreciate and enjoy using large-arbor, disk-drag reels, I often use an older, simpler reel that I like or that brings back good memories. Top, left to right: *Seamaster double-handle Salmon model and my circa-1960 Hardy Zenith. Both these reels have landed more bones than I'll ever remember.* Bottom, left to right: *Ross Canyon 4, Scientific Anglers Mastery, and Abel Super 8.*

circa-1955 Seamaster is still as smooth as silk. Good fly reels are a source of enjoyment all your life. Between trips, your bonefish reel might sit on a shelf with all your other reels, and every now and then you'll take it in your hands to crank it or feel its smooth drag. So, after you've narrowed the search to a few, get the reel that you just plain like best. The shape, the color, the knob material, the feel when you crank it, the feel when you pull against the drag, the sound of the clicker, the perforations in the spool—they all count.

As long as it is anodized, a reel's color does not matter. Perforations in the spool do not make a reel significantly lighter, nor do they help dry the line much faster, but they sure are pretty, and they have no drawbacks. I like the way they look. So have a soul and select a reel that you really like, because being too practical is impractical.

REEL CASES

Most reels come with cases. If yours didn't, be sure to get one. The best case is one that can be put on the reel while it's attached to a rod. This way, as the outfit bounces around during a rough crossing to the flats, it will not get nicked or scratched. Some skiffs do not have rod racks, and your rods simply lie in the bottom of the boat as the guide runs from place to place. A padded, wraparound case will not only keep your reel from getting banged around, but will also protect it from salt spray during a rough ride.

Take care of your reels. Flush them with plenty of fresh water after every trip. If you submerge a reel in the salt, then take it apart, clean it, and reassemble it with the proper lubrication (check the paperwork that came with the reel for instructions on lubricating it). Corrosion is your enemy, and, as we all know, rust never sleeps. If you store a reel for an extended period, loosen the drag—but be sure to check the drag adjustment the next time you put the reel on a rod.

Chapter 9

Miscellaneous Gear

. . . [S]o buy lots of miscellaneous fishing stuff. Some of it is useful or necessary, and the rest is what entertains you while fishing is poor.

—a casting student

Besides all the basic tackle, fly fishers accumulate loads of paraphernalia. Some of this stuff is necessary, and some can add to the pleasure of a bonefish trip. Although much of this peripheral equipment does not relate directly to hooking a bonefish, it is indispensable to a successful trip.

This chapter contains my checklist of miscellaneous items to bring on a bonefish trip. If your list is missing some of these (and you have a list in your computer, right?), you may want to add them. Of course, you might not need everything that I bring. Every angler develops his or her own list of things that make a fishing trip more enjoyable. For instance, from time to time I bring my clarinet on a trip so that I can practice. You probably will not want to bring one, or hear me play mine.

ALARM CLOCK

Sometimes I think that I should have been a jazz musician, because I can easily stay awake half the night. But when it comes time to get up to go fishing, I need help. If you are like me, bring a battery-powered alarm clock. Get one that uses AA batteries, which last longer than the AAA size.

BANDANAS

Norman Duncan, one of the great innovative fly fishermen of the 1960s, taught me to wear a folded bandana, bandit style, while fishing. Since then, I always carry at least one and use it quite often. An all-cotton bandana provides great protection on the flats. First, of course, it keeps the sun off your skin, especially your nose, which is often the part that is most exposed. On flat-calm days when the entire surface of the ocean acts like a mirror, and in mid- to late afternoon when you have to fish facing into the sun, a bandana shields your face. A bandit-style bandana also guards against the severe windburn caused by long rides in a skiff at 30 to 50 miles per hour. And just as football player applies dark grease under his eyes to cut glare from his skin, so can a bandana (as long as it's not white) reduce glare from the tops of your cheeks, helping you see fish better.

BELT (FOR FISHING ONLY)

Use a dedicated fishing belt with your fishing and wading pants. Most fishing pants are made to be worn with a belt, and a belt gives you a place to attach a sheath for your pliers and maybe a file. I prefer cloth or nylon material for my fishing belts, leaving my leather belts for dinner at the lodge.

BINOCULARS

The longer I fish the flats, the more I realize how useful a pair of binoculars can be. For years, I have been carrying compact Zeiss 8 x 20 binoculars that fold into a small package and fit easily in my tackle bag. As soon as I started carrying them, I found a million interesting things to see on the flats. I can see birds and all kinds of wildlife much better and can easily spot bonefish tails at a distance. If we are looking for a marker to find a channel and get home late in the afternoon or looking for a companion skiff in the distance, binoculars can save the day.

If it's not your turn to fish, you can scan the water with the binoculars to help your guide find a tailing bone for the caster. This can make a real difference in the day's results. A few years ago, my son, my wife, and I went fishing on a flat-calm afternoon. Tailing fish were few and far between. Marilyn took the binoculars, and even though she was in the lowest part of the boat, she spotted most of the fish that day, beating my many years of experience and my son's 20/20 vision. Just don't get binoculars that are too big or you will not carry them with you.

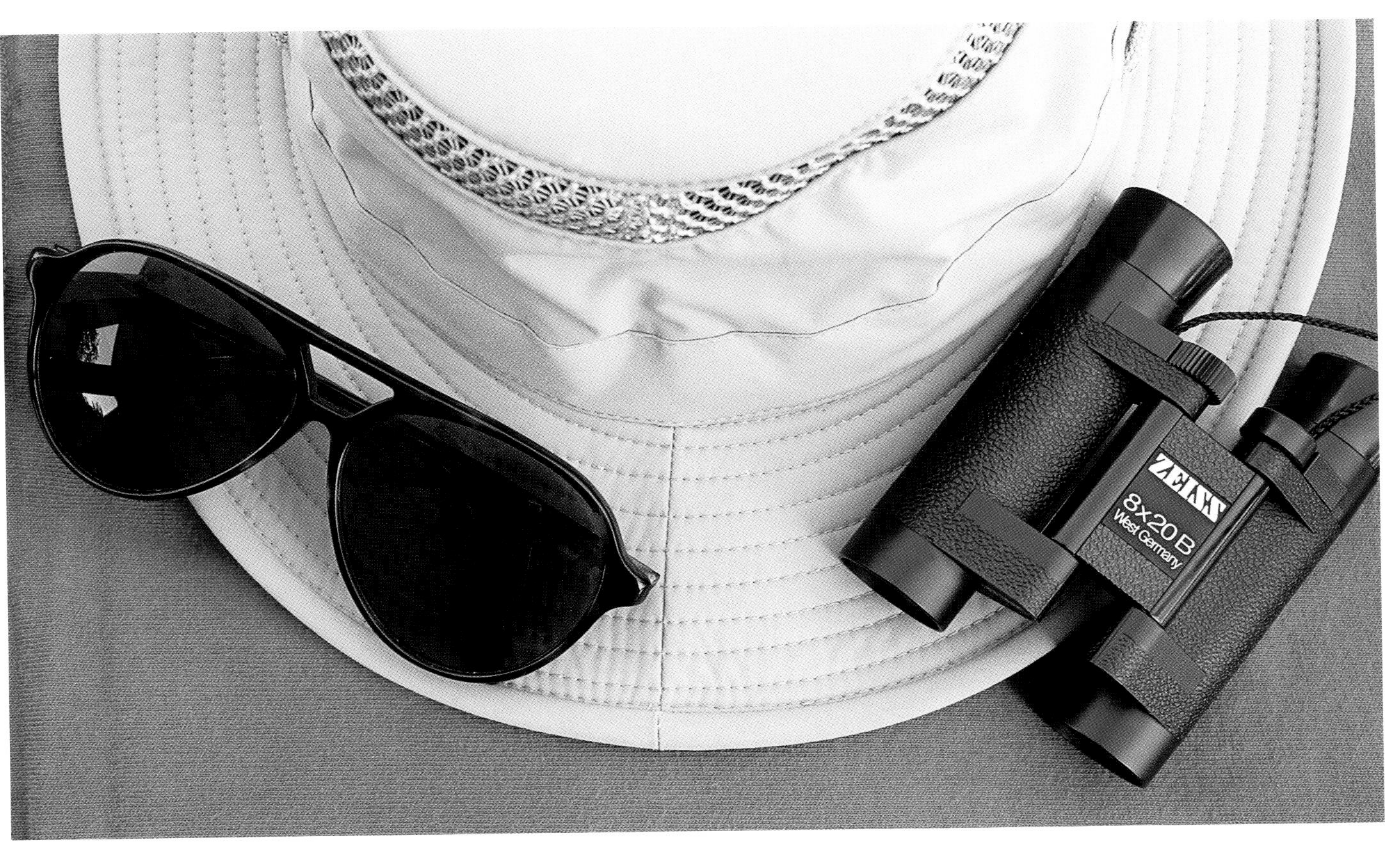

Binoculars, a hat, and polarizing glasses all help in finding bonefish.

CAMERA

A bonefish trip is a special experience, and for many people a rare one. You will come back with memories, but why not return with photos, too? In chapter 19, "Traveling for Bonefish," you will find a detailed treatment of camera equipment and how to carry and protect it.

CLOTHING

If you fish on the flats, you will get wet, whether from spray on a rough day, rain, wading, or even falling off the skiff. I've done it all. You want pants and shirts that dry quickly. Jeans definitely will not do. As a matter of fact, if you take a pair of long jeans to the islands, the humidity alone will make them feel soggy. No jeans.

If you want to wear short-sleeved shirts and short pants, you will have to set aside some extra time every morning to cover all exposed skin with sunscreen. Your choice.

Your shirt does not need a dozen pockets. It does not need to carry all of your tackle, plus lunch and a camera. When you're in the skiff, you can reach your tackle bag in a hurry. When you wade, wear a belt pack. I prefer a shirt with two pockets and will put up with four, but I will not wear a shirt with any more. Flats-fishing clothes should be simple.

I like my shirts a little on the large size. Looser shirts are cooler and not as restrictive when I'm casting or reaching for a fish. As to color, I prefer a light pastel shade. Dark colors can be downright miserable in the tropics and subtropics. I don't wear white shirts out of concern that they can scare fish in very shallow water, though I really can't prove this. But since white is a poor color for photography on the flats, I avoid it. These days, I alternate between long and short sleeves during a week's fishing.

I do most of my bonefishing in long pants. They protect my legs from the sun and save me the trouble of applying sunscreen to them. From time to time, especially if I'm going to wade a lot, I wear shorts. Shorts have the advantage of making less noise when wading. Sometimes I carry a pair of shorts in my fishing bag, and when the tide is right for wading, I switch to them. Later, I go back to the long pants for the rest of the day in the boat.

Incidentally, the combination of bare feet and short pants, when possible and safe, makes for the most quiet approach. Keep this in mind.

CLIPPERS

While I often use my scissors forceps to cut and rig leaders, clippers cut closest to a knot and make the smoothest connections. I always have one in my tackle bag and one in my wading bag.

FILE

The best files are made of extremely hard steel, but the harder the steel, the faster it rusts. Oiling a file cuts down on the rust, but it also reduces how much metal the file cuts with each stroke. It's a compromise, but a file remains the most popular tool for sharpening bonefish hooks.

A hook stone can't rust, but it removes very little metal with each stroke. Sharpening a hook with a stone can take forever. Some anglers carry stones for touching up hook points.

Lately, I have been using large, heavy-duty diamond-coated hook files. They can take a lot of metal off the point of a hook, and they do not seem to rust. I don't know why diamond files aren't more popular; they work great.

FIRST-AID KIT

It's not a bad idea to pack Band-Aids, pain medication, cold medicine, antacids, antibiotic ointment, and so forth in a small first-aid kit. Get a headache when you don't have an aspirin and you'll soon give up your best fly reel for two of them and a glass of water. Your prescription medications can also go in this kit. Your doctor or pharmacist can help you pack the right items.

Don't check this kit at the airport. Put it in your carry-on bag so that you will still have your medicines if your baggage gets lost.

FISH TAPE

You have to be brave here, risking disappointment and even heartbreak, but if you really want to know how big a bonefish is, then use a tape measure. Be prepared: your fish will never be as big as those caught by people who don't use tapes. A fly fisher's imagination will always outperform a tape or scale.

Since I like to know the lengths of fish, or at least the better ones, I usually carry a plastic measuring tape and bring it out when a bonefish seems worth measuring. The table in chapter 2 listing bonefish lengths and weights will help you estimate weight fairly accurately. If you want more accuracy, or if you are looking for world records, use a certified scale. If you'd rather estimate, don't bring the tape; you'll catch bigger fish that way.

You can measure a bonefish's full length, but fork length has proved more accurate for estimating weight. A bonefish's tail, which weighs practically nothing and adds substantially to its overall length, can vary greatly from one fish to the next.

FLASHLIGHT

A small flashlight comes in handy when you are in a strange location. I prefer one that uses AA batteries, which last longer that AAA. If you also bring an alarm clock, make sure that it and your flashlight use the same batteries.

FORCEPS

Over the last few years, scissors forceps have replaced my fishing pliers. Their long, thin shape lets me reach deep inside a bonefish's small mouth to remove a hook quickly and with minimal damage to the fish, allowing me to return the bone to its home that much faster. The scissors portion of the tool easily cuts any size of monofilament, unlike some pliers. Since they're made of stainless steel, these tools withstand salt water well. I use the medium 6-inch size for most fish and the large 8- or 10-inch model for sharks and big barracudas.

The down side of scissors forceps is that they don't crimp barbs quite as easily as pliers. And I can't seem to find a sheath that is comfortable to wear on my belt. Still, these are my favorite tools on the bonefish flats. I always have both the medium and the large one with me.

GLASSES CLEANERS

Water, salt, and dirt inevitably find their ways onto your glasses while you fish. Bonefish are hard to see under the best circumstances; smeared, dirty lenses make spotting a fish practically impossible. Yet I meet anglers who pay no attention to their sunglasses and then wonder why everyone else saw the big bonefish that they let go by.

Check and clean your glasses several times a day, and give them a good cleaning at night. You'll catch more fish, guaranteed. Drugstores, opticians, and sunglasses companies sell a variety of cleaning solutions. Some of these formulas also have good water-repellent qualities that help when you go on a boat ride on a rough day.

GLOVES

It seems that no matter where you are in a skiff, whether you are fishing or sitting down eating a sandwich, the backs of your hands are almost always exposed to the sun. If your skin is very sensitive to the sun, wear light gloves with the tips of the fingers cut off so that you can tie a fly to your tippet or file a hook. You might not need to wear gloves all day, but wearing them for just a few hours can save your hands.

A tape measure, diamond file, and scissors forceps are always part of my fishing gear.

HAT

You need a hat not only for sun protection, but also to reduce glare on your glasses. For sun protection, I prefer a hat to a cap. A full brim shades your ears and neck as well as your face, whereas a ball cap shades only your eyes. If you prefer caps, get a Keys-style fishing cap that has a flap to cover your ears and shade your neck.

While a full brim provides lots of shade, one that's too wide will flap in the wind and drive you crazy while running in a skiff. A wide, stiff brim will simply cause the hat to blow off your head. I prefer a brim from two to just under three inches wide, depending on the style of the hat.

A hat or cap needs to be soft so that you can sit on it, fold it up and store it in the console, or flatten it to pack in your suitcase. Make sure that the underside of the brim is a dark color to help cut down on glare. It really makes a big difference in seeing fish.

As I do with shirts, I prefer my hat to be a light pastel color to white. Maybe a gleaming white hat won't spook bonefish, but I don't want to take the chance.

INTERNATIONAL GAME FISH ASSOCIATION RECORD APPLICATIONS

If you have ever hoped to catch a world-record fish, you should bring the I.G.F.A. book and a couple applications. The record book comes out annually and contains some great articles as well as the record listings. While you're at it, join the association; I've been a member for years.

INSECT REPELLENT

You will need insect repellent at some bonefish destinations, especially during the hotter, wetter season. Bugs are not often a big problem, but bring some repellent anyway.

I usually carry both a spray can and a bottle. Twice, I have run out of bug spray when the outboard broke and we had to pole back. One time we poled for an hour; the other time we poled for more than four hours. The mosquitoes had us for lunch and later dinner. Those hours of poling are still vivid in my mind—and so is the sound of the spray can running out of juice. A spray is easy and convenient, but with the bottle you always know how much is left. It seems like a silly detail, until you are caught without it.

Remember that insect repellents containing DEET can damage your fly line. Wash the palms of your hands before touching the line.

NOTEPAD

There are always reasons to take notes during a trip—the addresses of people you meet, things that you want to bring next time, records of fish, and so on. You could bring a laptop computer, but that's too much like bringing the office with you. Instead, bring the Chico Fernández Adventure Travel Word Processor. It never breaks, always writes, does not need to be programmed, does not crash, and does not cost much. For an explanation of how to make one, see chapter 19.

PASSPORT

Make sure to put your passport on your list so that you never forget it. It can be a real hassle if you do. I know. Make a habit of having a couple copies of the front page, the one with your photo and all the information. Keep one in your wallet and another in a bag other than the one that contains your passport. This way, if you lose it, you'll still have all the information. That can help a lot, especially when traveling these days.

PLIERS

As mentioned earlier, I now use scissors forceps instead of pliers to cut mono, take hooks out, flatten hook barbs, and perform other tasks. If you want to carry pliers, make sure that the jaws and cutting edges are perfectly aligned and that there is no gap between the jaws.

RAIN GEAR

Many anglers try to predict the night before a trip whether it is going to rain, hoping to avoid bringing their rain gear, which weighs practically nothing. These anglers get soaked a lot. Most anglers can predict the weather about as accurately as they can predict the stock market. Enough said.

Please make top-quality rain gear part of your fly-fishing equipment. Bring the full suit, jacket and pants, and not just the jacket. Besides keeping you dry during the frequent tropical showers and squalls, good rain gear will also make a long, rough boat ride much more comfortable by keeping the spray from soaking you. Some early morning and late-evening runs can feel quite cool, particularly at 40-plus miles per hour, but good rain gear doubles as a wind breaker. It's part of the equipment and I *never* go on a trip without it. If the last leg of a trip to a remote fishing camp is by boat, make sure you have packed in such a way that you can instantly get your rain gear out.

I have fly fished all over the world and have even fished in the snow, which is crazy, yet the coldest I have ever been was in Florida. We were running away from an afternoon storm in February at 40-plus mph. The temperature had dropped into the 50s, and all I had was a pair of shorts and a T-shirt. The trip lasted almost an hour, but it felt like we ran all day. I still shiver when I think about it. That was more than 30 years ago, and I've never left the dock without my rain gear again.

SANDALS

If you are going to wear sandals, such as the Teva type, make sure that they have a good arch support. You are going to be standing most of the day. If you don't wear socks with them, make extra sure that you put lots of sunscreen on your feet. The tops of your feet are very sensitive to sunburn. I have seen a full week's fishing ruined because of it—and the angler couldn't even put his shoes on for the plane ride home.

I like fishing in good sandals. You can even do some light wading in them if the bottom is sandy and fairly hard, though they are no substitute for wading boots. After a day's wading in salt water, wearing open sandals in the evening gives your feet a chance to dry. I generally wear sandals to dinner at bonefish camps.

SUNGLASSES

Most of the time, the bonefish flats are one big sea of glare. It is imperative that you use polarizing sunglasses, mainly to spot fish, but also for your own eye protection. Most anglers today prefer glasses with amber, tan, or brown lenses because these colors seem to work best for spotting fish. On a cloudy day, you will probably do best with yellow. Bring an extra pair in case you lose or break your everyday sunglasses. You just can't fish without them.

SUNBLOCK FOR YOUR LIPS

If you don't have a mustache, you'll need a tube of sunblock. Your lips need the protection because they are especially sensitive to the sun. Carry a tube of sunblock in your tackle bag and make certain to apply some to your lips, or grow a large mustache (recommended for men only). I use both methods.

SUNSCREEN

Don't try to predict how sunny it will be or tell yourself that you are only going to fish for a couple of hours in the morning (we all know that means eight hours). Use sunscreen every time you fish. Skin damage from the sun is cumulative.

Apply liberal amounts while you are still in the comfort of your room. I apply sunscreen until most of it has

more pressure with a given tippet size, and it is usually then that connections begin to fail. So, it is important to know which connections are the strongest.

To test various connections, I called fly fishermen Frank Steele and Bob Stearns. Both of these anglers have played with leaders and knots for many years and really know their stuff. Frank uses a Chatillon test scale, model TCG-100, the same official scale that Scientific Anglers/3M uses for fly-line and backing tests. It is infinitely more accurate than I needed for these tests. Bob's scale was another Chatillon, a PPLG model balanced for this type of work.

Over the course of several weeks, we broke a lot of Dacron, fly lines, and connections. We then used our data to compute the average breaking strengths of various connections. In all of these tests, we joined the backing to a floating, weight-forward 8-weight line.

Nail Knot. This is a very popular connection, and it works, but it is not ideal. If you use a nail knot to join the backing to the fly line, you cannot change fly lines without tying another knot. It's also not the strongest connection. The connection between a weight-forward 8-weight floating line and 20-backing-test broke, on average, at 12.3 pounds. Average breaking strength: 60 percent. This will surprise many anglers.

Needle Knot (seven turns). This makes a very smooth connection, but you can't change lines at will. Like the nail knot, a needle knot is not as strong as most anglers believe. Tied with 20-pound backing, the knot broke at an average of 12.4 pounds. Average breaking strength: 61 percent.

Nail Knot with a Bimini. This is done by making a Bimini twist in the backing, and then tying a nail knot with the double line produced by the Bimini. It still doesn't permit instant line changes, but it's stronger. It is a bit hard to tie correctly because of the double line involved. The connection failed, on average, at 15.6 pounds. Average breaking strength: 76 percent.

Albright Special. Many anglers use this knot to attach backing to a fly line. It is bulky, but it still passes through the guides. Again, you cannot change fly lines at will. Strength is poor. When used to join 20-pound backing to a weight-forward 8-weight floating line, the Albright Special broke at an average of 11.4 pounds. Average breaking strength: 57.

Loop to Loop. To make this connection, first tie a Bimini twist in the backing to make a long loop. Bend the end of the fly line over to make a loop about 3/4 of an inch long, and secure the loop by whipping it with fly-tying thread or using 8-pound-test mono to tie two nail knots about 1/2 inch apart. Then connect the backing to the fly line with a loop-to-loop junction. You can undo the connection in seconds to change to another line. The junction slides through the guides with ease, and its breaking strength is always close to 100 percent. In my opinion, this is the ideal connection. Usually, the fly line or the backing breaks before the loop-to-loop junction fails. I use this connection on all my outfits, even my freshwater trout reels. And check the strength test: the backing broke, on average, at 19.5 pounds. Average breaking strength: 96 percent.

What happens with the other knots is that the backing, which is very abrasive, easily cuts through the coating of the fly line and then slides off the core. It doesn't take much pressure, either. So use a loop-to-loop connection; it's stronger and it lets you change lines quickly and easily.

FLY LINE TO LEADER

It is surprising to me how many anglers pay little attention to this important connection. The knot that joins the end of the fly line to the butt of the leader must not only be strong, but it should also be as small as possible so that it can run through the rod guides easily and smoothly.

If you keep in mind that the average bonefish leader is 10 or more feet long (and it keeps getting longer as fish get more pressure) and that you almost always have to reel several feet of leader into the rod to land a bonefish, then you realize that every knot that comes into the rod must be as small and slick as possible. Not only must the leader-butt knot come into the rod easily, but it also needs to go back out very quickly when a bonefish makes one last run in an effort to get away.

In looking at the connections offered below, you may wonder why the same knot that I did not like for connecting Dacron to a fly line is now fine for connecting mono to a fly line. The reason is that the mono, unlike the Dacron, does not cut through the coating as easily, so it holds well under pressure. Here are some of the most popular methods.

Albright Special. This is the knot that Capt. Jimmy Albright, one of the greatest Keys guides, invented to connect tippet material to a heavy shock tippet for tarpon. It can easily connect a 12-pound class tippet to an 80-pound shock tippet. But it was not designed for connecting the fly line to the leader butt. It is too bulky, especially for a bonefish outfit, and it goes through the guides with too many bumps and thumps. It holds fine, but it's just too bulky.

Nail Knot. This is the single must popular knot to connect fly line and leader, and rightly so. It is easy and quick to tie, fairly strong, and small. Six to seven turns is about right, depending on the core of the fly line; more about this later. Just make sure that all turns are tight and even when you pull the knot all the way tight.

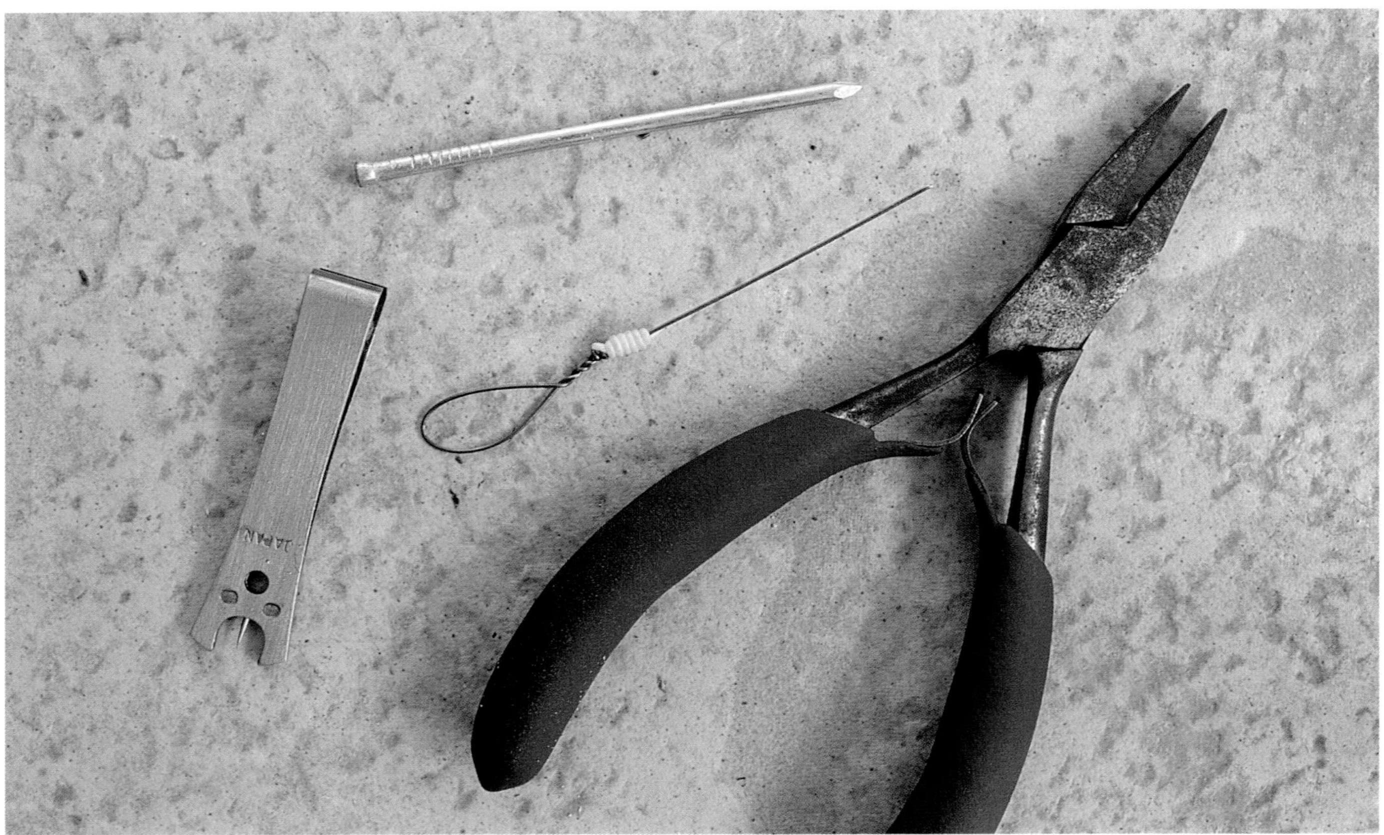

Rigging kit: A nail and a piece of No. 10 wire with a haywire twist to be used as a "stiffener" when making a fast nail knot; clippers to cut tag ends close to the knot; and a pair of flat-jawed pliers for pulling on mono while tying Duncan loop knots or pulling a stiffener that is too tight to remove from a nail knot.

Needle Knot. This connection is simply a nail knot in which the butt section of the leader, after having been shaved to a point with a razor blade, has been inserted through the middle of the fly line with the help of a large needle (thus the name). Then a regular nail knot is tied a short distance behind the tip of the fly line. The result is a nail knot on the fly line, with the leader butt coming out of the tip of the line. It makes for the smallest, slickest knot you can find. And because the leader butt goes through the fly line's core, a needle knot is a bit stronger than a regular nail knot. This may not seem important because both are more than strong enough, but the needle knot's greater strength means that you can tie it with fewer turns—five, say, rather than seven—and make the connection even smaller. It does take a few minutes to tie, and it can be used only with fly lines that have braided-nylon (multifilament) cores, not with braided-monofilament or single-strand mono-cores. If you have the time and inclination, and the right line, it's worth the effort.

Loop to Loop. The other method of attaching a leader is by a loop-to-loop connection. Take the end of the fly line and make a very small loop, about 1/4 of an inch or so. Secure the loop either by serving it with fly-tying thread or, better yet, by tying a six- or seven-turn nail knot with 8- or 10-pound mono and cutting off both leftover ends of the mono. If tied properly, the nail knot will partially bury itself in the fly line's coating. Then make a 1/2-inch loop in the butt section of your leader, using any loop knot. Join the leader to the line by interlocking the loops. For this connection to work properly, both loops must be kept very small and all tags must be cut flush. When it's right, though, it slides through the guides just fine, even though it looks like it shouldn't. The advantage of this method is that you can change entire leaders in a few seconds to deal with changing conditions such as wind and visibility. It works with any type of fly line. A loop-to-loop junction does not slide through the guides quite as easily as a needle knot, but then, nothing does.

DIFFERENT LINES, DIFFERENT REQUIREMENTS

All the connections we've looked at will work with standard fly lines that have braided-nylon cores (or multifilament cores, to use another name for them). They will not all work with other types of lines. Some lines with braided-monofilament cores and single-strand mono-cores will not hold a regular nail knot very well; the knot and the fly line's coating slide off the core. You can't slide a needle up the middle of a line with a solid monofilament core. Nor can you use the needle knot with most lines that have braided-monofilament cores because they do not have hollow centers.

You have several options with lines that have braided-monofilament cores. Obviously, you can use the loop-to-loop method.

A nail knot also works, but tie it with seven to ten turns. It will hold well.

Another way is to strip an inch or so of coating off the end of the line to reveal the braided core. Tie a figure-eight knot in the exposed core, insert the butt section of the leader through the figure-eight knot, and then tighten it. Tie a regular six- or seven-turn nail knot with the leader butt. As you pull the nail knot tight, make sure that it lies right against the figure-eight that you tied in the fly-line core. The nail knot can't slip off the end of the line because the knot in the core will stop it. Works great.

Lines made with single-strand monofilament cores (the Scientific Anglers Monocore and similar designs) present fewer rigging options. Under pressure, a nail knot will slide off the end of the line because the line's coating and core will separate. You have only one choice with these lines: the loop-to-loop connection. It's by far the strongest connection, good enough even for tarpon and billfish lines.

Some anglers strip about six inches of coating off the end of a mono-core line (no easy task) and then use a blood knot to tie the exposed core to the leader butt. It works, but it takes a lot of effort and makes a big, clunky connection. With these lines, use the loop-to-loop method.

COATING THE KNOTS

It's not absolutely necessary to coat line-to-leader connections with some type of cement, but I always do. Coated knots slide through the rod guides more easily. The coating does nothing to increase the strength of the connection; its purpose is just to make the knot smoother and less likely to hang up on a guide or the tip-top.

Nearly any self-leveling cement will do the job. The old favorite is Pliobond, and it still works fine. However, it is quite heavy; an overly thick coat can make the tip of the fly line sink. Besides, its brown color is ugly on a fly line.

I use clear fly-tying head cement, applying a very light coat—just enough to make the knot a little smoother. I've also used clear nail polish. Some anglers give line-to-leader knots a thin coat of Loon Outdoors UV Knot Sense, which cures in seconds by ultraviolet light.

MY CHOICES FOR RIGGING

When I rig a line with a conventional nylon core and know that I am not going to make many changes in the leader, particularly the butt section, I'll probably select the nail or needle knot, depending on whether I feel like taking the time for the needle knot. But if I feel that I am going to change leaders often, then I will rig the line with a loop-to-loop connection.

With a line that has a braided-monofilament core, especially the newer ones that seem to have better adhesion between coating and core, I lean toward a seven-turn nail knot. Again, though, if it seems likely that I will change the entire leader fairly often, I use the loop-to-loop method.

With single-strand mono-cores, there is no option but to loop.

ARRIVE COMPLETELY RIGGED

Always have all your reels fully rigged, right down to the tippets, by the time you arrive at a fishing camp or destination. If you arrive in the middle of the day, you might have a chance to fish for a few hours before dinner. If you haven't rigged your tackle, that's how you will spend those hours.

Some anglers show up with the rod that they plan to use most fully rigged and their other rod (or rods) not ready for action. They go bonefishing and spot a big, hungry permit to which they cannot cast. Don't make this mistake—have everything ready to go.

Even though I tell my groups to arrive fully rigged, someone usually shows up at breakfast the first morning with a new, empty reel, a large spool of backing, a fly line in a box, a half-dozen spools of leader material, and a fly box. It would take the better part of an hour to set up everything the way it should be rigged. The angler sits down near me and puts all his new, unconnected possessions on the table.

That's when I say, "Oh, for me? A present? Oh, you shouldn't have." He'll fish with borrowed tackle that first day.

Step in the boat with every rod rigged all the way to the fly. If you have a light and heavy rod for bonefish, then rig the light outfit with a smaller fly and the heavier one with a larger, weighted fly. If you bring a 9- or 10-weight for barracudas, have the leader, wire, and 'cuda fly tied and the hook sharpened. If you have a 9- or 10-weight for permit, then have a crab fly tied on and sharpened.

I take a few big fish every year just because I was fully rigged. Believe me, you will catch more fish if you always arrive at the dock with all your outfits in working order.

Chapter 11

Leader Logic for Bonefish

Having problems with your fly turning over? Take me to your leader.
—Joe Brooks, at the Rod & Reel Club, circa 1960

The leader is a translucent extension added to the end of the fly line. It has several vital functions in fly casting and fly fishing. During casting, a leader slows the line at the end of every false cast, helping smooth out the process and letting the angler feel a uniform control throughout the whole cast. A leader should behave like an extension of the fly line it is attached to, and it should turn over against the wind and still land softly on the water. It should be long enough to let the fly come down as far as possible from the splash of the fly line, so as not to alarm the fish. In the water, the leader should be able to move the fly so naturally and innocently as to create the illusion that it is food swimming freely in its environment.

A well-designed leader does all those things. Before making leaders for bonefish angling, you should understand what goes into a good one.

LEADER THEORY

During the cast, the energy in the line is constantly being transferred from the bottom to the top of the loop. When the loop reaches the end of the fly line and the beginning of the leader, its shape and energy should continue into the leader; that is, the leader should pick up where the line leaves off. For the fly line to transfer energy to the leader, there must be a similarity in weight and to some extent stiffness between the end of the fly line and the portion of the leader tied to it—a continuity, in other words. This is why a good leader acts as an extension of the fly line.

In chapter 6, we noted that the decreasing mass of a fly line's front taper helps slow the speed of the unfurling cast and produces a quieter presentation. In the same way, the leader continues that taper all the way to the fly and helps the fly turn over, even in the wind, while still producing a quiet, natural presentation.

For that to happen, the portion of the leader attached to the fly line—the butt section—must approximate the weight and to some degree the stiffness of the tip of the fly line. Then the leader should gradually decrease in diameter all the way down to the tippet section, where the fly is attached. How quickly or gradually the leader's diameter decreases, and exactly where it decreases, is determined by something called a leader formula. We'll look closely at leader formulas in a few minutes.

The most efficient type of leader is tapered, progressing from fat, stiff, and heavy at the fly-line end to thin and supple at the fly end. If the leader has no taper or very little taper, it will do a poor job of delivering the fly, especially in the wind.

There are still a few advocates of level leaders who claim a finer, more delicate presentation. An example would be a 10-foot bonefish leader made of a single length of 10-pound-test line. But to make a delicate presentation, one must first turn the leader over, often in the wind. That's an almost impossible task for a level leader, even in the mildest wind. On a flat-calm day when one may be able to make such a leader straighten at the end of the cast, the uniform, thin diameter will decrease control and therefore accuracy.

You could tie this 10-foot level leader with 30-pound line and get it to turn over, more or less, but the end would be much too thick to tie to the fly and too stiff to let the fly swim naturally. With a tapered leader, you have it all: good turnover and a supple tip to let the fly swim as if unattached. You need a tapered leader.

ANATOMY OF A LEADER

A leader is composed of three sections: the butt, the midsection, and the tippet. Each part has a function in the overall performance of the leader. By changing any section's length and/or thickness, you can change the performance of the leader. As you become more knowledgeable, you can fine-tune a leader to perform best according to conditions and your casting style.

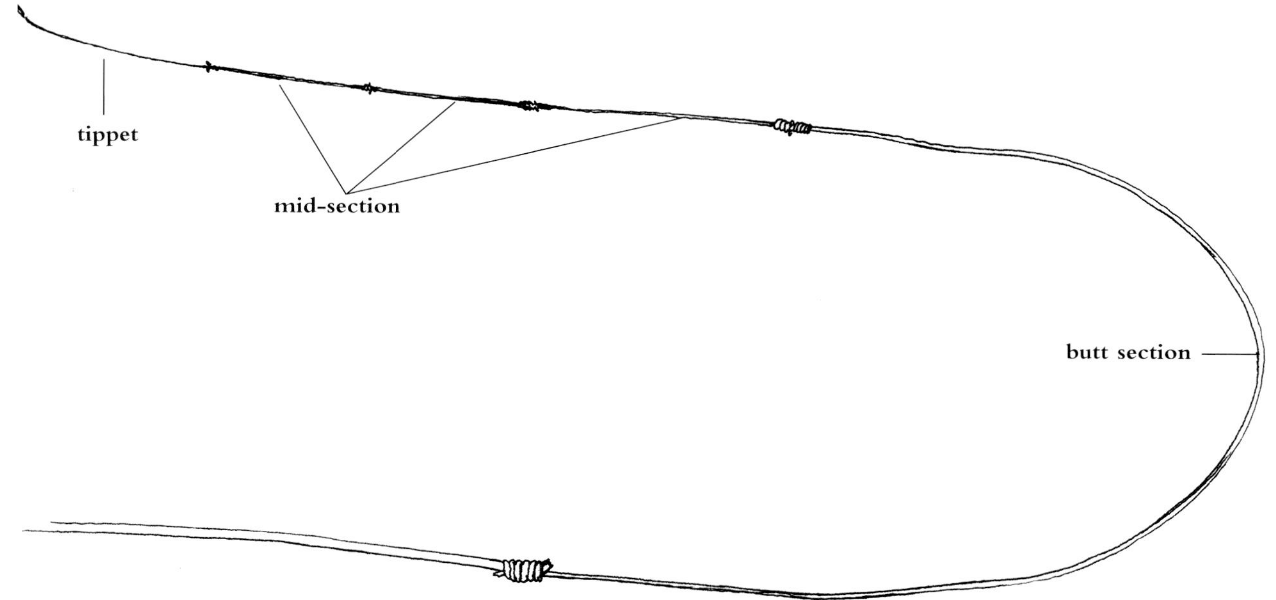

A long butt section is essential in turning over a leader.

Butt Section

This is the section tied to the fly line. Its length and weight determine how well the leader will turn over. It should be the longest, stiffest, and heaviest section of the leader. The leader's butt has the largest influence on accuracy and your ability to cast in the wind. It is truly the backbone of the leader.

Selecting the butt section for a particular fly line is probably the single most important decision affecting its performance. Just remember that when you choose a larger diameter for the leader butt, you are also selecting a heavier and stiffer piece of line.

Since monofilament is heavier (that is, more dense) than a floating fly line, the leader butt needs to be a bit thinner than the tip of the fly line. How much thinner? Use a piece that is 60 to 70 percent of the diameter of the fly line and you are in the ball park. Let's say that you have a typical 8-weight saltwater fly line with a tip diameter of about 0.040 of an inch. You decide to use a leader butt with a diameter 65 percent of that of the fly line's tip. Do the math: 65 x 0.040 = 0.026, or $^{26}/_{1000}$ of an inch. With many nylon monofilaments, that works out to around 40-pound test. Remember, though, that one manufacturer's 40-pound line might be much thinner or thicker than another manufacturer's 40-pound mono. Good anglers go by diameter when they build leaders, regardless of the line's breaking strength.

If you start with a leader butt about two-thirds the diameter of the tip of the fly line, you are probably close enough. I know that this is a great generalization because of the many variables in fly lines and leader materials, but it's at least a good starting point.

Here are some guidelines for leader-butt sections for fly lines from 5-weight to 10-weight that will be used for bonefishing. Guide yourself by the diameter, which is generally marked on leader spools. The pound-test rating is provided just to give you a rough idea of what you are looking for; it will vary greatly from very soft to moderately stiff leader materials. With softer materials, you can generally use a larger diameter than with harder materials.

5-weight line: 0.023 (about 30-pound test)
6-weight line: 0.023 (about 30-pound test)
7-weight line: 0.023 to 0.026 (30- to 40-pound test)
8-weight line: 0.024 to 0.027 (30- to 40-pound test)
9-weight line: 0.025 to 0.028 (40- to 50-pound test)
10-weight line: 0.025 to 0.029 (40- to 50-pound test)

The following materials are among those I have used for the butt sections of bonefish leaders with 6- through 9-weight outfits. If you select one of these lines for the first section of a leader, use the same brand (in smaller diameters, of course) for the middle or taper section of the leader. Naturally, the heavier butt sections go with heavier fly lines.

30-pound-test clear Ande monofilament
30-pound-test Rio I.G.F.A. leader material
30-pound-test clear or Ultragreen Maxima monofilament

30-pound-test Scientific Anglers fluorocarbon
30-pound-test Scientific Anglers clear nylon
40-pound-test Rio I.G.F.A. leader material
Umpqua 7–9 Weight Butt Material
40-pound-test Scientific Anglers fluorocarbon
40-pound-test clear Ande monofilament
40-pound-test clear or Ultragreen Maxima monofilament

Midsection

This part of a leader tapers the fastest and is usually made of several sections of monofilament, each smaller in diameter than the last. It is attached to the butt section at one end and the tippet at the other. The middle is the last section of the leader that has any real power to help turn over the fly. By necessity, it is much shorter than the butt section because by the time the casting loop reaches the middle of the leader, the cast has spent most of its energy.

Bonefish leaders are typically longer than those used for other saltwater fish, and they progress from fairly heavy butt sections to relatively light tippets. Accordingly, a bonefish leader's midsection generally contains more pieces of monofilament than the middles of other saltwater leaders have. The transition from butt to tippet requires two to four short pieces of mono.

You could tie a leader for bonefish with no midsection, using, say, 6 feet of butt and 4 feet of tippet. It would work, but not well. It would not roll out smoothly and would therefore lack control and accuracy. On a windy day, our two-piece leader would collapse at the beginning of the tippet section, letting the tippet and fly land in a tangled pile. A good midsection provides a very smooth transition from butt to tippet. It will turn over much easier in the wind and give you more accuracy. The midsection is a vital part of a bonefish leader (or any long leader, for that matter). Some anglers call this part the hinge section, but I disagree with that term because there should not be any hinge effect in your leader.

Tippet

This is the thinnest section in the leader and the weakest link in your tackle. One end connects to the midsection, the other to the fly. Since bonefish do not have teeth, we don't need to tie shock or bite tippets as we do for tarpon, snook, or barracudas.

While a leader's butt and midsection are selected by diameter (or weight, if you prefer to think in those terms), the criteria for the tippet, which is too thin and light to help turn over the fly, are strength and suppleness. In selecting tippet strength, you must take the size of the fly into account. A small bonefish fly will not swim very naturally when attached to a heavy, stiff tippet, while a large or heavily weighted fly will not cast well with a thin tippet, and the tippet will tend to get wind knots. A tippet should be heavy enough to avoid getting wind knots when you cast, supple and thin enough to let the fly swim in a natural manner, as inconspicuous as possible, and strong enough to hook and hold a bonefish. All these factors must be taken into consideration. Like many other things in fly fishing, an ideal tippet is an ideal compromise.

Tippet materials from three manufacturers might have the same diameters but different breaking strengths. Similarly, three materials with the same strength may differ in thickness or stiffness. Still, we can find some guidelines for selecting tippet materials. With few exceptions, my usual range of tippet strength for bonefish is from 8-pound test to 12-pound test. Occasionally, when using a 6-weight rod on a calm day and for smaller bones, I may use 6-pound test, but not often. I never go heavier than 12-pound test. Ten-pound material is what I use most often.

In the Florida Keys and the Miami area, where some of the biggest bonefish in the world are found and where the largest bonefish flies are used (weighted, size 2 patterns are standard), I often use a 12-pound tippet, dropping down to 10-pound-test material on very calm days. In most other places where the average bonefish is smaller and the average fly is a size 4, a 10- or 8-pound tippet is usually my choice, depending on the outfit I'm using. With very small flies such as sparsely tied size 6 and size 8 patterns, I fish 8-pound tippets and sometimes go as light as 6 pounds.

Remember that if you use too thick a tippet with a small bonefish fly, say a 12-pound tippet and a size 6 pattern, the fly will not swim well. You will probably get lots of refusals, some follows, and very few takes.

Here are some of the materials that I have used for the tippets of bonefish leaders. The diameter of each material is given in thousandths of an inch; you can see how diameters vary among manufacturers.

8-pound-test clear Ande	0.0117
8-pound-test Rio I.G.F.A.	0.012
8-pound-test Maxima	0.0125
9-pound-test Scientific Anglers fluorocarbon	0.0117
10-pound-test Scientific Anglers clear nylon	0.012
10-pound-test clear Ande	0.0126
12-pound-test Rio I.G.F.A.	0.0135
12-pound-test Scientific Anglers clear nylon	0.013
12-pound-test clear Ande	0.0145
12-pound-test Maxima	0.0155

My micrometer might differ slightly from yours, so regard the numbers as close approximations. A larger or smaller diameter does not necessarily mean better or worse, at least with bonefish tippets. With time, you'll develop a preference for a particular brand or brands of material.

My favorite all-around tippet diameters for bonefish are 0.012 for most locations and 0.014 for the Keys and Miami area, give or take a little. There is a real difference between these two diameters; you can touch the leader and feel the difference in thickness and suppleness.

LONG LEADERS

The first time I used an extra-long leader, I didn't know it. It was just a matter of necessity on that flat at that time. But I have been using long bonefish leaders ever since my accidental discovery of them in the early 1960s.

For the third day in a row, I had set my alarm clock for 5 A.M. and, after a quick cup of coffee, driven across the then-small city of Miami and over the three bridges to Key Biscayne. After parking under a bunch of sea-grape trees, I followed a sandy path lined by sea grapes, Australian pines, and coconut palms to a spot on the northeast shore of the key that faces a large, open flat. This outside flat, still productive after so many years, is mostly turtle grass, with just a few shallow, sandy potholes at its deepest end, where it is closest to the ocean.

During the low incoming tide on the previous two mornings, I had tried to cast to several large bonefish that came up onto the flat to feed. I'd watched their big tails waving in the air as they looked for a variety of crustaceans on the bottom. Even my best casts spooked them. I added an extra foot of tippet, but it didn't help.

Now, on the third day, having added quite a bit to the leader again and knowing that this would be the last day for another two weeks that the tide would let me fish for these bones early in the morning, I waded slowly onto the flat to give it one more try. When I finally made a cast to the first tailer, I was pleased that it did not scare him. A bit agitated, the bonefish followed the fly for a few feet and then took it. Or at least I thought he did. But when I tried to set the hook, the fly came out, and the fish, having felt the steel, headed for deep water in great fear. I was trembling a bit myself.

Encouraged by my limited success, I waded toward the next tailing fish. This one, feeding at the edge of one of the sandy potholes, was far away. When I finally positioned myself within casting range, I could see that he was very large. That made my casting a bit more difficult; I think hunters call it buck fever.

The fish ignored the first couple of casts and kept rooting in the bottom, his tail and sometimes even his dorsal fin out of the water. But on the next cast, the small *splat* of the fly must have caught his attention, for he quickly came over for one of those thorough inspections that only an old, experienced fish can make. He followed close behind the fly, interested but not convinced. No matter what kind of action I used, I could not get him to take it. Knowing that I was running out of retrieve, I simply stopped the fly and let it sink to the bottom, a trick I had learned from an old-timer in the Keys.

Slowly and deliberately, the fish tailed. Through my line and rod, I could feel his mouth bumping on the fly. When I set the hook, the fish's great weight and power put a deep bent in my bamboo rod. The bonefish reacted by turning abruptly and disappearing from the flat into deep water, leaving a large swirl of foam and mud behind him. Following behind him were my fly line and eventually what looked like 150 yards of backing.

When he finally stopped, my hands were sweaty, my throat was dry, and my reel was almost out of line. It was a long time before I could bring him back to me and walk him to the sandy beach. After holding him for a few long seconds, I released him and watched him swim away. I've always figured that he weighed 12 pounds, but however big he really was, I know that the experience surpassed the weight.

By now it was nearly 8 P.M. I could hear the sounds of traffic, reminding me of a college class I had to attend. I clipped the fly from the leader as I trotted back to the car. But as I was reeling the leader onto the reel, I noticed that it seemed very long. That evening, I pulled the leader off the reel to measure it, and to my surprise it was almost 14 feet long. It was hard to believe that such a leader would turn over as it had that morning. Ever since, my average bonefish leader has been much longer than my rod.

If anything beyond rod length intimidates you because it's hard to turn over, chances are that you are not constructing your leader correctly. Most competent fly casters can turn over a properly tapered 12-foot bonefish leader with ease.

A longer leader can make a huge difference. When a bonefish comes onto the flats to feed, he spends most of his time looking for food on the bottom or feeding with his nose on the bottom. At the same time, he must be on the lookout for sharks, barracudas, and birds of prey. Mr. Bonefish is one nervous fellow on the flats. The shallower the water, the more jittery he gets. As fishing pressure has increased almost everywhere, bonefish have become more nervous than ever. So, you must try to keep the splash of the fly line far from where the fly drops. That means using a long leader. Fortunately, the flies that properly imitate bonefish food are mostly very small, making the use of these long leaders much easier.

On the other hand, a day's fishing might present many different scenarios. Early in the morning, with calm winds and bonefish tailing in nine inches of water, a

12-foot leader is barely long enough. By mid-morning, the wind has picked up and you are casting weighted flies to mudding fish in two feet of water, and a 9-foot leader does a good job of turning over the heavier fly in the wind. Later that afternoon, after a summer shower, the winds might calm down again, making a long leader just the ticket for bones cruising in a foot of water. The situation is always changing.

Most bonefish leaders fall between 9 and 14 feet in length. I see no reason for a shorter leader because even on the windiest days you ought to be able to turn over a well-constructed 9-foot leader. I also see no reason for a leader longer than 14 feet. If you are in a situation of flat-calm weather with bonefish tailing in super-shallow water, and you still spook fish even after switching to a very long leader, then change rods. Put down the 8-weight and pick up a 6-weight with a 12-foot leader that has a fine tippet at least a yard long. This change will make a much bigger difference than merely lengthening the leader on your 8-weight outfit. In shallow water on a calm day, the angler with the lighter rod often takes more fish than the guy with the 9-weight. Sometimes, the angler casting a 6- or 7-weight takes all the fish.

My average bonefish leader, if there is such a thing, is about 11 feet long. The range of my leaders is probably 10 to 13 feet. For more finesse, I go to a lighter outfit.

A bonefish leader has a long, very powerful butt section for defeating the wind, and a long, very thin tippet that allows the fly to drop softly in shallow water with the delicacy of a rose petal. Between those two parts, the leader's midsection uses several pieces of monofilament to reduce the leader's diameter and transfer the energy of the cast.

LEADER FORMULAS

A leader formula expresses the length of the butt section, midsection, and tippet as percentages of a leader's total length. For example, a 40/30/30 formula refers to a leader of which 40 percent is butt section, 30 percent is midsection, and 30 percent is tippet. If the leader is 10 feet long, 4 feet is butt, 3 feet is midsection (this will consist of several pieces of mono), and 3 feet is tippet.

Generally, the longer the butt section in relation to the overall length of the leader, the more easily the leader will turn over in the wind and the harder it will land on the water. The shorter the butt section, the harder it will be to make the leader straighten into the wind. A formula with a very long butt section, such as Charles Ritz's 60/20/20, will fight wind very well but turn over a bit too hard for bonefish angling. A formula with a 30-percent butt section might land softly on a calm day, but it will have a very hard time turning over the other 70 percent on a windy day.

I feel that a 40-percent butt section is the minimum length to fish the flats. As you will see in great detail below, my own bonefish-leader formulas are 50/30/20 and 50/25/25 for most days. On windy days, I tend to use a longer butt section, and my leader may be a 60/20/20 design, which really turns over in the wind.

Bonefish-Leader Formulas

I find that my best leader formulas usually have around 50 percent butt section. The formula I most often use is the 50/30/20. On calmer days, the formula may be more like 50/25/25, which sports a bit shorter midsection but a longer tippet for a quieter presentation. Still, both have the long, powerful butt section to turn over the fly.

Super-windy days will see me use a 60/20/20 leader. The extra-long butt will help greatly in turning over the fly. While windy days often let you get away with a shorter leader, on some days you are better off with a 12-foot leader even if the wind is blowing. Use a long butt section in the wind.

A 10-foot 50/30/20 leader would have a 2-foot tippet, but with the 50/25/25 formula it would have a 2½-foot or 30-inch tippet. On 12-foot leaders, the tippets would be 29 and 36 inches, respectively. I feel that this is just right for most fishing situations.

Some anglers, looking for a more quiet presentation, use a 33/33/33 formula, or one third butt, one third midsection, and one third tippet (e.g., 4 feet of each in a 12-foot leader). They do get a bit more delicate presentation, but I feel that the shorter butt and longer middle and tippet are very hard to cast into an average wind, let alone a stiff wind. On a calm day, the 33/33/33 leader is less accurate because of the shorter butt section.

Rather than make radical changes in leader formulas, such as going to the 33/33/33 on a calm day, I find it better to change leader length while sticking with the same proven formulas (50/30/20 and 50/25/25). This way, even if I get caught with a long leader when the wind picks up, I still have the long, powerful butt section and superior accuracy.

Do keep in mind that the proportions in these formulas do not have to measured to the inch, but rather serve as close approximations.

LET'S MAKE A BONEFISH LEADER

With all this information behind us, let's get the necessary materials and make a leader from scratch. The explanation might seem long, but once you learn what to do, you can make a good leader in twenty minutes or less. I often make a few the evening before going fishing, or tie several a few days before going on a week-long trip.

There is a great variety of good leader materials on the market today. I prefer leader material that is soft to medium in stiffness.

Materials

I prefer leader mono that is soft to moderately stiff. The softer material makes a tighter loop when you cast, stretches and straightens more easily when you start fishing, and ties easier in smaller knots. The old recommendation to use a stiff leader in the wind has not proved true for me.

Unless you feel like doing a lot of experimenting, stick with one brand of material as you construct a leader. That is, don't mix one manufacturer's line with another's because they will have different properties, particularly stiffness. The only exception here may be with the tippet section; you might use a fluorocarbon tippet on a nylon leader, for example.

The best color, and by now I have tried them all, is clear. Its translucent quality seems to help it blend with any light level and any surroundings. Very pale green is a close second—but *very* pale, okay? Darker tippets have not done well for me on the bonefish flats. They look too conspicuous over any bottom color. My percentage of strikes went way down every time I tried them. A medium-green material might look good when it's above turtle grass, but when the next cast is over white sand, the material really stands out from the background. The multicolor camouflage lines show up even worse on light bottoms. Give me clear.

Get a pair of clippers or any other tool with which you can trim the tags very close.

Use a saucer with water to wet the knots before you tighten them. I know that everybody wets knots in their mouths, but you'll find that water is a great lubricant. Try it. When fishing, I will dip a knot that is ready to be tightened under the water or into the cooler.

If you want to get a little more serious about tying your own leaders (for bonefish or anything else), get a micrometer. It won't cost much and will last practically forever. A micrometer is accurate and, like a scale, it has no opinions—just the facts, ma'am, just the facts, as Joe Friday used to say. A mike will help you immensely in following leader formulas, changing leader designs, and especially selecting butt sections. If you don't want to get a micrometer, you can generally find the diameter of a material on the spool's label. Be aware, though, that the specifications on labels are not always perfectly accurate.

During the cast, the butt and midsection are what turn over the leader; the tippet is too soft to help. You select the butt and midsection by diameter so that they will have enough weight. But the tippet you choose by strength.

Because every piece of a leader is a different thickness than the pieces on either side of it, you need to join them with a knot that can secure dissimilar diameters. The best connection is the blood knot. The blood knot is strong, yet it is also small and symmetrical, inconspicuous in the water, and less likely than some other knots to get stuck in a rod guide. It also uses a minimum amount of material if you need to retie a knot.

Other knots, such as the double Duncan loop and the surgeon's knot, also work. In my experience, though, they are not as strong as the blood knot, at least with bonefish-leader materials. Tying them requires more material, which can make retying a portion of a leader difficult or impossible. The surgeon's knot is also fatter than a blood knot. After trying countless leader connections, I still prefer the blood knot.

The Butt Section

Let's make a 10-foot bonefish leader tapered to a 10-pound-test tippet. For the butt section, use a piece of soft to moderately stiff mono with a diameter about two-thirds that of the end of your fly line. As we noted earlier, this is usually about 40-pound test for a 7- to 9-weight fly line. Cut a piece about 6 feet long. Using the 50/30/20 formula, the leader butt will be about 5 feet long (50 percent of 10). Cut 6 feet because you will lose some length in tying it to the fly line on one end and to the midsection on the other.

Attach one end of the mono to the fly line. Chapter 10 described several ways to do this. With the butt tied to the fly line, you are now ready to add the pieces that make up the midsection.

The Midsection

According to our formula, the midsection constitutes 30 percent of the leader, or 3 feet. Within that distance, the leader needs to come down in diameter enough for you to attach the 10-pound tippet.

To make it simple, let's use three 12-inch pieces of mono. So, to the 40-pound (0.025 or so) butt section, tie a piece of 30-pound (roughly 0.023) line. Then add a foot of 20-pound (around 0.019) mono and a foot of 15-pound (about 0.016) material. Because a bonefish leader has a heavy butt and a thin tippet, the midsection often needs at least three pieces to make the transition in diameter.

Now we have 5 feet of butt and 3 feet of midsection composed of three sections of monofilament. The last piece of the midsection is thin enough to attach the tippet to.

The Tippet

To complete the formula, you need 2 feet of tippet, so cut about 3 feet. This will give you enough to tie the tippet to the midsection and later to attach a fly, and still have about 2 feet.

There are several ways to tie the tippet to the midsection. One, of course, is to use a blood knot. That's fine, except that if you use a blood knot to attach the tippet, it will be the weakest link in the leader. That's right: the weakest place in a bonefish leader is usually not where you attach the fly, but at the knot where the tippet meets the midsection.

You can improve the strength of that connection by using an improved blood knot. This is tied just like a regular blood knot, except that you double the thinner line (the tippet) and then tie the knot. In other words, tie a blood knot with the single strand at the end of the midsection and the doubled line of the tippet. The doubled line solves the problem of joining two lines of substantially unequal diameters. I use at least seven turns of the light, doubled line and two or three turns of the heavier midsection. This produces a much stronger knot, long but compact, and it's usually the knot I use to tie my bonefish and permit tippets.

But you might want an even stronger connection. Maybe you want to use a fairly light tippet for big bones, or you are looking for a world-record fish in a particular line category. In either case, you want all the tippet strength you can get. There is a way to get a 100-percent connection between the midsection and tippet. Tie a Bimini twist in the tippet material; a Bimini turns a single line into a double line, and it retains 100 percent of the line's strength. Then take the double line that the Bimini produces and attach it to the midsection with a blood knot. Presto, a connection with 100-percent strength. I have used this knot combination for light tippets and big fish for years.

Tippet Length

I know that the formula dictates tippet length, and normally you can just follow the formula. However, some conditions call for a change. On a very calm day when fish are easily spooked, but turning over a leader is not hard, I will often lengthen my tippet section to 3 or 4 feet, or even more. The fly lands almost as softly as if it wasn't attached to a leader (almost).

Another situation where I use extra-long tippets is on deeper flats with three to six feet of water. Here, the long, thin tippet will help get a weighted fly down in a rush. It can make a big difference.

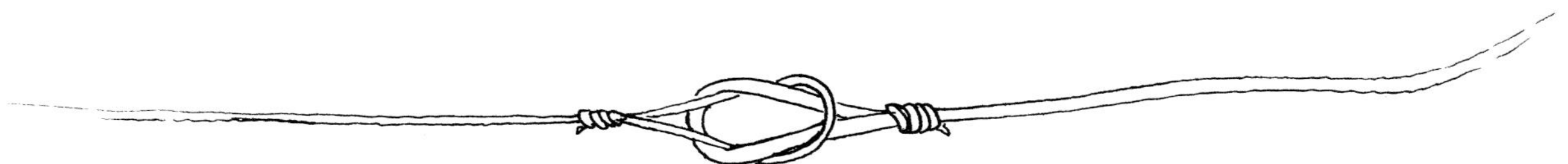

The right loop-to-loop connection (top) *will hold, but made the wrong way* (bottom), *the loop-to-loop will easily be cut and break off. It's the same loop-to-loop, the difference being how you tighten it.*

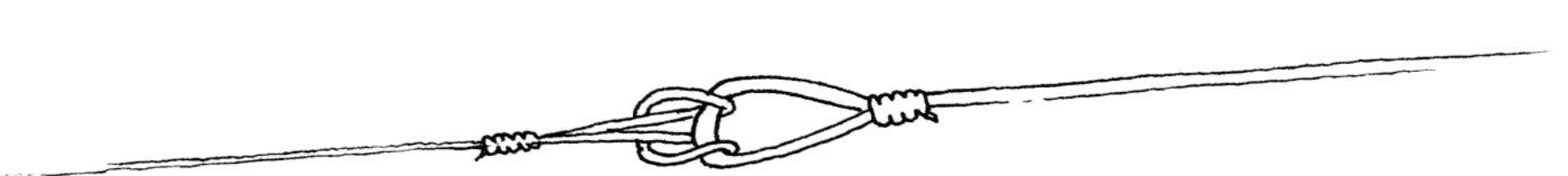

JORGE MARTINEZ

QUICK-CHANGE OR LOOP-TO-LOOP CONNECTIONS

This is not a change in your leader formula, but rather a way to create a quick disconnect at any point within the leader. With a loop-to-loop junction between the midsection and tippet, you can very quickly replace one tippet with another, changing from, say, a 10-pound-test bonefish tippet to a 12-pound tippet with a wire trace and a barracuda fly.

Or you could make the loop-to-loop connection between the butt section and the midsection. This would let you swap 5 feet of midsection and bonefish tippet for a 15-pound tippet rigged with wire and a shark fly. Now you are ready to cast to a shark you saw while looking for bonefish. In making the change, you have also shortened the leader because you replaced 5 feet of midsection and tippet with a shark rig that's only 3 feet long. You've not only changed flies, but also altered the leader to make it better for casting a heavy fly and a wire bite tippet.

You can also use a loop-to-loop connection between the fly line and the leader, looping the butt section to a loop on the fly line itself. This way you can interchange whole leaders. The variations are endless.

My favorite loop knot is the Duncan loop. It's smooth and small when tied correctly. Some books call it the uni-knot, but it was created by engineer Norman Duncan in the mid-1960s. I know; I was there.

Another choice, but not mine, is to tie a 6-inch butt section to the fly line and put a loop on the end. This, too, lets you replace the entire leader without having to tie any new knots. But the short butt comes off the reel with a pronounced curl, and it's impossible to straighten because it's too small to hold and stretch.

As neat and useful as loop connections are, they are more visible and more wind-resistant than blood knots. Not much, perhaps, but enough. I use loops when they serve a purpose, but otherwise I like a nice "clean" leader.

My biggest use of loops on the bonefish flats is with my 9-weight outfit, because I often change from a 10-pound tippet for bonefish to a 12-pound tippet with a permit crab fly, or to a 15-pound tippet with wire for a big barracuda or shark. My 9-weight outfit nearly always has a loop-to-loop disconnect at the end of the leader's midsection.

REDUCING THE LEADER'S LENGTH

Let's say that you are fishing early in the morning when it's very calm. You are using a long leader, and it's working great. But by mid-morning the wind starts to kick up and the leader no longer turns over as well. You want to keep the proportions of the leader, but you need to make it shorter. No problem. By simply cutting and retying each blood knot in the leader, which takes only a few minutes, you'll make the leader shorter but retain roughly the same proportions.

Later that evening, the wind calms down and you need a long leader again. You'd better have a spare leader in your bag, or you will take a fifteen-minute break to tie one. And believe me, you don't know how much your hands can shake until you spend fifteen minutes constructing a long leader with bonefish tailing all around you as the sun sets.

THE CURLY LEADER

Just like your fly line, your leader always comes off the reel with a curl in it, especially if the leader has been on the reel for a while. Monofilament has "memory," and it remembers the diameter of the spool on which it was stored. This has several drawbacks. To perform best, a leader has to be as close to perfectly straight as possible. Any curl, particularly in the butt section, will hurt your casting, your ability to manipulate the fly, and your percentage of hookups.

When you cast, a curly leader will not turn over well, if at all, because the fly line cannot transfer the cast's energy to it. A leader has to start out straight before you can make it straighten at the end of the cast.

Once the fly hits the water, a leader with curls will not transmit the action you are trying to impart to the fly. The curls are slack, and they act like a spring to absorb the movement you try to create by stripping line.

If a fish does eat the fly, that same slack will keep you from feeling it and will delay your strike. Again, the curly leader functions as a spring that absorbs rather than transmits energy.

Every time you stretch your fly line to straighten it, stretch the entire leader, too. Make sure that it's perfectly straight before you start looking for fish. Stretching the leader takes only a few seconds, and it is of the utmost importance.

TIPPET-TO-FLY KNOTS

To loop or not to loop—that is the question. In the past twenty years, I have published three articles on the subject of tying a fly to a tippet. In looking back, I see that I have been moving slowly toward the loop school of thought with every subsequent article.

Before choosing a specific knot for attaching a bonefish fly to a tippet, you first need to decide whether you want a loose, free-swinging connection or a knot that cinches tight against the hook eye. There's no question that a fly attached with a loop has more action; whether this is always better is a matter of opinion. And a looped fly will definitely sink faster. Sometimes, though, a looped fly will tangle more often during casting, particularly in windy conditions.

A fly attached with a rigid knot sinks much more slowly and darts rather than hops during the retrieve. It's also less likely to tangle or foul during the cast. However, if the knot is not drawn tight enough and it moves even a little to one side of the hook eye, the fly will swim awkwardly. When that happens, your chance of getting a strike is almost zero.

Each method has advantages and drawbacks. These days, I attach most of my bonefish flies with a loop knot. I feel that a loop lets the fly move freely, with a more natural swimming motion, even on a steady retrieve. When you are imparting action during a retrieve, the looped fly is much more sensitive to each little movement of the fly line. The natural and most effective movement of most weighted bonefish flies is to dive between strips. A loop knot facilitates this. For action, there is no contest between loop knots and cinched-to-the-eye knots.

But in extremely shallow water, you may not want the fly to sink too quickly, but rather to stay almost suspended in the water column when retrieved. When

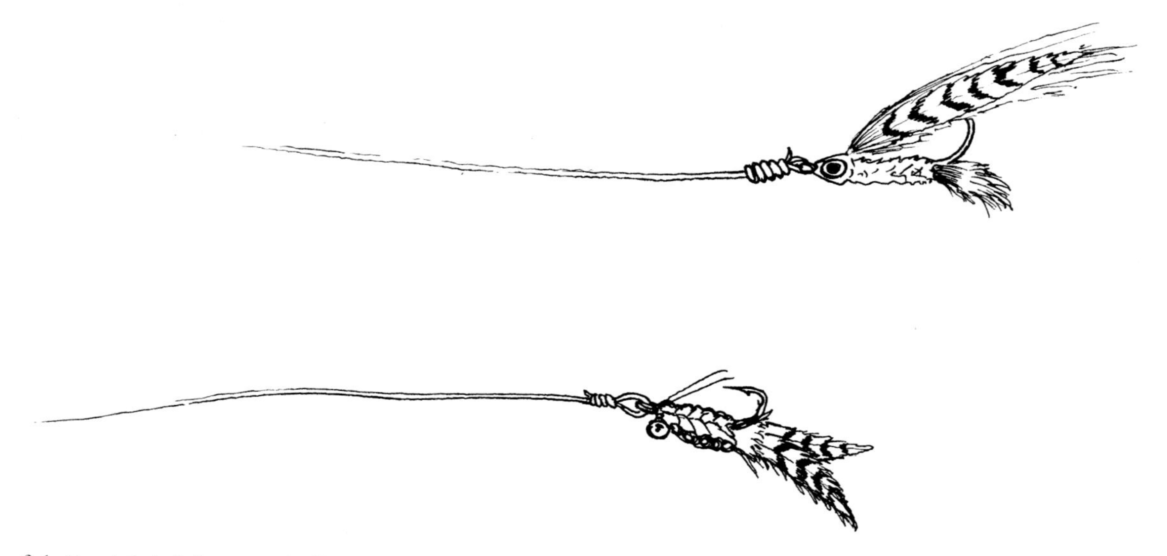

JORGE MARTINEZ

Top: *a Bonefish Special tied for very shallow water with a clinch;* bottom: *a crab fly tied with a loop to help it sink fast*

bonefish are feeding in just inches of water, you want the fly to move not with an up-and-down jigging action, but with a darting motion. Here, I use a tightly cinched knot.

When I want a loose connection between the fly and tippet, I use the Duncan loop. Tied with six or seven turns, it holds very well and usually tests at 90-plus percent of the line's strength. My biggest bonefish, a 14-pounder, and some of my biggest permit have all been taken with this knot. I have used it for forty years, which is about how long I have known Norman Duncan.

To cinch a bonefish fly, I used to tie an improved clinch knot with six and a half turns or so. Over the past few years, however, I have gone to a plain-vanilla clinch knot tied with seven, seven and a half, or even eight turns (lubricated with water, of course). This knot is simpler than its "improved" version and, with seven or more turns, it tests higher. An eight-turn clinch knot tests at 99 to 100 percent. Since drawing up eight turns is very difficult with some tippet materials, I often use seven turns; the knot is still more than strong enough.

DRESSING THE FLY LINE AND LEADER

Any knot connecting the fly line and leader—nail knot, needle knot, loop-to-loop, whatever—weighs more than the tip of the fly line. The heavy knot pulls the end of the fly line and the beginning of the leader a few inches below the surface, making the fly a little harder to manipulate and the line a bit more difficult to pick up from the water. Maybe this is just a minor annoyance, but bonefishing is hard enough without extra challenges, even small ones.

Whenever you dress your fly line, apply dressing to the leader knot and some of the butt section of the leader. In very shallow water, dress the whole butt section and maybe even part of the midsection. The end of your fly line and the leader butt will float higher, letting you pick up the line from the water and impart action to your fly just a little bit easier. If you bring a big bonefish to the boat and he decides to make one last lunge after the leader knot has passed through the tip-top and one or two guides, the line dressing on the knot will make it just a little more slippery and less likely to get stuck on a guide.

FLUOROCARBON

Fluorocarbon materials come in many varieties, with new ones hitting the market every few months. So far, though, I haven't found one that I really like for bonefish angling. True, fluorocarbon is less visible in the water than nylon, but the difference doesn't seem significant in a leader with a relatively thin tippet. Besides, bonefish aren't particularly leader shy.

Since fluorocarbon sinks much faster than regular mono, a leader tied completely of fluorocarbon is harder to lift from the water when you need to make a quick second cast. In super-shallow water, an all-fluorocarbon leader drags on the bottom.

You can tie a regular leader and use fluorocarbon for the tippet, but it is stiffer and the fly does not seem to work as well, at least to me. Fluorocarbon's stiffness also makes knots much more difficult to draw tight.

Manufacturers have been improving fluorocarbon lines over the last few years, making them softer and easier to tie knots with, and I will keep testing them. So far, fluorocarbon materials are not my choice for bonefish leaders, but they are getting close.

KNOTLESS LEADERS

Only a few years ago, most if not all knotless leaders for saltwater fishing were, in my opinion, very poor. They had fairly thin, short butt sections, which, as you know by now, will not turn over very well. All that has changed, however, and today most of the better manufacturers make knotless leaders for bonefish with butt sections from 0.024 to 0.027 of an inch in diameter, which is just about right. The butt sections today are 5 to 6 feet in length, which is also good. These leaders work quite well in most situations.

I didn't tell you about this at the beginning of the chapter because you need to understand leaders whether you tie them or buy them. And you still need to know how to tie and use knots, even with a knotless leader. Besides, I feel that you can make a better leader by hand. More important, you can customize it to suit the ever-changing conditions on the flats.

Whether you use multipiece or knotless leaders, the main knot that you need to know is the blood knot. The tippet section of a knotless leader becomes steadily shorter as you change flies, and eventually you must add new tippet. When you land a bonefish, quite often you will see that the tippet has been frayed by rubbing against the fish's body or any of a variety of hazards in the water. Tying knots in an originally knotless leader is an everyday chore on the flats. Of course, you could discard a $5 leader every time the tippet is too short. Your guide wouldn't mind, I wouldn't mind, and the guys at the fly shop will love you.

Most knotless leaders for bonefish come in 9- and 12-foot lengths. In deciding which you need, keep in mind that these leaders are usually exactly the lengths stated on the labels. By the time you tie it to the fly line and attach a fly, the 9-foot leader that you bought for windy days has shrunk to 8 feet or less. You probably don't want a leader that short. Maybe you should have

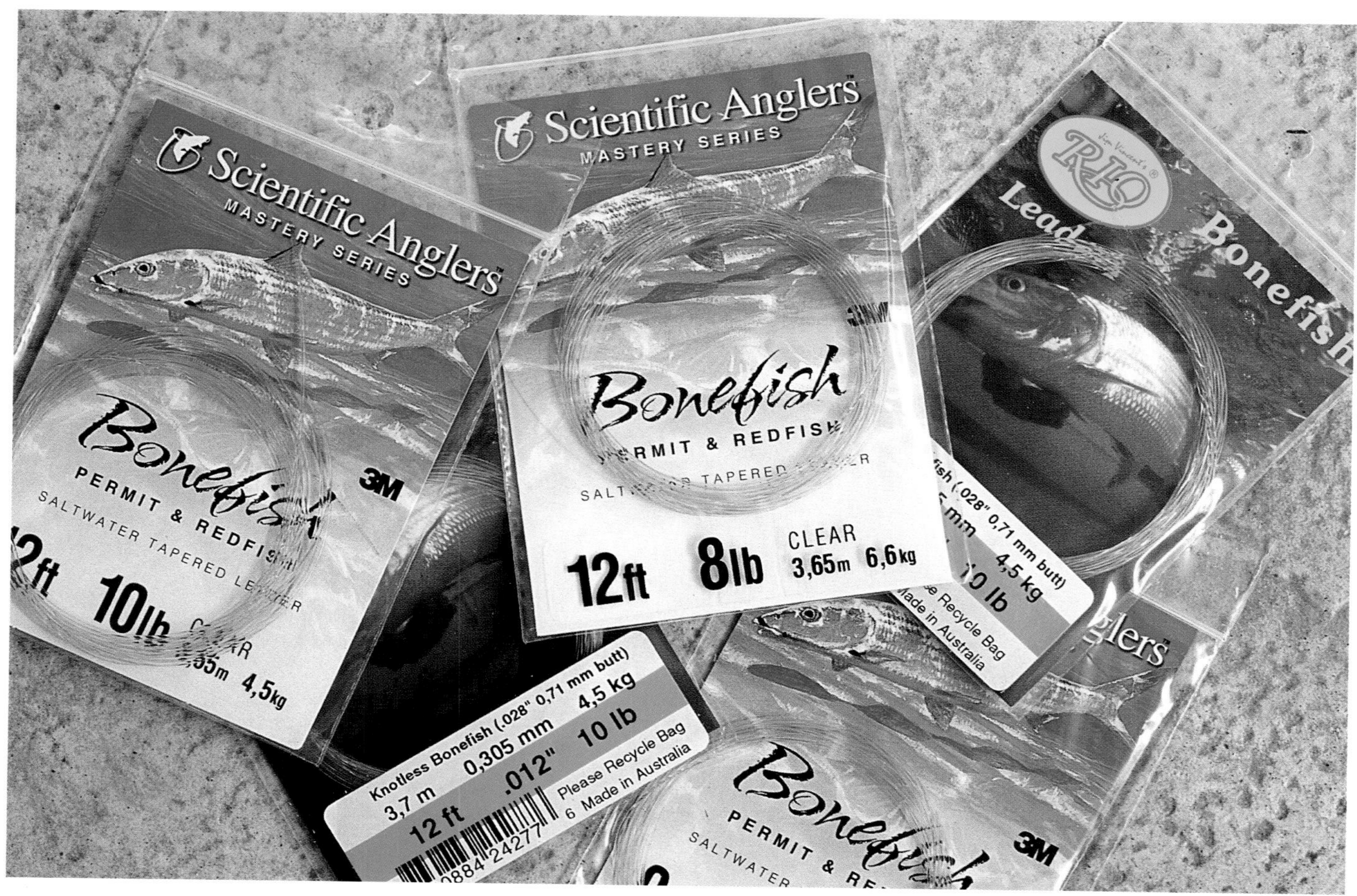

I still feel that I can make a better leader than I can buy, and a leader made with several pieces can easily be modified to suit changing conditions. But knotless leaders for bonefish have improved greatly, and I must confess that I am starting to use them quite frequently. Many follow the 50/30/20 formula described in the text.

bought the 12-footer and trimmed it a little. Knotless leaders can work fine, but you've got to remember that the length in the package is not the same as the length on the water.

The most common way to attach a knotless leader to a fly line is by looping it to a foot of butt section nail-knotted to the tip of the line. In this way, you also add a foot, or more if you want, to the leader. Indeed, you can make the permanent butt 3 feet long. Add a 9-foot knotless leader to that, and you have a 12-foot leader. Or loop on a 12-foot leader and have a 15-footer for flat-calm days. It works because the resulting leader has a very long butt section.

If you prefer, you can tie a short butt section to the fly line and then attach a knotless leader with a blood knot. I like this method because it's fast and it produces a clean leader. Another way is to make a small loop in the end of the fly line and a loop on the butt section of the leader, and then simply interlock the loops.

You have a lot of options with knotless leaders—but not quite as many as you have with hand-tied, knotted ones. No matter which kind of leader you use, you need to understand how it works (or why it refuses to). A badly designed or completely inappropriate leader can spoil your casting and presentations, but a good leader can make your fishing much more pleasant.

PART III

Catching Bonefish on a Fly Rod

Chapter 12

Casting for Bonefish

In the poetry of motion that is fly casting, I see elegance, rhythm, and change, not unlike great jazz improvisations. Two very different worlds for which I've always had great passion.

—the author

It happens all the time. A good guide, knowing that he has little time, works hard poling a skiff to bring his client within reasonable casting range of a tailing bonefish. Then, having poled the skiff halfway across a flat against the wind, he finds out that his well-dressed, properly outfitted client has taken care of every detail except learning how to cast. And you can't buy a tight loop, any more than you can buy a backhand in tennis.

The biggest complaint I hear from guides all over the world is getting a fly fisherman who did not take the time to learn to cast in a windy, ever-changing environment like that of the bonefish flats. Believe me, casting is the one thing you *have* to bring to the game.

If you fish with conventional bluewater tackle, a good captain can troll baits in the right area and hook you a fish. When you fish over a reef, a good chum line can bring fish almost within a rod length of the boat. But on the bonefish flats, the most a guide can do is get you within casting range and then, in a low voice, say those two words that can make so many anglers nervous: "Go ahead." And then it's up to you, and only you. That's what makes it so exciting, so challenging. You can buy your way for hundreds or thousands of miles from your home to a remote bonefish flat, but you can't buy the last 60 feet between you and the fish.

In many cases of heartbreak and frustration, an angler simply did not understand the degree of skill and the type of skill that he or she would need on the flats. The angler might even be a pretty good trout fisherman or may be able to cast 80 feet while fishing for steelhead or salmon, given enough time. On the bonefish flats, though, things are different. The wind can be strong, the fish often move a little faster than anticipated, the time to make the presentation is only a few seconds in most cases, and the little bonefish fly, often weighted, is not all *that* light.

Still, if you take the time to learn, you can do it, and do it well. As an added bonus, you will find that after you learn to fish in the bonefish's world, you will have become a better angler in any environment, fresh or salt water.

WHAT YOU WILL FACE

Besides the facts that bonefish are easily spooked in shallow water (the shallower it is, the spookier they are) and that you usually have only a few seconds to make an accurate cast (while judging the fish's speed and direction, the depth of the water, and the force and direction of the wind), you must contend with one more important factor: fishing pressure. Fishing pressure is increasing everywhere, making bonefish harder to catch. Casts are becoming just a bit longer in some areas, and anglers are using lighter lines for more quiet presentations. In many areas, 7- and 6- weight lines are becoming common; at destinations with lots of small bones, some experts have gone to 5-weight outfits. Although the flies cast with these outfits are small and light by saltwater standards, they're big and heavy by trout-fishing standards. With any outfit, you still must get a 10- to 12-foot leader to turn over and straighten.

If you go down to the Florida Keys looking for those extra-big bonefish, you will have to be a *much* better caster than if you go to a camp in the Bahamas or Central America, where the bones are more plentiful and not as heavily fished, though they're also usually smaller. Many anglers who have caught all kinds of fish all over the world have been humbled by a few days in the Keys.

I learned to cast a fly on my own because there weren't that many fly fishers to ask for help forty (or more) years ago. It was mostly trial and error. And I can tell you lots of stories about that, some funny and some not so funny. These days, a beginning or intermediate

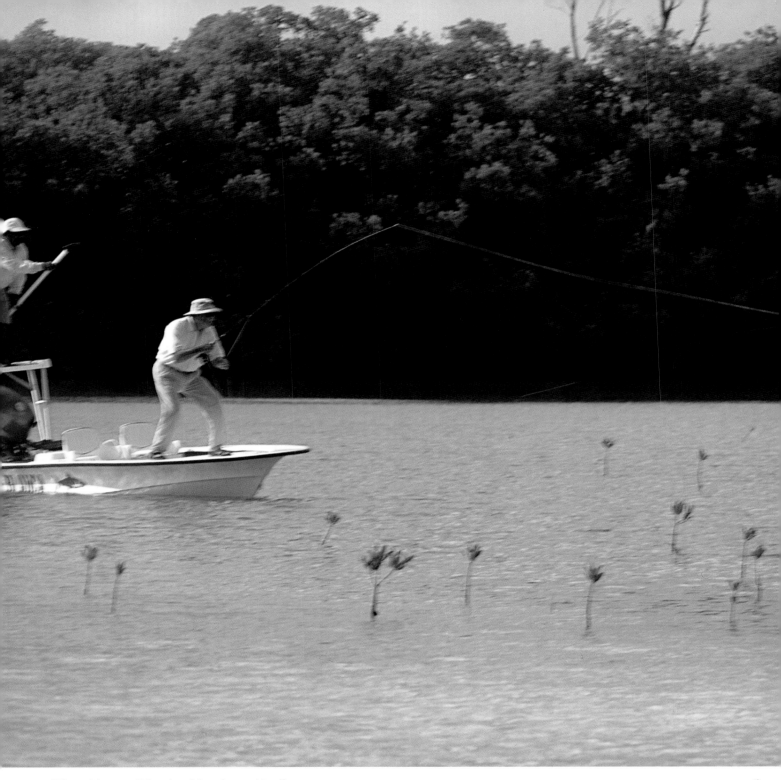

The guide says, "Go ahead," and now it's all up to you.

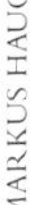

angler doesn't have to learn by trial and error like I did. You can take classes; you can even go back to school. My recommendation is that you enroll in a reputable school (such as the Florida Keys Fly Fishing School or one of the many schools that I conduct at fly shops around the country) or take private classes from someone who knows how to *teach* fly casting. That someone can throw an entire fly line does not necessarily mean that he or she can teach. Please understand this.

HOW MUCH CASTING ABILITY DO YOU NEED?

No doubt you realize that the better you cast, the better your chances of hooking a bonefish. The question here is how well you *must* be able to cast before you pay hard cash for a guided trip and finally face the bonefish that you have been dreaming of.

I feel that the following requirements are essential if you want to take bonefish consistently. Try to meet them, or even surpass them. True, you could get away with less if you are lucky, but I would not count on luck. Besides, I really want that long-awaited trip to be a great experience for you.

Distance

Only we fly fishermen, with our great ability to embellish, would need a definition of something that we can measure, but we do need it. In my view, fly-casting distance is *the length from your most forward toe to where the fly lands*. The fact that you finally got the tail end of a 90-foot fly line partway up the rod (but not out of the tiptop), while backing a little with the rod at the end of the cast to help it along, does not mean that you have made a 100-foot cast, even counting the 10-foot leader. If you don't believe me, measure and suffer.

When you talk about distance, do take the time to measure from your toe to where the fly landed, so that when a guide tells you to cast 60 feet at 11 o'clock, you'll know how far he means.

Regardless of all that has been said about not needing to make very long casts for bonefish (which is generally true) and about most casts to bonefish being medium or short deliveries (which is also generally true), I feel very strongly that you should strive, at least on dry land, to cast the whole fly line or close to it. I feel this way for a reason. Ask several of the top bonefishermen in my area (Miami and the Florida Keys) how far they usually cast for bones, and the answer will be somewhere between 30 and 60 feet. But ask any of these anglers if he can cast the whole line, and the answer will probably be a casual, "Yes, sure." These anglers can easily make short and medium-range casts to bonefish because they have learned to cast much, much farther. For them, a 60-foot cast is simple. All they have to concentrate on is accuracy.

If your maximum cast is 60 feet on grass without a fly (more than enough distance for bonefishing, right?), then your real distance on the water, with the wind and a weighted fly and a bit of buck fever when you see those big tails, is 40 to 50 feet. Maybe. Of course, that assumes that the situation isn't forcing you to deliver the fly with your backcast. How far can you cast that way—with a weighted fly and with a rocking skiff under you? Besides, if merely reaching the bonefish takes all your effort, you will not be thinking about accuracy.

However, if you practice until you can cast close to the whole line—more than 85 feet, say—on the grass, then you should be able to cast an honest 45 feet in the real bonefish world while concentrating on accuracy. So, yes, I think that you need to learn to make a long cast. Besides, casting a long line will also help you in other saltwater endeavors that I just know you'll get into. And it's fun. Casting should be fun for you, not an obstacle that you must overcome to catch a fish. I have been fly casting since about 1956, and I still love to cast just for the pure pleasure of it.

The typical casting distance when sight-fishing for bonefish ranges from 20 to 65 feet. Maybe an average cast, whatever that means, is 35 to 55 feet. In some low-visibility conditions, however, all the casts could be around 25 feet long. On a sunny, flat-calm day when the fish are in eight inches of water, the average cast could easily be over 65 feet. So learn to cast well and enjoy yourself. Some days casting is all we get.

Accuracy

You need a good degree of accuracy in your presentation, whether it's 15 feet or 60 feet. Increase your accuracy and your hookup rate will increase tremendously. Don't underestimate the value of a quick, accurate, short cast; I have taken many bones with such casts, both from a boat and while wading. I've even hooked quite a few bonefish right at the boat or at my feet. A bonefish can sneak up on you in even the shallowest water, forcing you to make a quick cast. It happens all the time, especially on low-visibility days.

The secret to accuracy is control. You will have the most control when you learn to false-cast most of the line the cast needs and then shoot the last few feet. If you try to false-cast a small amount of line and shoot a lot, you will not be accurate or smooth.

Being able to cast a controlled loop at a variety of distances will give you consistency and accuracy. The loop does not have to be extremely tight. It can be a few feet high, but it needs to be smooth, symmetrical, and controlled. Today's bonefish lines have longer heads, usually about 45 feet, in keeping with the "hold lots of line in the air" instead of "shoot a lot of line" philosophy of most successful anglers.

The little line that you do shoot should also be controlled. That is, do not completely let go of the fly line, but instead let the line run through your hand. If the cast is going a bit too far, you can stop it by closing your hand.

When the fly drops on the water, you should have a minimum of slack in the line. The instant you start to strip, the fly should start moving.

I feel that you probably will be the most accurate when you learn to cast with your hand at shoulder level, instead of casting with your arm raised all the way up so that you look like the Statue of Liberty. If you do want to cast with your arm high, then do so by casting over your

Being able to cast a controlled loop is essential to good accuracy.

head so that the fly line is aligned with your eyes to give you accuracy.

We are programmed to hit what we are looking at, whether it's a basketball hoop or a catcher's mitt. When you are trying to drop the fly a few feet in front of a bonefish 50 feet away, you must, in the last few seconds, take your eyes off the fish and look at the place in front of him where you want the fly to land. If you keep your eyes glued to the bonefish, you are very likely to hit him right between the eyes. And he is likely to leave his scales behind on the way off the flat.

Practice accuracy with a leader at least the length of your rod or a bit longer and with a fly; cut off the hook for casting on grass. Use a stick or a fish dummy as a target so that you can practice casting in front of a fish. Do not cast to a hoop.

The Fast Draw

My friend's complete concentration was on the 60 or 70 feet of fly line he was false-casting and the tight loops he was forming. He looked almost enchanted by the line's flight in the air. Every time he let one go, he would hit 90 feet, easily. He looked good. But he was doing it the easy, unrealistic way. Casting on the lawn the evening before our fishing trip, holding the ideal amount of fly line for a long cast with his rod, with no fly, without having to take his eyes off the fly line and with all the time in the world to reach that distance—well, he wasn't really practicing. The only thing he was gaining was false confidence.

I suggested that he was a good caster and no longer needed much practice with the long cast, but should perhaps concentrate on the fast-draw cast at short and medium ranges, with the highest degree of accuracy possible. But a man who can easily cast 90 feet will seldom feel that he has to practice 30- or 40-foot casts.

The next morning was fairly calm and a bit hazy, with lots of glare and heavy cloud formations accumulating as the morning progressed. The fishing forecast was for poor visibility that would get steadily worse through late morning.

The tide was almost halfway in, and most bonefish on the flats were cruising rather than tailing, and not pushing much of a wake, if any. By the time we could spot a bonefish, we were usually within 30 feet of him. Sometimes, we were much closer. The casting forecast for the day was fast, short, and accurate.

Every time my friend spotted a bonefish, he would start to false-cast over and over, desperately trying to get enough line out to feel the load he was used to casting. By the time he had 35 or 40 feet of line out, the bone was within 20 feet of the boat and very disturbed.

My friend had been practicing for long-range shooting on the prairie, but a bonefish angler also needs to practice for a fast-draw gunfight in the saloon. In other types of fly fishing, you cast while you fish. As you work a shoreline, for instance, you cast and retrieve, cast and retrieve as you move along. In sight-casting, though, you spend most of your time looking and hunting. While you hunt, the line and rod are idle. You are waiting to make a fast-draw cast at a moment's notice.

You have to know how to make this cast to catch bonefish. You must set things in motion and get off a shot in just a few seconds. It takes practice, but it's not all that hard to learn.

These days, a typical fly rod works best with 30 to 40 feet of the designated line and the leader out of the tip-top (depending on the taper of the line and the philosophy of the rod's designer). With that much line out, you will feel the rod bend as it pulls against the line, and you will be able to cast easily and comfortably. But try to make a fast cast when you are holding the fly in one hand, and you'll find that the leader and the few feet of fly line out of the tip-top do not weigh enough to load the rod.

It takes some practice to develop a feel for those first several false casts made with very little fly line. If you are already a caster, a few half-hour sessions of fast-draw practice will put you well on the way to better sight-casting.

The trick is to hold the leader and as much fly line as possible out of the tip of the rod. This amount will vary with wind conditions and how high you are off the water. You can usually hold more line out of the rod while standing on the casting platform of a skiff on a calm day than you can while wading on a windy day. You must adjust for the situation. But the more line you have out of the rod, the more weight you start with and the faster you will make the cast.

Note that fast does not mean furious. Stay smooth. Be efficient, not rushed. Frantic movements, especially if made with your casting arm up high, tend to spook bonefish. You've got to stay cool.

There are two ways to be in a ready position while sight-fishing. One is to hold the fly with your line hand, and the other is to hold the fly and a loop of line. You should learn both, because each has its own uses.

Holding only the fly. Assuming that you cast with your right hand, hold the fly by the outside of the hook bend with the index finger and thumb of your left hand; a good trick is to barely hold the bend and some of the fly's wing or tail. Make sure that the point of the hook is visible outside your grip. As a skiff moves along a flat, the line or leader will often catch on a small mangrove shoot or other protruding structure. If you have the sharp point of the hook between your fingers when the line catches on something, there is going to be a hookup, but not one involving a bonefish.

While holding the fly, let as much fly line slide out of the tip of the rod as you can comfortably handle in the situation. You will find that you can easily carry a rod-length of fly line and the leader beyond the tip-top, giving you close to 20 feet of leader and fly line with which to make the first false cast. That's a much better way to get started than having only a few feet of line outside the rod. One false cast and a short shoot will let you put the fly at least 25 feet away; another false cast or two will extend the cast to 45 feet.

Holding the fly and a loop of line. Not many anglers use this method, but I do, at least on a fairly calm day. On windy days I usually go back to holding just the fly.

This method works on the same principle as the first, but instead of holding just the fly with your left hand, you hold the fly and a single loop of line. You have even more line out of the rod, and therefore can get off a cast much faster.

Here's how it works. Start by holding the fly with your index finger and thumb, taking care that the hook point can't accidentally end up in your flesh. Then make a loop consisting of the whole leader and a foot or two of fly line, and hold the fly line by trapping it between your small and ring fingers and the palm of your hand. It's more complicated to explain than to do.

When you have to make a quick cast, start your backcast and let the fly line and then the fly leave your hand. That's all there is to it.

You'll find that with this method you can carry 30 feet of leader and fly line beyond the rod tip. With a single backcast, you can easily put a fly 35 feet away. Pretty effective, really. With 30 feet in the air to start, a couple of false casts can put you past 60 feet. This style of fast draw can quickly turn into long-range shooting.

A shorter leader for speed. One of the things that makes the fast draw difficult is that the leader does not have much weight and therefore does not help much in loading the rod during the first false casts. On most days, you cannot afford to make any changes in the rod, line, or leader to accommodate a short cast because the next cast may well have to go longer than 60 feet. You simply need to practice to develop the feel for making a short, quick cast.

Sometimes, though, you can safely assume that most (if not all) of your casts will be short. On a windy, overcast day with poor visibility, you can count on making mostly short casts, if only because you won't be able to see bonefish that are far away. In this case, shortening the leader will help you get the fast draw started. You are simply substituting heavier fly line for lighter leader. You will feel the rod load much sooner.

If the day is windy and overcast, chances are that you will be able to get away with a shorter leader without spooking bonefish. You might go from a 12-foot leader to a 9-footer, and while this may not seem like much, it will make a difference in the fast draw.

Handling the Wind

Be able to contend with the wind, not only physically, but mentally, too. The minute they feel the wind, some anglers change their otherwise good strokes and start swinging. Their loops become bigger, the wind grabs them, and the casts fall apart. As their casting deteriorates, the anglers say, "I just can't cast in the wind." Nonsense. If you can make tight loops without the wind, you can make them in the wind.

A smooth, tight loop will cut through most wind. Lengthening your stroke to pick up some of the waves and slack in your cast will help a lot. If you feel that you need to add more power, do it smoothly with a long stroke.

Remember that the wind is not always your enemy. Usually, the windier it is, the closer you can get to your prey and the less likely you are to need an extra-long cast. At places like Islamorada in the Florida Keys, I pray for a bit of wind so I can get close to those monster bonefish. If it's flat calm, you don't have a chance.

The wind can blow from any angle, and you must be able to deal with it. Just as bonefish can appear behind you and force you to present the fly with a backcast, sometimes the wind blows from the same side as your casting arm—your right side, if you're a right-handed caster. Coming from that side, the wind will blow the line (and the hook) into you if you try to make a normal cast. You'll have to turn around and deliver the fly with a backcast or use an off-shoulder cast made by angling the rod across your body so that the line passes over your left side rather than your right. It pays to learn both casts; you'll use them on the flats.

Some anglers even learn to cast with either hand. They tell me that it's not as hard as it seems, though I confess that I haven't done it. But an ambidextrous caster will have more opportunities.

The Pickup

You cast to a bonefish, and the fly doesn't land where you wanted it to. Maybe you simply missed, or perhaps the fish changed direction as you came forward with the presentation cast. Either way, you have to make another

MARKUS HAUGG

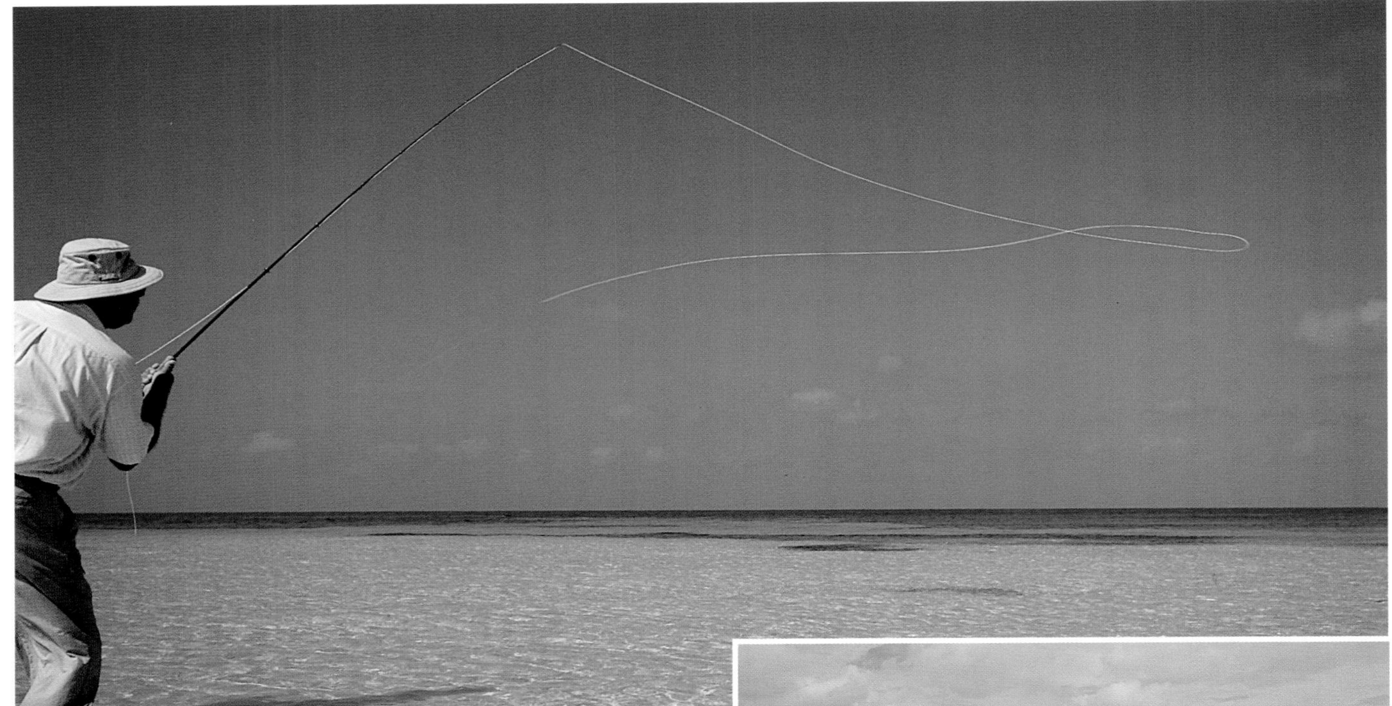

Learning to make the cross-body or off-shoulder cast can help you outsmart the wind.

Capt. John Donnell and I with a 14-pound bone taken in 20-mph wind. It's worth learning to fish in the wind.

SUE MORET

cast and reposition the fly as soon as possible. The best and most efficient way to do this is to pick up all or most of the line and drop the fly back in front of the fish.

With a bonefish right in front of you, the natural tendency is to rip the fly line off the water and hammer a cast in the fish's direction before it sees the boat or moves out of range. That's always a mistake. Ripping line off the water kills your timing and shocks the rod. Even if you do get the cast under control, you've probably already spooked the fish by making such a commotion.

Another tendency is frantically to strip line until you have the fly within 30 feet of the boat, and then start false-casting to set up another presentation. By then, of course, the fish has fled or at least moved out of range.

The smoothest, fastest, and most accurate way to reposition a fly is to learn to pick up all the line on the water, make a false cast or two, and drop the fly softly in place—without ripping line, without making noise, without losing control. Start by lifting the tip of the rod higher and higher, until only a few feet of line and the leader remain in the water. Without pausing, start the backcast with an exaggerated, long, smooth stroke; with most of the fly line out of the water, you can pick up the rest without making a sound. The bonefish will never know. Now false-cast once to restore your aim and drop the fly in place. The whole procedure looks almost like a slow-motion cast. Very civilized. And very effective.

The Double Haul

I can't think of any way that you could accomplish all these casts without knowing how to double-haul. But I

MARKUS HAUGG

MARKUS HAUGG

Top: *Picking up the whole cast to attempt a better presentation is an essential bonefishing skill.*

Left: *Saltwater fly casters need to know how to double-haul.*

don't mean the violent, rip-your-shirt hauls used by many casters. Each haul should be a smooth, fairly short, but perfectly timed movement. If you double-haul smoothly, you can do it all day.

This technique of pumping with your line hand while casting has several advantages. It adds speed to the cast, which helps the line cut through the wind better. It increases distance by a large margin, speeding up your delivery. A good double haul makes casting smoother, actually reducing the effort required to throw a long line. Good double-haul technique is essential to all saltwater fly fishing.

The Parallel Cast

Another technique that will serve you well is the parallel cast, in which the rod moves more or less parallel with the water—that is, in a horizontal plane—so that the line remains lower. This delivery comes in handy when a bonefish suddenly appears so close to you that a normal cast with the rod approximately vertical will surely spook him. A parallel cast keeps your rod, casting arm, and line below the bonefish's window of vision. Very often, you will crouch while making this cast. I use the parallel cast all the time, particularly in a skiff, where one is so much higher in the bonefish's window.

PRACTICE, PRACTICE, AND PRACTICE

After you have learned the basics of casting and a few types of casts, you must practice until those casts are committed to memory. When you face a bonefish, you must be able to focus on the fish without thinking about your casting technique or, worse yet, watching the line move back and forth. Your casting has to become almost subconscious; you need to develop something called muscle memory. After learning the basics, most anglers need about twenty hours of practice to develop some kind of muscle memory. Only then do you really start to cast.

I know that you are in a rush, but do not try to accumulate these twenty hours by practicing much more than twenty minutes at a time a few days a week. Eventually, you can work up to thirty-minute practice sessions. If you try casting for a few hours, you'll find that your wrist, the weakest link in the chain, will take only so much before it starts to collapse. Once your wrist gives out, your timing and stroke deteriorate rapidly. From then on, you will only develop bad habits.

Keep a practice rod rigged and ready. If it's going to take you fifteen minutes or more to find the rod and reel, assemble the outfit, and tie on a practice fly, you will rarely take the time to practice. Keep a fully rigged rod in your house or car, ready to cast. Then you will practice often and enjoy it.

Practice with your bonefish rod. Casting with a 4-weight trout rod will not teach you what you need to learn. Use a 12-foot leader with a 10-pound tippet and, of course, a fly. Take an old bonefish fly, size 2 or 4, and cut the hook at the end of the shank, right where the wire starts to bend. If you don't have any old bonefish flies that you can sacrifice, perhaps you can get one from a friend. I want you to get used to the weight of the fly. A little piece of yarn attached to the tippet will only give you false confidence.

If possible, practice during the hottest part of the day to replicate the conditions in which you will fish. Always wear glasses and a hat to protect your eyes and head.

Sometimes practice will become frustrating. Everyone has bad days. Generally, though, it should be fun. Casting well simply feels good. Resolve to practice, and you will learn to cast well.

CASTING AROUND THE CLOCK

After you have practiced all the basics until they've become almost instinctive, it's time to add another ritual. I call it casting around the clock. No more casting in the direction that's comfortable for you, which is usually downwind. The bigger bonefish always seem to come from the upwind side.

Casting around the clock requires a large, open lawn. If your own yard isn't big enough, find a place in a park where you can practice. Go there on a breezy day. Cast in any direction, varying the lengths of your casts and making sure that the fly turns over every time. Then turn a little and make a few more casts of various lengths. Turn again (just a little) and cast some more. By the time you've turned 360 degrees, you will have cast with the wind, sideways to the wind, against the wind, sideways to the wind again (but from the opposite side of your body), and at every angle in between.

Your distance, accuracy, and comfort will vary greatly as you change your angle to the wind. That's natural. If you cast around the clock regularly, your overall ability to cast in any direction will improve immensely, and you will become a better angler for it.

Later, you must practice on water to learn to deal with the added tension on the pickup. Casting on water will also teach you not to let the backcast drop.

If all of this conveys the impression that you need to do some work before becoming a good fly caster, then I've made my point. But you can't fish a fly until you can cast it, and you can't hook a bonefish until you can cast well.

Casting is great fun that only becomes more enjoyable as you become better. I love it. The fly line in the air really is like poetry in motion. It's good for my soul. It is such a large part of being a fly fisherman that I would not want to fly fish if I did not need to fly cast to do it.

Chapter 13

Preparing to Fish

Tomorrow you will try to catch a bonefish, but tonight you are making decisions and checking gear.

Which rods will I need? Which flies should I bring? Does every fly line have a good leader with a fresh tippet? Do I have enough spare leaders? Are all my lines clean and slick? Will I need flies and leaders for permit or barracudas? Have I forgotten anything? What else do I need to bring to the dock in the morning?

The possibilities are many. Too many. If you were to rig for all possibilities and bring all the extra tackle that might come in handy, you'd need two skiffs to carry the load. Yet you want to arrive at the dock with the right stuff.

The most effective way to narrow down what you'll need is to find out what the conditions will be tomorrow, particularly at the first stop of the day. Will you wade or fish from the skiff? This may determine which outfit you need. Will the tide be high or low? This may determine fly size and weight. Have the fish been extra-spooky lately? If so, you will need an extra-long leader. The list goes on.

Talking with your guide will provide answers to many questions. You could chat by telephone, but it might be better to meet him for a drink. All kinds of information flow over drinks. Many of the big fish that I have taken were partly the products of good conversations the night before. Whenever I visit a fishing camp, I try to have a meeting with my guide the night before our first day of fishing. Even a short meeting helps us make plans for the next day and the week ahead, and it helps me show up with exactly the right tackle and flies.

Some preparations don't change from trip to trip, and the night before you fish always includes certain rituals. Combine the basic preparations with your guide's observations, and you will always arrive ready.

CHECK YOUR LINES

If you didn't do so before starting your trip, make sure that your fly lines are clean. How often a fly line needs cleaning depends on where you fish, where you practice your casting (you do practice, right?), and even the condition of the boat in which you last used a line. Modern lines, particularly bonefish lines, don't need to be cleaned very often. Eventually, though, any fly line gets dirty.

If you need to clean a line on a trip, you can do it either of two ways. You can fill the sink in your room with warm (not hot) water, add a little mild soap, and then strip the line from the reel and submerge it in the soapy water. Let it sit for a few minutes, and then drain the sink and rinse the line with cold water. Remove the line from the sink and gently pull it through a folded paper towel, taking off the last of the dirt. The other method is to use a cleaning pad made for the purpose, such as those sold by Scientific Anglers. These do a very good job. Fold the pad around the dirty fly line and strip the whole line through it two or three times. You will notice the dirt left on the pad.

After cleaning a line, dress it with the appropriate product. You could wait to do this until the next day, when you're in the skiff, but you might forget. It's easy to get distracted on the flats. Better to dress your lines the night before you fish. Pour some dressing on a rag or applicator and pull the line through it. Don't forget to dress the butt section of the leader, the leader knot, and the connection between the fly line and the backing.

You might need to dress your line again while fishing, particularly if you make a lot of casts. Carry your dressing kit in your tackle bag or, better yet, a pocket. Dressing does several things for your fly line, all of them good. The line will slide through the guides much easier, double-haul with increased ease and speed, shoot much farther, and float just a tad higher. Regular dressing also dramatically increases the life of the line.

The first few minutes of a day often produce the best fishing. Be ready.

LEADERS AND RIGGING

It is amazing to me how often a guide has to delay fishing during the great early morning light to construct a full leader for a client. This time is precious—don't waste it. Step onto the skiff with your rods rigged and ready.

First, of course, you must settle on which outfits you will bring. As noted earlier, a single 8-weight rod will do everything pretty well, but many anglers, including me, prefer to have a lighter rod for wading. Where most of the fish are on the small side, such as in the Bahamas or Belize, you might want a 7- or 6-weight outfit for wading and an 8-weight to use in the skiff or on a windy day. In the Keys, your wading rod might be a 7 or 8 and your skiff outfit might be a 9-weight. If you expect to cast to permit or barracudas, you will certainly want a 9-weight outfit, or maybe a 10. Each destination has its own requirements. At any destination, it pays to have two rods in the boat so that you're ready for shallow or deep water, windy or calm conditions, bonefish and other species.

Your guide can help you decide which outfits you will need. He understands the local conditions and knows what to expect the next day. Then it's up to you to make sure that your gear is ready. If your guide expects tailing fish and cruisers in very shallow water, rig your outfits (or at least one) with a longer leader; 12 feet is a good length for casting in skinny water. If the forecast is for cruisers and mudding fish in deeper water, rig at least one outfit with a slightly shorter leader, say 11 feet. You'll want to go even shorter if you expect to spend the day fighting the wind.

If you need to, or even suspect that you should, tie new leaders for your lines or attach fresh knotless leaders. Don't merely hope that an old, beat-up 9-foot leader will do the job with tailing fish or that a 12-footer will miraculously turn over in the brisk wind forecast for the next day.

If possible, rig all the way to the fly. Again, your guide can suggest the best fly for the conditions expected the next morning—a light fly for shallow water, a weighted pattern for deep water, or whatever. Arrive at the dock the next morning with your outfits fully rigged. When the boat stops at the first flat, you'll be ready. I can't count the times when those first few minutes early in the morning produced the best opportunity, the biggest fish, or the only bonefish of the day.

After rigging an outfit, pull the entire leader out of the tip of the rod, run the leader down and around the reel, and then bring the fly up to one of the stripping guides. Hook the fly on the frame of the guide, not on the ceramic ring through which the line passes. If you hook the fly to the ring, two bad things can happen. One, the fly will be half an inch or more away from the blank, and you might hook yourself while grabbing the rod the next day. Second, the hook might chip the ceramic ring. A damaged ring will eventually damage your fly line, and it could cut the backing when a fish runs.

If you don't know which fly you might need, then rig to the tippet. I pull the leader and some fly line through the guides, bring the leader around the reel, and

MARKUS HAUGG

A good angler and guide become a team that can perform magic on the flats.

then tie the end of the tippet with an overhand knot to one of the stripping guides. When I get to the first flat and find out which fly I need, all I have to do it untie or pull the tippet from the guide and attach the fly. And with the rod rigged in this matter, the leader's butt section stays straight all night. That saves a little time the next morning.

WHAT TO BRING

You will be fishing from a skiff, not a yacht. These days, with fishing pressure increasing, bonefish skiffs are getting shorter, narrower, and lighter, and often have little in the way of spray rails. No doubt these skiffs are better fishing boats than we generally had in the old days, but they have less dry space for tackle than bigger boats have. This is a problem only for those who bring way too much stuff. Several rigged fly rods, a tackle bag, a wading or belt bag, rain gear, and a big lunch and drinks for two anglers will all fit out of the way in almost any skiff.

Put your fly rods (each fully rigged to the fly, right?) out of harm's way in the rod racks. Except for *very* short runs, put them back in the racks every time you move to another location.

Your tackle bag should not be much bigger than 18 by 12 by 10 inches. It should have a wide shoulder strap so that you can leave your hands free for carrying rods, lunch, and so forth. A bag that size has plenty of room for extra reels, fly lines, leaders and leader material, clippers, forceps, fly boxes, a camera and film, and much more. Put your rain gear somewhere in or on the bag where you can grab it instantly. Your tackle bag will go in one of the skiff's storage compartments; the captain decides where.

You might also have a wading bag or belt pack. One of these is essential when you wade for more than a few minutes or wander far from the skiff. In many places, one can get out of the skiff and wade for hours. Your belt pack or wading bag holds leaders, tippet material, flies, clippers, and maybe even a point-and-shoot camera. It, too, goes in one of the skiff's compartments.

Lunch and drinks (bring plenty of water) go in the boat's cooler.

See? You don't need to bring the kitchen sink with you. Your guide will really appreciate your showing up with a light load. He's got to push the boat all day.

YOUR GUIDE'S EXPECTATIONS

A good guide spends extra time researching where to fish before he sees you. Then he poles a skiff several miles to hunt for bonefish, constantly calculating the changing tides and weather to decide where to try next. The guide's job requires great mental and physical effort, and I feel that the poler has a right to expect certain things from you in exchange for his or her efforts. Yes, the guide is going to get paid, but that's not enough, at least for a good guide. He is not into it just for the money. Like an artist, he works for rewards besides cash. He really wants you to catch a fish.

That brings us back to casting skills. I travel all over the world teaching the art of fly casting and fly fishing, and I find that many anglers want to go fly fishing for bonefish, but have *zero* casting skill and little interest in learning. They expect the guide to stop the skiff on the way to a flat and give them a few tips on casting so they can get the hang of it or learn the "tricks." Then they fully expect to head to the nearest bonefish flat for a full day of great fishing. Some guides lose their hair early; others turn gray prematurely.

Casting is the quintessential skill that you have to bring to the game. Without it, you can't play. No one can help you reach that last 60 feet to a bonefish.

You can't do much to improve your casting skills during the boat ride to the flats. So, before you get on the airplane, learn to cast a bonefish fly 50 feet in some wind and with some accuracy. That's a good start. Today's rods are so good that it doesn't take long to achieve this goal. Casting lessons and good saltwater fly-fishing schools are worth every penny.

Casting well pays off in many ways. When you spend enough days fishing with the same guide or friend, the team gets better and better. Soon, you are better than the sum of the parts. You start to anticipate the poler and he starts to fish through your hands. In this team relationship, communication becomes almost telepathic. You start to take fish that you couldn't have caught a year earlier. I know many of these team relationships. Some last for generations, with a father bringing his son or daughter into it. Eventually, the family starts to fish with the son of the guide. It's a beautiful thing.

But none of it can happen if you can't deliver the fly. Your guide expects you to be able to cast. Make him happy by being prepared.

Chapter 14

The Hunt

He is the wisest, shyest, wariest, strangest fish I ever studied.
—Zane Grey, in Tales of Fishes

So far, you have learned about the bonefish's environment, the fish itself, tackle, rigging, flies, and casting technique. Now let's put it all together—let's go bonefishing.

On your next trip to the flats, you might fish with a professional guide, with an experienced friend, or by yourself. Even if you go after bonefish with an expert, you still should know what to look for and how to hunt. Once you learn where, when, and how to look for bonefish, you can fish for them on your own. Much more important, however, you and a guide will become a better, more efficient team.

GETTING READY TO HUNT

As you step onto the skiff's casting deck, look around for any loose items—tackle bags, camera cases, shoes, sandals—that can catch the fly line while you're trying to cast. Built-in hazards such as cleats and pushpole holders that don't retract can be covered with duct tape so that they can't snag your line. A fly line will catch on almost anything within several feet of you. Shoes with stiff leather laces or sandals with protruding tabs can also be a nightmare for a caster, particularly in the typically windy conditions of the bonefish flats. Do your best to eliminate line-grabbers. Bonefish don't need any help to elude fishermen.

His sunglasses, cap, and bandit-style bandana help this angler to distinguish fish from bottom.

If you didn't wear your hat and sunglasses on the boat ride to the flat, put them on now. Some anglers carry more than one pair of glasses. Medium or medium-light polarizing lenses in a warm color, such as tan or amber, cut through surface glare and let you distinguish shades better than gray or blue glasses. On cloudy, overcast days, yellow polarizing glasses let in more light and help you see fish much better.

The dark underside of your hat's brim reflects little or no glare to your glasses. You can help your eyes even more by pulling the brim of your hat down so that it almost touches the tops of your glasses, forming a dark tunnel. When fish are very difficult to spot, this can make the difference between seeing or not seeing them. If you want to go one step further, and I always do, wear a bandana bandit-style on your face. You'll find that it cuts glare and reduces sunburn.

Make sure that the point of your hook is needle sharp. Test it by touching the point to your thumbnail to see if it sticks easily. If the point slides across your thumbnail, touch up the hook with a file or stone.

Check your reel's drag setting. You should have kept the drag loose between trips, but now it's time to fish. The amount of resistance that you apply to a fish should be divided between the reel's mechanical drag and the rim control of the spool. When a fish makes a sudden lunge, you can instantly take your hand off the spool and let the fish run against only the resistance of the drag. You'll break off fewer fish this way and still apply maximum pressure when you need it. It is the best way to fight any fish with a fly rod.

For bonefishing, I like to set a drag to a couple of pounds or so, just enough that the reel will not overrun, or maybe a tad more. Later in the fight, as the bonefish starts to get tired and his runs are not as fast or as long, you can add a little more drag. But always remember that the drag should not do all the fighting for you. You must use your hands to add or subtract pressure in an instant. There is a great difference between the resistance that you should apply when a bonefish is making one of his many high-speed runs (this is when you need light pressure) and when you are in a tug-of-war later in the fight (this is the time for maximum pressure).

Check the drag, but don't overtighten it. You can always increase the pressure during a fight. You can't do anything when a bonefish breaks the tippet.

You're almost ready to begin looking for fish. But you still have one very important job to do.

This fly line is lying flat and tangle free, ready to shoot through the guides.

STRIP AND STRETCH

Strip line off your reel by pulling it straight out—that is, toward the stripping guide—without the line touching the fly reel. If you strip downward, the fly line will scrape against the reel's frame or a pillar, and that can only shorten the life of the line.

As it comes off the reel, the line will fall to the deck in coils. All fly lines have memory. The stiffer the line, the more memory it has; lines made for the tropics, such as your bonefish lines, have a lot of memory. Straighten the line by stretching it a few feet at a time. A straightened, stretched fly line will lie flat on the skiff's deck. It's far less likely to tangle than a line full of coils, and the wind won't catch the line and push it around. When you cast, a stretched line provides better loop control, shoots farther, and transfers the energy of the cast to the leader, all of which add up to better presentations. It will float flat and high on the surface, making a smooth pickup much easier if you need to make a quick second cast. And since a stretched line lies straight on the water, it will fish better; the slightest twitch of your line hand will impart action to the fly, and the most subtle strike will be transmitted to your hand.

Always take a minute to stretch and straighten your line before you start looking for fish. A coiled fly line is a nightmare to cast. It fishes poorly, too, because it's full of coils that absorb any action you try to give the fly. If a fish picks up the fly gently, you won't even feel the bite.

While you're at it, make sure that your leader is straight. Pay particular attention to the butt section. If you prepared your rods as described in the last chapter, the leader butt should be fairly straight. Check it anyway, and stretch it as needed.

You might have to repeat this ritual every time you resume fishing after moving to a new spot. Don't be lazy; stretch the line and leader before you start to fish. It will pay off in better performance and more fish.

How much line should you strip off the reel? Less than many anglers think. When I started fishing for bonefish in Cuba in the late 1950s, tackle was very different from the gear we have now. I used bamboo rods, a Cape Cod fly line, big flies tied on size 1/0 hooks, and 8 feet of 10-pound-test line for a leader. We would pole or wade to within 30 to 50 feet of a bonefish and start flailing away.

Now, tackle is infinitely more sophisticated, we can make much longer casts, and flies for bonefish are smaller, further helping in the distance department. But because we still need to see the fish, cast accurately, control the fly's movement and action, and be able to lift the fly line to make another cast, we are still fishing more or less within that range. Some things have not changed all that much.

Most anglers, particularly those who have learned to cast most or all of the fly line, strip too much line off the reel when they are getting ready to fish. That's a recipe for trouble. You don't need more line than you will actually cast, and that distance depends on wind conditions, visibility, and your own ability. The more line you peel off the reel, the greater the likelihood of getting a tangle while casting to a fish or clearing the line after you hook one.

If it's windy, cloudy, or both, your guide might suggest that you strip off 50 feet of line or less. On a bright,

As you look for bonefish, you become a hunter. More of the day is spent hunting than casting.

calm day, when visibility is good and the fish are spooky, you might want to strip off 65 feet—provided you can cast all of it.

When you need to cast far, you usually have a little more time to do so. If you have only 50 feet of line off the reel when you spot a target 70 feet away that you cannot get closer to, you will probably have enough time to strip off the extra line. Successful long casts are rarely made in a hurry.

Just before starting to fish, I like to make a few practice casts in various directions to reestablish my feel for the complete outfit. Even if I fished the day before, I now have a new leader and a different fly. Sometimes I discover that the leader is too long for conditions or that the line needs a quick dressing. If everything is just right, I can start fishing with confidence.

If you don't often fish in the tropics or with a saltwater fly rod, you definitely should make a few casts to get the feel of your outfit. Believe me, it can't hurt.

WADING FOR BONEFISH

The trout fisherman usually prefers to use a dry fly. The bass angler, a popper. The backcountry snook fisherman, a surface fly. And so the bonefisherman usually prefers to wade. It is the purest way to fish for bonefish, partly because it takes place in very shallow water, often at short range, and it demands excellent fly-rod skills. But I think there is even more to it. You see, when you get off the skiff and wade, especially when you are alone or a good distance from others, it's just you. When to cast, where to cast, how to retrieve—every judgment call is yours. If everything goes right and you finally slip your hand under a big, fat bonefish, you know that *you* caught him.

A few years back, on a hosted bonefish trip, I fished with an angler who had taken sailfish on flies, giant tarpon, and many other big fish. After catching a couple of bonefish from the skiff early in the morning, he had to leave the boat to wade after a big bonefish in water too shallow for the skiff's draft. He waded more than 100 yards stalking the fish while the guide and I stayed on the skiff and watched. The angler had to make two or three presentations before he hooked the bone. He sustained the long run, fought the fish well, and eventually landed him. I waded over with a camera to take a few photos. When I got there, the angler's first words were, "I feel this is the first fish I ever really caught." He was beaming. I understood exactly what he meant.

Wading is best on a hard bottom and at low stages of the tide when visibility is good. Tailing fish are usually easy to see, even at a distance. On very windy days, when the fish show just the tips of their tails as they feed, they can be hard to spot. Normally, though, they're not hard to see.

Cruising fish often give themselves away by showing the tips of their dorsal fins or tails. On a cloudy day or on a dark bottom, you might have to look for a wake or "nervous water," a slight surface disturbance moving in a direction different from that of the rest of the water. Nervous water says that there is something alive and moving in that area. It can often be very subtle, and spotting nervous water is among the skills that come with experience.

You can usually get a lot closer to a bone when wading than you can in a skiff. Most bonefish skiffs make some kind of noise, particularly when they move against the wind, and the portion of the hull that is underwater pushes a bow wave that fish can feel. A wader also pushes a wave, but it's much smaller. When you wade, you can usually get within casting range.

It helps to crouch a little and present a lower profile to the fish while you cast. Keep the loop low to the water. This is not the time for your Statue of Liberty imitation, especially on a calm day when bonefish have a large, unbroken window on the surface and seem to see everything around them. Stay low.

As you wade, you will drag some fly line behind you. This is usually not too big a problem. You might have 50 feet of line off the reel, but the rod takes up about 8 feet of line, and you have another 10 or 12 feet out of the tip-top. That leaves about 30 feet of line in the water, but since the line forms a long loop, you're dragging only 15 feet of doubled line. It's manageable. When you're ready to cast, flip the loop of line forward so that it's closer to you. You can then make the cast without any trouble.

You don't need a stripping basket. Baskets are great in the surf, where one often has to make long casts and contend with breaking waves. On the flats, you won't cast as far as a surf fisherman does, and you can let the line lie on the nice, calm water at your feet. A stripping basket is no help here.

You do need wading boots to protect your feet from sea urchins, chunks of coral, and other dangers. I bring mine on every bonefish trip. A few places, such as the south end of Exuma, have flats of pure sand where you can shed your boots and wade very quietly. And believe it or not, wading barefoot can make a big difference.

A few years ago, my son and I were fishing out of Peace and Plenty in Exuma. Our guide took us to a large flat made entirely of white sand. Bonefish were everywhere in the low outgoing tide. They were also very hard to approach that day. Some days are different than others; I don't know why.

We were making casts well over 70 feet and using leaders in excess of 12 feet, but the bonefish knew we were there. Their body language showed it. We spooked fish right and left.

Then the guide asked my son to take off his boots and change to a pair of shorts that he had brought. He asked me to do the same, but I decided to wait and see.

My son and the guide, barefooted and in shorts, started a strange walk. They would lift each foot carefully

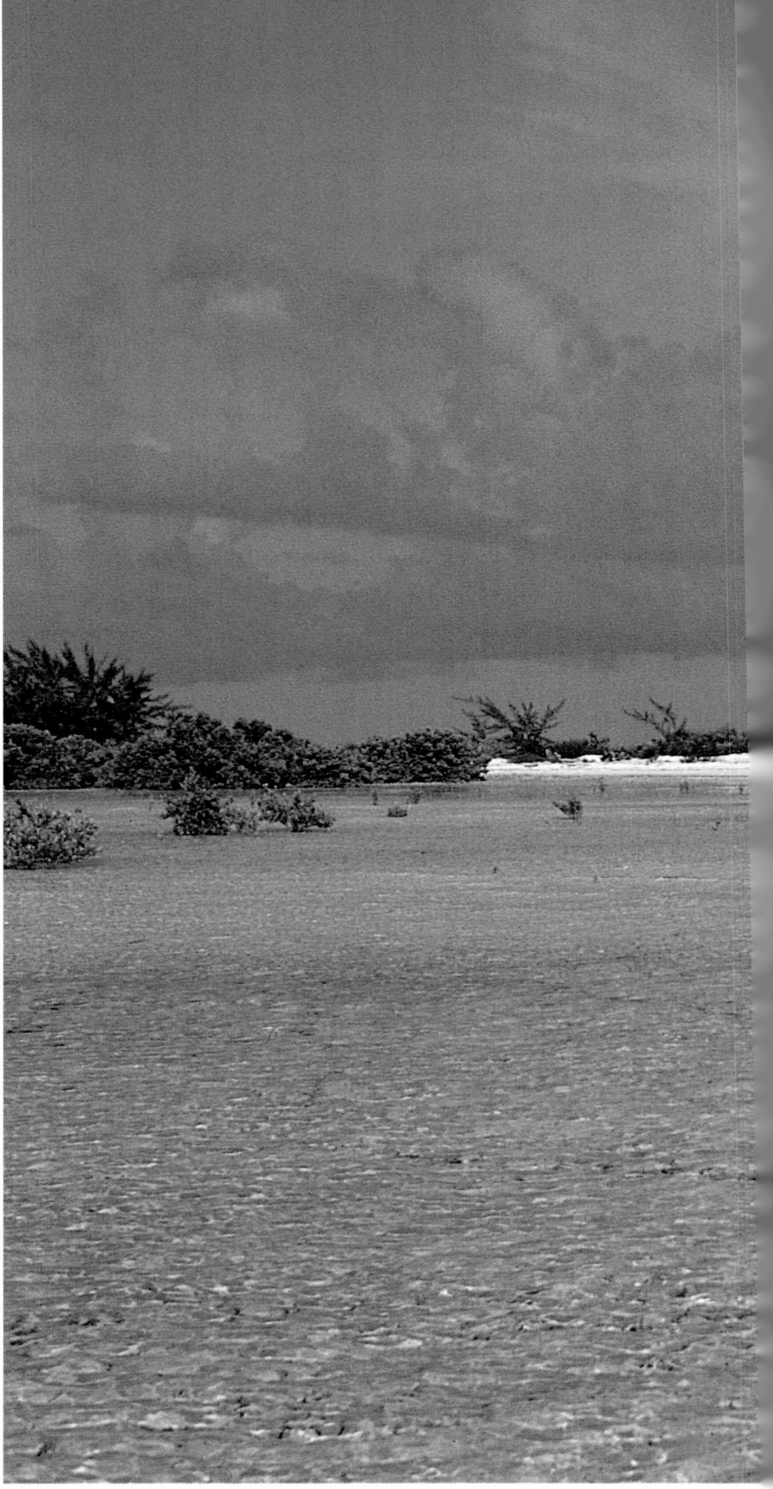

and then slide it back into the water toes first. They looked quite funny and I started to take photos just for laughs.

Suffice it to say that by the time Stephen had landed his third bonefish, I was copying their funny walk. The difference was that great. Now, when a similar situation arises, I don't hesitate to begin the "blue heron walk." I don't care about looking ridiculous—I'm hunting bonefish!

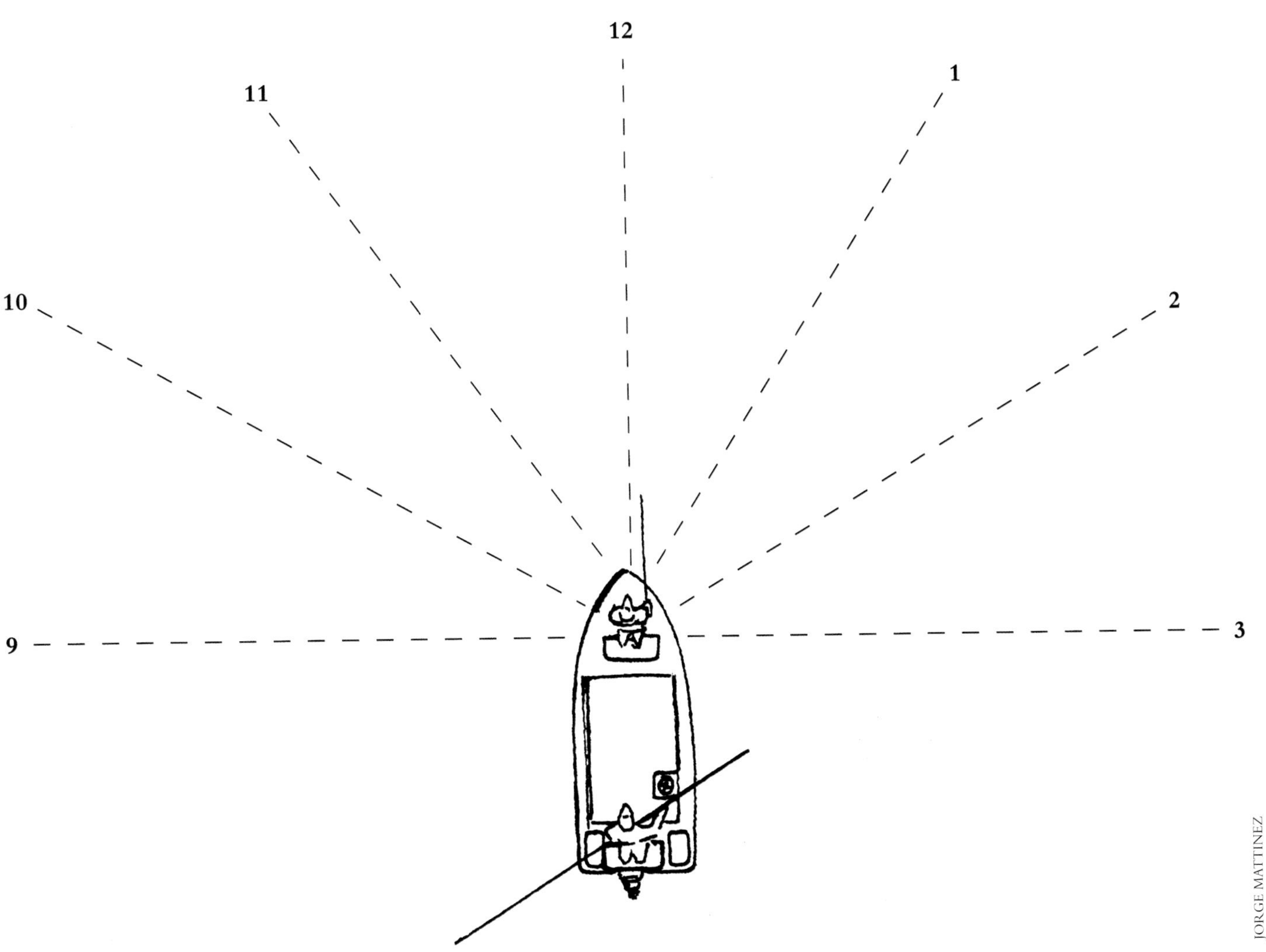

Once a poler has spotted a bonefish, the clock method is the best way to tell the caster where the fish is. Keep in mind that the clock goes all the way back to 6 o'clock on the engine, because sometimes a fish is somewhere behind you.

requires him to take his eyes off the fish, he will ask you to keep an eye on the bone so as not to lose sight of him.

TIME AND PLACE

As you know, the best stage of the tide for bonefish varies with each flat. On any tide, I always look for two important signs: a good flow of water and life on the flat. A good flow of water across the flat moves both the bonefish's food (crustaceans and baitfish) and the food's smell. To a fish, current serves the same purpose that wind serves to a predator on land. I generally stay away from a flat that is at a dead-low tide or full flood. Look for flats where water is moving. The great guides can move from flat to flat and hit the right tide on every one. Many years of experience go into that skill, and guides have always had my deepest respect.

Still, you may not be sure if you are on a good flat, even if the current is moving well. There are other clues that most anglers do not notice: the amount of life you see while poling or wading. Small sharks looking for food, a mudding ray feeding on the bottom, baitfish and small snappers around structures and potholes, the occasional small school of inch-long fry spooking away from you—all these indicate that a flat is in a very active cycle of the tide stage. You've probably found an ideal time to fish it. If all the signs of life are there, sooner or later Mr. Bonefish will come to the party.

If you are looking for a flat to wade, try the lower stages of the tide, both incoming and outgoing. You should find some tailing fish on either stage.

GETTING TO KNOW THE NEIGHBORHOOD

You've found a flat that you want to learn really well. Maybe this particular flat is convenient for you to fish, or perhaps it seems to attract a lot of big bonefish. The reason doesn't matter; you've decided that you want to become an expert on this little piece of the ocean.

Here's how to go about it. Check the times of the tides on the flat and arrive extra early, when the fish are sure not to be there; that is, get there when the flat is dry. Now walk as much of the area as you can. Notice the depressions, the edge of the flat where the drop-off will be when it is full of water, and the areas with the most turtle grass, which usually contains more food and may attract more fish. Learn the flat before it fills with water, because then you will not be able to see all its secrets.

Soon the water will start to trickle onto the flat. As soon as the water level approaches half a foot in most areas, a few bonefish may appear at the edge of the flat, eager to be the first customers in the supermarket. They may be tailing, cruising, or mudding. As you wade to them, you will have the advantage of knowing that flat much better than someone who just got there, even if he has been visiting that flat for years.

If a flat does not go completely dry at its low stages, or if it's too soft to wade, then pole the flat—the whole flat. Don't merely pole across it, but zigzag until you have felt most of the bottom with your pushpole. When you do this, you truly learn the area. You see where the hard and soft areas are, which usually correspond to more or less current. You find the areas of turtle grass and the potholes. It's the difference between walking in the woods and riding through them on a motorcycle. Which person knows those woods better? Obviously, the walker.

The best guides I have ever fished with never run a flat to see what's there. Never. They pole the flat and get to know it well. You can run a flat fifty times over as many fishing days and learn nothing. But take a day to pole a big flat on both the incoming and outgoing tides, and you will know that flat pretty well. Just one day can make you a local expert.

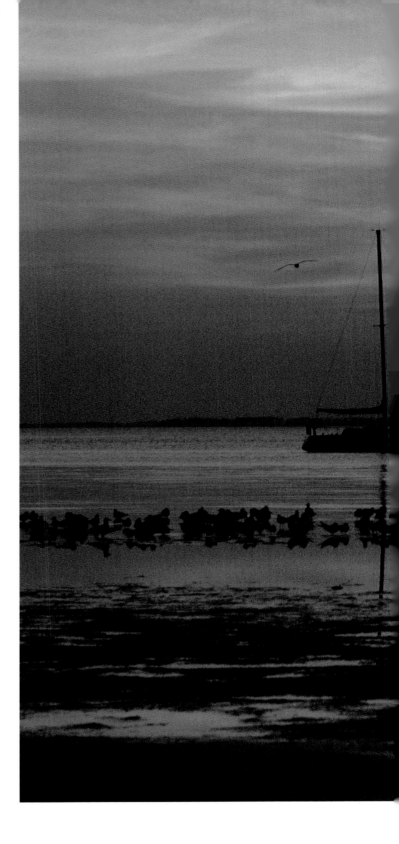

PREDICTABLE MOVEMENTS

When a hungry bonefish enters a flat with the first few inches of water of an incoming tide, he has no choice but to move with the tide. On a very low outgoing tide, fish that are trying to feed as long as they can will be forced out with the last few inches of water, again moving with the current. But when a flat has enough water, a bonefish will swim and feed into the tide. It's simply more efficient because the current brings food or its scent to the bonefish, and by moving into tide he soon finds his prey.

Bonefish prefer to move into the tide for another reason. As a bonefish feeds, he does a lot of digging in the bottom, blowing away sand and debris to uncover shrimps or crabs hiding under the sand or around marine grass. In doing so, the bonefish makes the water around him cloudy, creating the mud that anglers look for. With the tide running into him and past him, soon the mud moves behind the fish, leaving the prey uncovered and visible. The bonefish eats it and keeps moving, always moving.

Checking a flat at dead low tide, before the bonefish get there, and watching it slowly come alive is one good way to learn the neighborhood. Another is to pole every square foot of it—but hardly anyone takes the time to do this.

SUE MORET

This 14-pound bone, my largest to date, was tailing in over a foot of water.

If you lose sight of a bone or a school of bones for a moment, look uptide from where they were a minute ago. You'll probably find what you're looking for.

THE AREA OF AWARENESS

As a bonefish, or any other gamefish, moves along a flat looking for food, he focuses completely on an area in front of him. This area, which changes in size depending on what the bonefish is eating and where, is commonly called the fish's area of awareness (some call it the window of opportunity). It is a triangle with the point at the nose of the fish. It might extend out only a few inches, or it might be a few feet long; its size depends partly on the water's depth. Tailing, cruising, and mudding fish each have different areas of awareness. A tailing fish, for instance, focuses on a small patch of bottom, sometimes only a few inches wide. A cruiser sees more of his immediate environment.

The area of awareness is three dimensional: besides length and width, it also has depth. You must keep all three dimensions in mind as you place the fly and decide how long to let it sink before beginning the retrieve. When you cast to a bonefish, your target is generally somewhere in the area of awareness—it is not the fish itself.

COMMUNICATION

I can't stress enough how important it is that you have great lines of communication with your guide. Year after year, major bonefish tournaments are usually won not by a great angler, but by a great team, a guide and a fly fisher who have fished together for many years. They communicate very well, each anticipating what the other is going to do when a fish is seen. They know each other's strengths and weaknesses. And together they are more than the sum of their respective abilities. That's why they win tournaments.

I have known guides who have fished an angler all his life, and then fished his son. By the time the angler passes away, the now-old guide is fishing the son and grandson. Such teams catch fish that a boat containing two or three strangers cannot catch. And it's beautiful to watch.

If you're fishing with him for the first time, do your best to communicate with your guide. He can't read your mind (yet). And when he offers advice or makes a suggestion, listen to him.

Chapter 15

The Approach and Cast

And finally the equipment becomes part of you, and you start fishing only with your hands and your eyes, as you should. —*Sandy Moret*

The ideal approach is one in which the fish never knows that something is wrong until he feels the hook. This is what you are striving for, and when you make it happen, it is most satisfying.

As you cast to a bonefish, pay attention to his constantly changing "body language." A bonefish's attitude, movements, and even appearance change as he faces new predators or finds new prey. One reason for these changes is a shark or barracuda on the hunt. Birds flying overhead will also change a bonefish's attitude. You can't do anything about predators that suddenly appear and make a bonefish nervous; a big 'cuda that spooks the fish you've been stalking is part of the game. But you can control one factor that can change a bonefish's attitude and appetite: your approach.

Repeated false-casting, especially if you keep your casting hand well above your shoulder, acts as a warning flag to bonefish. Each unnecessary false cast is another chance to alert the fish to your presence.

Noises from a boat travel through water very fast. The slap of waves against the hull, a pair of pliers dropped in the cockpit, or even a hatch closed too loudly can scare a bonefish. Any noise coming from the skiff can spoil your approach.

Some anglers develop a habit of rocking back and forth as they cast, perhaps in an attempt to help themselves keep rhythm. But as you rock, so does the light bonefish skiff, creating waves with every false cast that you make. Believe me, the bones can feel this very well, and they don't like it. Don't rock the boat.

If you fish without a guide, don't run the boat all the way to the edge of the flat. A lot of anglers figure that they can roar onto a flat, shut down the outboard, and immediately see tailing bonefish all around. The fish were gone while the boat was still up on plane. Good anglers and guides stop at least 100 yards from a flat and pole the rest of the way. Those few minutes of poling also give the angler time to stretch his fly line, check the hook point, and generally get ready. The edge of a flat is an excellent place to find feeding bonefish, but finding them doesn't accomplish much if the angler isn't ready to cast. Don't be too lazy to pole a little bit.

THOSE OLD SPOOKED-BONEFISH BLUES

There are spooked bones and then there are spooked bones. That is, there are degrees of spooked. Not every fish that senses the skiff or your presence leaves the flat in a rush. Often a fish or an entire school suspects that something is wrong, but keeps on feeding more or less normally. The fish might even keep moving toward you as they feed—but they're on high alert. Cast carefully, keeping the line low and dropping the fly a few feet outside the fish's area of awareness so that the splash doesn't spook them. As the bones get close to the fly, start your retrieve.

At other times, nervous bonefish continue to feed, but only as they move away from you. If you wade or pole a little faster, they move a little faster. You increase your speed a bit more, and so do they, always keeping just beyond your casting range. How do they know? And even if you do manage to put a fly close to the fish, it's more likely to spook them or quicken their pace than to get a strike. In these cases, it's often best to shrug your shoulders and go look for some "happy" fish. Those nervous bones have your number.

When you spot a bonefish that's feeding away from you, your best course might not be to chase the fish, but rather to try to go around and get ahead of him in order to make the first cast a good one. This often works better than slapping cast after cast behind him as he swims away. If a big school of fish is moving in the wrong direction across a large flat, you might even want to pole to a safe distance, fire up the engine, and run the skiff in a semicircle to get in front of the fish. Your first cast is usually

You must be absolutely quiet during the last few seconds of the approach.

MARKUS HAUGG

your best shot, so it's worth making the effort to set it up properly. If, however, a fish working on an outgoing tide is approaching the end of a flat, he will soon drop into the channel on his way to another flat. In this case, you have no choice but to chase him. If the fish is feeding happily, a cast to his right or left—but never over him, of course—might catch his attention.

A fish or an entire school will often appear at the other end of a flat, well beyond casting range but headed your way. You get ready but do nothing else, waiting for them to come into range. The fish might be tailing or just pushing a nice, pretty, relaxed wake as they head your way. Cool.

Suddenly, while they're still more than 100 feet away, the fish change speed or stop tailing. The wake disappears, though the bones are still coming toward you. But they no longer seem relaxed and happy. Somehow, they know. I would lead them a bit more than usual on the presentation and hope for the best. If this sort of behavior continues, switch to a leader at least 12 feet long with a 4-foot tippet. Sometimes that helps with jittery, alert fish, though sometimes nothing helps. Welcome to bonefishing.

Early and late in the day, you and your boat will cast a longer shadow that tends to spook bonefish. In the morning and evening, take your shadow into account as you plan your approach. Bonefish will occasionally tolerate a shadow, but they're more often terrified of it.

The approach, then, involves much more than pushing the boat or wading until you're within casting range of the fish. You must consider the fish's direction, his speed, his location on the flat, his behavior, the angle of the sun, the length of your shadow, and other factors. Very often, more work goes into setting up a cast than actually making it.

WHEN TO CAST

Knowing when to start casting to an oncoming fish calls for precise judgment. I can give you some guidelines, but ultimately you will have to develop a feel for it by computing a variety of factors. You will have to weigh your ability to cast in the present conditions, wind and visibility, the speed of the oncoming fish, the boat's position, and more. You have to learn how to read each individual fish. It's a judgment call, and every situation is a little bit different from the last one.

First, know your casting skills and have no illusions that at this moment you are going to cast farther than you have ever cast. You won't. If your best cast under these conditions is 45 feet, then try to intercept the fish at that distance. This will tell you how soon to start your cast.

Starting too early causes either of two problems. You might have to drop the fly well ahead of the fish, which means that you'll have to pick up the line to make a second cast. That might spook the bonefish, and besides, the second cast is rarely as good as the first. Or you might keep false-casting as you wait for the fish to come nearer. Each extra false cast is another opportunity for something to go wrong.

Start casting too late, and you risk having the bone come close enough to see you or the boat. You might also end up with 40 feet of line in the air and a bonefish that's only 30 feet away, in which case you will surely line the fish.

Within reason, different distances will work in the same situation. That is, a good caster might start earlier and cast 65 feet, while a novice might start later and end up casting only 40 feet. Both might catch the fish. Day in and day out, however, the better caster will spook fewer fish and hook more by keeping the fish a bit farther from him as he works the fly. A better caster always has the advantage.

I don't mean only the ability to false-cast on the lawn without a fly. You need to master the fast-draw cast described in chapter 12. Remember that you are hunting, not casting, when you spot a bonefish. If you cannot quickly go from holding the fly in your hand to putting it in the air to dropping it within the bonefish's area of awareness, you will not have a lot of success on the flats. Practice the fast draw.

As you false-cast, you will continue to see the fish and follow his movements, adjusting the cast as necessary. If you need to false-cast a few times (but not too many) to get your loop tighter and adjust your aim, keep the line and leader at least a few feet short of the target. False-casting right over the top of a bone will almost certainly spook him. On the last cast, shoot the final few feet to the target. This trick gives you good accuracy (because you're shooting only a little line) while keeping the line away from the fish. Get in the habit of false-casting outside the fish's area of awareness. If you are going to make a 50-foot cast, false-cast 40 or 45 feet of line and shoot the last few feet on the presentation cast. It works great.

The ideal distance is the closest distance at which you can see the fish well enough to present the fly in front of him, study his reactions and body language, and still not be seen. In most situations, this falls between 30 and 65 feet. But I have taken fish 15 feet away while wading on windy days, and I have caught bonefish with casts over 90 feet when I couldn't move any closer to a school and I had a tailwind to help. By and large, though, you will make 30- to 65-foot deliveries.

WHERE TO CAST

To improve your accuracy, try to stop looking at the fish on the last cast and look instead at the area of awareness where you want to place the fly. At the last second, shift your vision from the bonefish to the area in front of him that you actually want to hit.

We humans are programmed to hit what we see, and it's very difficult to stare straight at a bone and drop the fly a yard ahead of him. If you keep looking at the fish, chances are that you will throw the fly right between his eyes and spook him. Your target is not the fish's head, but a spot in front of him. Make this target as small as you can—a target within a target, as it were. You will cast more accurately.

Remember that a presentation consists of showing the fly to the fish in a natural manner. There's more to it

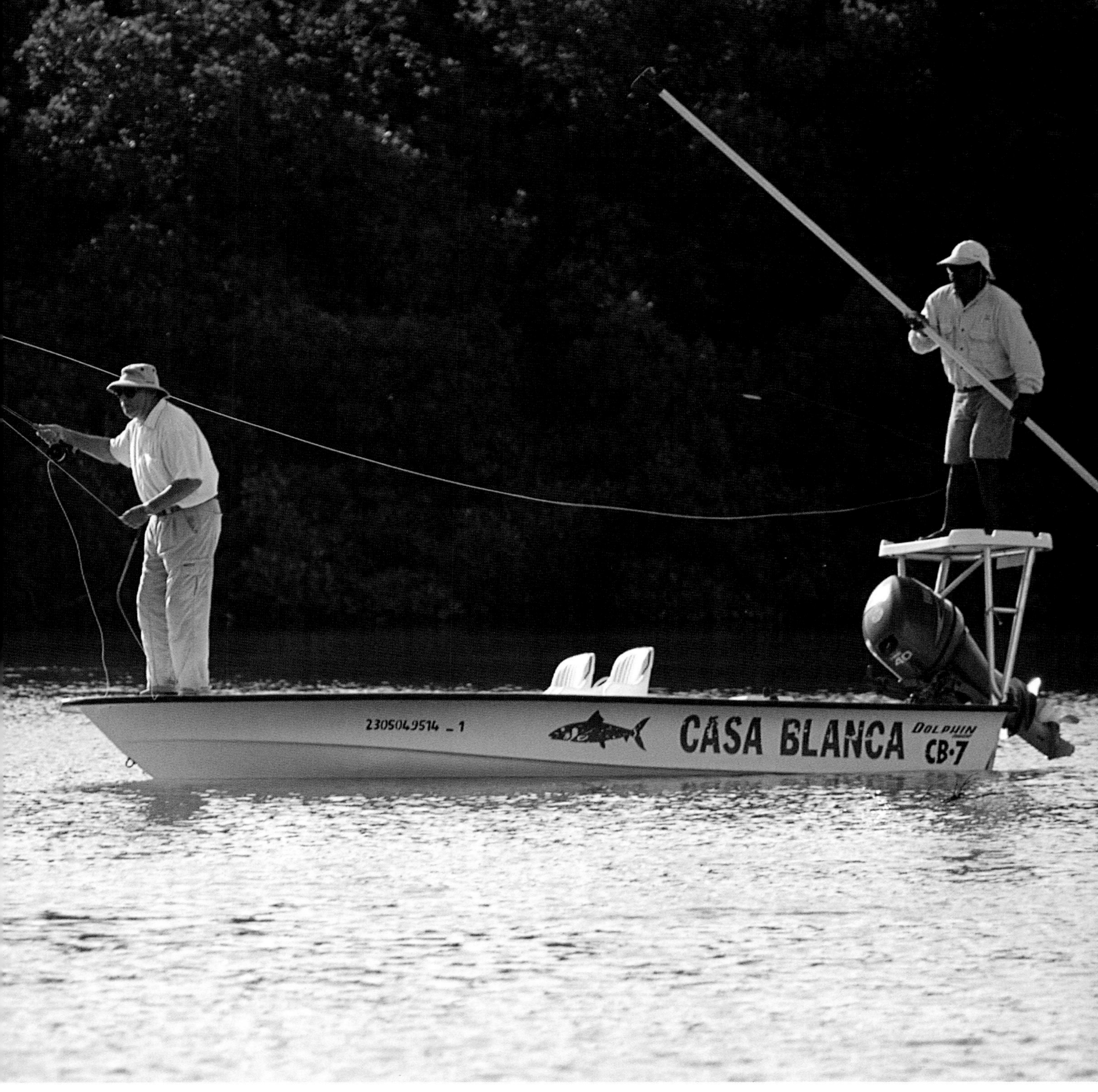

MARKUS HAUGG

With enough practice, your casting becomes automatic and all your concentration is on accuracy.

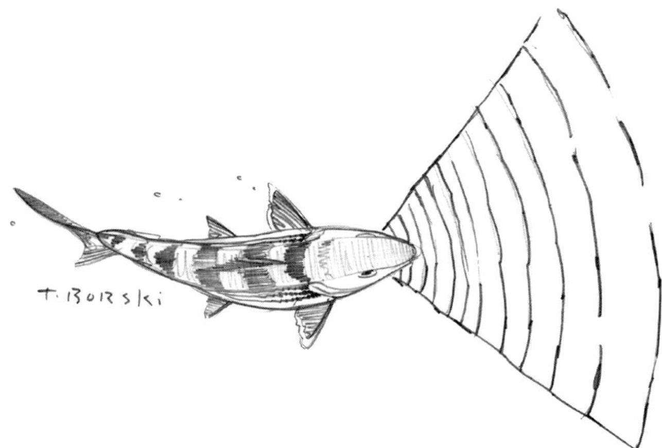

A bonefish's area of awareness is not necessarily his full vision, but instead the area where he is most concentrating when feeding. The angle widens and contracts, shortens and lengthens, as he looks for prey in different depths and terrains. It seems to be shorter in turtle grass and longer in sand.

than merely putting the fly in front of him. The fly also has to be at the right depth, and for a bonefish that's usually at his level or lower. Unlike tarpon, which love rising to a fly, a bone does not like to come up for a fly, though he doesn't mind going down for it. The area of awareness has three dimensions. If you see a bonefish in more than two feet of water cruising your way but swimming right against the bottom, merely casting in front of him and retrieving is probably not going to work. The fly is too high in the water. So, how much you need to lead a fish depends in part on the depth of the water. In, say, three feet of water, you must give the fly time to sink, which means that you probably need to drop it a little farther in front of the fish.

The *plop* of a fly hitting the water too close to a fish will most often spook him off the flat. Yet there are times, quite often actually, when the same plop will make him rush over and take the fly. You can never be sure with bones. Generally, a fish is more likely to spook from a close cast on a calm day, and more likely to turn and take a fly that landed near him on a windy day, particularly on a deeper flat.

When a fish seems nervous and hard to approach, try to guess which way he is moving (it's usually at an angle into the tide) and then cast outside the range of his awareness. Let him move into the fly. Of course, the fish's area of awareness changes according to how fast he is swimming, whether he is looking at the bottom or tailing, and so forth. I might cast just a couple of feet from a tailing bonefish, but four to even six feet ahead of one that's cruising fairly fast.

My old friend Sandy Moret is a master at casting just outside the fish's area of awareness and letting the fish swim into the fly. The fly plops down far enough ahead of the fish not to spook him, but close enough for the fish to see it as he moves forward. Over the years, Sandy has won many bonefish tournaments in the waters around Islamorada, where many bones have advanced degrees and some even teach at the Ph.D. level.

Few people are as knowledgeable about the big bonefish in the Islamorada area and the Keys in general as Capt. Steve Huff, and few have as much respect for the fish. Steve's thirty-plus years of watching and studying these big bonefish have produced many tournament trophies and world records for his clients. Characteristically, Steve has his own way of tackling the problem of presenting a fly to these big, savvy bones. Instead of using feet to indicate how far in front of a bonefish the angler should cast, Steve measures the distance by fish lengths. He finds that it is a lot easier for an angler to think in terms of casting, say, two fish-lengths in front of a fish rather than five feet in front.

Steve likes to be aggressive with his presentations. "Cast close to a bone," he says. "One or two fish lengths, depending on the speed of the fish. And in a strong current, I put it a little farther ahead and let the fly drift to him."

The right presentation is difficult to make, but not complicated: You want to cast the fly close enough so that the bonefish will see it, but not so close as to scare him. It's a compromise that calls for fine judgment, and it's a compromise that changes with each fish. Experience is the best teacher.

TAILING FISH

A fish tailing on a very shallow flat knows that sharks and barracudas are looking for him in the water and that birds of prey are looking for him from the air. He generally has to feed by pushing his face against the bottom, which makes it hard for him to watch out for danger. No wonder tailing fish are jumpy. Anything that *might* be a threat sends him streaking off the flat.

To make matters even worse for us, a tailing fish is looking for prey right in front of his face. He generally doesn't look very far ahead—a few feet, maybe, or only a few inches.

When you cast to a tailing bonefish, keep in mind that his area of awareness is generally quite small. It often reminds me of a person reading an engrossing mystery book: his whole world is a page only a foot in front of him. A bonefish often acts in a similar manner. It's not unusual to place several good casts just inches in front of a tailing fish and get no response. But if you get too

MARKUS HAUGG

When you see many bonefish tailing, try to pick one. Don't cast to the general area; flock-shooting doesn't work.

close, the plop of the fly may spook him. The challenge can be even greater in tall turtle grass, where a bone with his face buried between blades of grass can see only an inch or two ahead. It often seems impossible to get the fish's attention.

The ideal solution is to determine in which direction he is feeding, and then cast just outside his area of awareness and let the fly sink. Don't move it at all. Let the fish move to the fly. When you judge that the fly is within his area of awareness, twitch it. Don't move it much—just a twitch to get his attention. We'll look at this and other retrieves more closely in the next chapter.

Sometimes a bonefish will tail intermittently, probably because food is scarce. In this case, wait until he finishes tailing. Watch the tail go down, and as he starts to swim again and is looking ahead, cast in front of him.

CRUISING FISH

A cruising fish, particularly one in deeper water, has a much larger area of awareness because he is looking ahead. Your target can be anywhere from a bit over two feet to more than six feet ahead of the fish, depending on depth.

If a cruiser is going to the left or right, cast in front of him, but no more than a few inches past him. Obviously, casting beyond the fish risks lining him. Even if you avoid spooking the fish, the fly will move toward him as you start the retrieve. That's almost sure to spook him. Prey moving toward the predator, as if attacking, is simply unnatural. Maybe it doesn't make sense for a ten-pound fish to spook from a one-inch fly, but it happens. I have seen plenty of 6-foot-long tarpon spook from 3-inch streamers moving toward them.

If you get a head-on shot, with the fish coming more or less straight toward the boat, you have a couple of options. You can cast a few feet in front, let the fish come to the fly, and then start to retrieve. This works fine if the fish is far away, but if he's already near the boat when you cast, your retrieve will draw him even closer, and he's likely to see the boat. A better way is to cast slightly to the left or right of the oncoming fish. When he does chase the fly, he will move to one side rather than continue toward the boat.

A heavily weighted fly took this cruising fish.

A fish quartering away from you requires a quick decision. If he's close, take the shot, being careful not to drop the fly line too near the bonefish. But if the fish is farther away, and particularly if he's out near the limit of your casting ability, it's better to let him go rather than risk spooking him and having him spook more fish as he rushes off the flat.

MUDDING FISH

A bonefish feeding on a soft bottom, such as an inside or bay-side flat, produces a visible, compact cloud of mud in the water. A school of bones can create a very large mud that's easy to see from a considerable distance.

When you fish for mudding bones, it's essential that you determine in which direction they are feeding. If you cast to the mud itself, your fly will land behind the

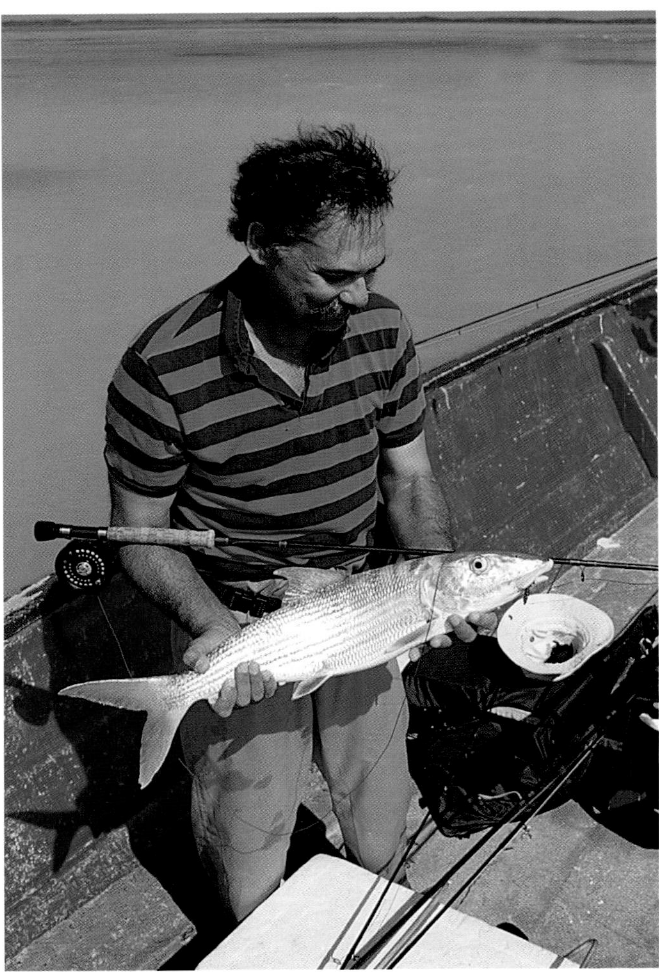

This bone was taken in six feet of water with a slow-sinking line. A sinking line can save a trip when conditions make shallow-water fishing impossible.

fish. Before making the cast, figure out where the fish are headed, and then lead the mud. Ideally, you will pick out an individual fish, which often appears quite dark against the immediate background. If you can't see the fish, cast a bit ahead of the mud. You may be surprised by a hard strike.

In many parts of the world, schools of bonefish will mud in six to ten feet of water. These schools, and the muds they make, can be immense; I have seen deep-water muds larger than an acre. Deep-water bonefishing is not like sight-casting on the flats, but it can be fun for a couple of hours. You simply cast into the densest, most active part of the giant mud and let the fly get close to the bottom before starting the retrieve. More than once, I've caught dozens of bones from a deep, mudding school in just a couple of hours. It's loads of fun, though not very challenging. But that's okay—we all need some relatively easy fishing now and then.

RULES OF THUMB FOR FLY PLACEMENT

How far to cast in front of a bonefish is a product of several factors: the fish's speed, his feeding behavior (tailing or cruising, for instance), the depth of the water, the size and weight of the fly, and the amount of wind. Every fish requires a new set of calculations and a judgment call, but we can simplify things a little by remembering some guidelines.

Swimming speed. The faster the fish is moving, the longer the lead. For a tailing fish that's moving very slowly, use a short lead and drop the fly close to him.

Feeding behavior. Cast farther ahead of a cruising fish, because he is looking up. A tailing fish is looking down; cast close to him.

Water depth. Cast farther ahead of a cruising fish in deeper water to give the fly time to sink to his level.

Fly size. The smaller the fly, the closer the presentation; the larger the fly, the farther away the presentation.

Windy versus calm. Cast closer to a fish on a windy day, and farther away on a calm day.

More than one fish. When casting to a school of bonefish, try to place the fly so that more than one fish sees it. Obviously, the more fish that see the fly, the greater the likelihood that one will eat, but there's more to it. When two or more fish see the same fly, they become competitive and less cautious. Each one wants to grab the food before another fish takes it. If you can show the fly to several fish, you will probably get a hookup. In bonefishing, it's a rare treat to see several fish rush your fly and to have one take it without even thinking twice. If you can, present the fly so that you have more than one customer.

LET IT SIT

When fish are very spooky, try casting 20 or more feet in front of an incoming bonefish and letting the fly rest. Don't move it. The fish will take their time feeding while you wait. It feels like bait fishing. Sooner or later, a fish will spot the fly (which is probably moving slightly in the current), come up to it, and take it. It sounds crazy, but this can be a good method. I rarely fish this way myself, but I have seen it done with great success in the Bahamas. Sandy Moret has seen the let-it-sit trick work very well in the Islamorada area, where the world's smartest bonefish live. Yes, it's a desperation tactic, but it's one worth knowing.

WHEN YOU MISS

No matter how good you are or how much you practice, you are going to miss with some of your casts. Actually, many of them will not hit the target. Sometimes it's your fault: you just plain missed. Other times, the cast was

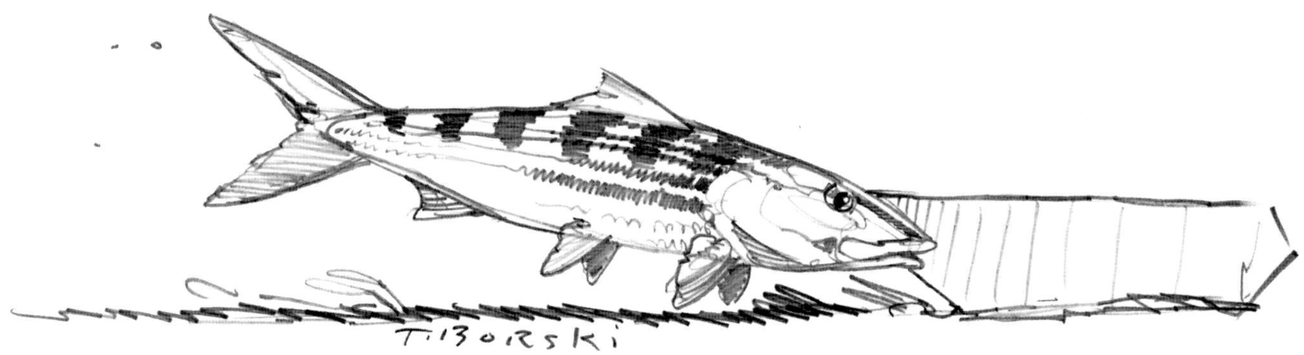

Remember that in most cases, a bone is looking for food at his eye level or below, and mostly below. Besides placing the fly in front of the fish, you must also let the fly sink at or below his level. This is most important and is the reason for taking several flies of the same pattern and color in different weights.

right where it had to be, but the bonefish saw something he liked at the last moment and turned in a different direction. He didn't spook, but he didn't see the fly. It happens all the time. And when it does, you have to pick up and cast again, quickly but without ripping the line off the water, which makes a lot of noise.

Here's what to do. Slowly lift the tip of the rod and raise most of the fly line off the surface, until only a few feet of fly line, the leader, and the fly remain in the water. Now start your backcast. You'll see that the fly line that remained on the water does not make much noise as you lift it from the surface. False-cast once or twice for accuracy, and drop the fly where it needs to be. Do all this without taking your eyes off the bone—if you turn your head to watch your backcast, you will never find that bonefish again. Never.

Sometimes you'll have to do this more than once before you finally hook up. Or, if luck is not with you, before you finally spook the fish. But don't worry if you spook him; it's all part of the fun. Besides, we learn more from our mistakes than from our successes.

It's hard to tell if you missed if you don't know where the fly is. Because it's relatively small, a typical bonefish fly is very hard to see during the retrieve. You can often follow a tarpon or snook fly as it swims, but a bonefish fly disappears when it enters the water.

How will you know if the fly is in front of the bone, or a couple of feet to the right or left, and therefore out of the game? If you did not watch for the plop of the fly on the water, you will not know. When you cast, try to note where the fly lands so that you can judge whether to retrieve and hope for a strike, or pick up and cast again. The tiny splash that a bonefish fly makes entering the water is often the last clue you will have about the relative locations of the fly and the fish.

THE EMERGENCY SHORT-RANGE CAST

Sooner or later, a bonefish, or even an entire school of bones, will sneak within 20 feet before you or your guide notice. They can do this even in very shallow water. We spend most of our time on the flats straining to see bonefish, but every now and then they take us by surprise, magically appearing so close that you could almost toss the fly to them by hand. Don't ask me how they do it.

You know that the fish have not yet noticed you or the boat. But you also know that they are going to spook any second now. What to do?

The natural tendency is to lead them by many feet so as not to spook them. In my experience, this approach rarely works. You only have a few seconds to get a strike. Working out enough line for a long lead will take too much time; the fish will probably spook first.

I would go for broke—make a quick cast with your rod as parallel to the water as possible and a minimum of false casts. Avoid placing the fly between the fish and the boat, which would require the fish to charge the boat. Instead, drop the fly to the side to force the fish to look away from you and the boat as he charges the fly.

Don't think twice in this situation. Keep the rod low and put the fly on one side of the fish right now. Either way, it will be over soon.

Chapter 16

The Retrieve, Hookup, and Fight

The fly landed in the right place. You let the small shrimp imitation sink to the proper level, and the bonefish seems to have noticed it. It's time to start acting like a shrimp. You begin a series of very short strips, trying to make the fly imitate the slow progress of a small shrimp that hasn't yet spotted the predator closing in on it. But the bonefish loses interest and turns away as if he never saw the fly.

What happened? My guess is that the fly never moved.

In trying to impart action to a fly, you must think of several factors besides the movements of your line hand. If you have any slack in the line while trying to give life to the fly, the movements of your line hand will only take up some of the slack. The fly, meanwhile, is sitting still; you think that you are moving it, but you're not. By the time you take up all the slack and the fly finally starts to move, the bonefish is long gone.

Slack has several causes. Even if you cast well, the fly line is not perfectly straight at the end of the cast. As soon as the line falls to the water, wind and waves start to push even more slack into it. The boat might be moving toward the fish. If you start the retrieve with the tip of the rod high above the water, you will create a big belly of slack that absorbs every movement of your line hand.

Get ready to impart action to the fly by lowering the tip all the way to the water if possible. All the way—touch the tip-top to the surface. If you are standing too high on the skiff to touch the water with the rod, at least get the tip as close as possible to the surface. Then strip until the fly line is nice and straight. You'll find that now the slightest movement of your line hand will cause a nearly equal movement of the fly. With no slack, you'll be able to feel the slightest, most subtle strike, and you will miss fewer fish.

Now you can make that shrimp walk and talk. Instead of turning and swimming away, the bonefish will respond to the fly.

SHALLOW WATER

Let the fly sink when you fish in water less than a foot deep, but not necessarily to the bottom. In very shallow water, bonefish often take a fly as it sinks, particularly when it gets close to the sand or grass.

If the fish doesn't react, maybe he hasn't yet seen the fly. Give it a bump or two. Just as a blinking light draws more attention than a light that's not blinking, a fly that twitches or darts catches the fish's attention. Be gentle with these bumps; a violent, jerky movement can scare the fish.

If he follows the fly without taking it, move the fly slowly and steadily—no bumps or jerks. Make long, slow strips. This type of retrieve might not seem very active, but the fly's materials wiggle and pulse as the pattern travels through the water.

Remember to fish slowly. Many of the foods consumed by bonefish, particularly crustaceans, move slowly and often awkwardly. Just as a man can't take a thirty-foot stride, a one- or two-inch shrimp cannot take a quick two-foot stride. It would look unnatural to the bonefish.

You have to become the food that your fly imitates so that the impostor, the fly, will play a convincing role. You are an actor imitating a shrimp or a baitfish. Become the food.

Because it is mostly white with some yellow in the belly, my Bonefish Special is meant to imitate a small schoolmaster snapper or yellowfin shad. At least I feel that it does; I don't know what the bonefish thinks, of course. As I strip a Bonefish Special, I *am* that small baitfish—until the bonefish takes it and the ruse is over. Then Chico the angler strikes back.

If a bonefish is within a few feet of the fly, you might want to leave it on the bottom for a few seconds before you move it, especially if it's a shrimp or crab imitation. Don't be in a rush to move the fly. It is not unusual to see a bonefish come from six feet away to pick up a fly sitting on the bottom.

DEEPER WATER

Shallow-water fishing is very exciting, but don't underestimate sight-casting in more than two feet of water. If anything, seeing and casting to bonefish in slightly deeper water is even more challenging than fishing on a very shallow flat. Besides, deeper flats often hold bigger bonefish.

When you fish in deeper water, make the presentation with a longer lead that gives the fly time to sink to the bottom or very close to it. Even though you generally use a slightly heavier fly than you would in skinny water, it still takes a bit longer to reach bottom. Don't start the retrieve too early.

It's important to develop a feel for how quickly (or slowly) a fly sinks. Before you start hunting, simply drop the fly in front of you and see how long it takes to reach bottom. You can count if you like—one-one-thousand, two-one-thousand, and so on. I do this with all flies, and I really think it helps. Remember that you want to stay at the fish's level or below, because practically all of his prey tries to hide in or on the bottom. Prey does not try to outrun a bonefish; it knows that it can't.

Since a fly for deeper water is usually larger than a skinny-water pattern, it probably imitates something that swims a bit faster. In deep water, I tend to use a faster, more aggressive retrieve.

MUDDING FISH IN DEEPER WATER

Although a mud gives me a pretty good idea where the fish are, I still try to spot an individual fish so that I can make the most accurate presentation possible. On a flat deeper than two feet, I try to determine the fish's level in the water instead of letting the fly drop all the way to the bottom; with all that mud around him, a bonefish might not see a fly sitting on the bottom of the flat. When the fish rushes the fly, I watch for the sudden stop that tells me he's got it.

As a rule, I fish minnow flies the fastest, though still not as fast as I'd retrieve a streamer for most other species. I fish crab flies the slowest, giving them little movement and keeping them on the bottom more than other patterns.

Even in deeper water, it's still important to match the retrieve to the mood and behavior of the fish. I move the fly a bit faster for a fish that's feeding quickly, and slower for a tailing fish that's making very little forward progress.

Remember *never* to work a fly toward a fish, no matter how deep the water is. They are not used to being attacked by their food. Even though the fly is so much smaller than the bonefish, it can still frighten him. The food should always look like it's trying to get away from the predator.

If a fish merely follows the fly, looking curious but passive, try changing speeds. Either accelerate your retrieve to make the prey look like it's fleeing, or stop and let the fly drop to the bottom as if it's trying to hide under the sand or grass. If changing speeds doesn't work, and especially if two or three fish in a row refuse to bite, consider changing flies. I can't tell you which fly the bones will want, but I have learned that changing size is usually more important than changing color.

Capt. Steve Huff fishes for bones almost exclusively with crab flies and shrimp patterns such as his Joe-to-Go, and he's among the great masters at reading the fish's attitude. "I try to get a recognition in the fish's behavior that he has seen or is aware of the fly," Steve says. "Then, if he is very close to the fly, say a fish length away, I may not move it. If he is a couple of fish lengths away, I may twitch it or move it slowly again, just trying to make sure I got his attention." That's good advice, and it underscores the importance of making sure that the bonefish has spotted the fly. If you know that he has seen it, then you can alter your retrieve—speed it up, let the fly drop, or swim the fly slowly and steadily—to make the fish bite. If you're certain that several fish have seen the fly, and if changing the retrieve failed to convince them, then think about trying another fly.

LEARN FROM REJECTION

Always take time to talk with your guide and discuss what happened with every fish. Guides are no different from other people; some are more outgoing than others. Very often, a guide who doesn't say much will, when asked, explain that the fly was just behind the fish, that the cast was great but the fish was already a bit nervous, or whatever. You will learn with every mistake and every opportunity. That's how you get better.

I have seen anglers spend several days missing fish, only to find out that the guide knew the reason but was just too shy to speak up. At the end of the last day, the guide finally says, "The fly wasn't sinking fast enough" or, "You need to lead them a little more when they are that spooky." No doubt it's good advice—but it comes too late to do the angler any good on this trip.

Don't assume that your guide has nothing to say. Maybe he's just shy. Ask for guidance and advice. I do all the time.

DID HE TAKE THE FLY?

Many fish hit a fly hard, or at least grab it with a solid pull, but the take of a bonefish can be subtle. Very often, you don't feel the take at all. Your only indication of the strike is the fish's body language.

Try to read the bone's reaction to the fly. If you understand it, his body language will tell you what to do.

MARKUS HAUGG

If a bonefish comes from the side and takes the fly hard, you will probably feel him. No problem here. You are more likely to feel a strike when you are stripping fast, or relatively fast, as you would with a baitfish pattern such as a Clouser Minnow or Bonefish Special. Bonefish usually take crustacean patterns very softly. The fish will come up behind the fly and take it as he is moving forward and toward you. If he is moving faster than your retrieve, which often happens, he is creating slack rather than pulling, and you won't feel the take. But you have a very short time in which to strike before he decides that the fly is not food and spits it out. To compound your difficulties, in many situations the skiff is drifting toward the fish, creating even more slack. So, how do you know if the fish has the fly?

Usually, you will see the fish following the fly and then rushing toward it and stopping, or stopping and wiggling. He's trying to eat it or he's got it—that's why he stopped. You've got to strip-strike now.

You might think that if you keep stripping, sooner or later you are going to tighten up and feel him. After all, the line has only a couple of feet of slack. Most often, though, the fish spits out the fly before you feel him. You will not know that you had a strike.

I've often heard a guide tell a client, "He's got it, he's got it!" The client stood there puzzled because he didn't feel anything. And since he wasn't looking for the fish's sudden stop, he didn't see anything, either. I've witnessed situations in which a bonefish took a fly two or three times on the same retrieve and the angler never struck once. Meanwhile, the guide and I were going crazy. Fun, isn't it?

When a fish that's right on top of your fly stops all of sudden, he's probably chewing on it. Strike. But even if the fish has the fly in his mouth, you can still miss him by striking the wrong way.

HOW TO STRIKE

This is one of those situations in which instinct does not help you. When you believe that a bonefish has picked up the fly, your natural reaction is to raise the rod, snapping it up and back. So that's what you do—and you get the first perfect backcast of the day. The fish, as excited as you are, rushes after the fly and comes face to face with you, a large boat, and a screaming guide with an eighteen-foot stick. Poof—he is gone.

Using the rod to strike a fish has several big drawbacks. For starters, it is too slow. Your rod tip is low to the water during the retrieve. To strike, you lift the rod up; then, when it is high enough, you start to bring the rod back until (you hope) the line comes tight and, eventually, the hook sinks in. It takes an eternity. Believe me, you will be late with the strike. And when you miss, the momentum of your long, sweeping strike yanks the fly out of the water and out of the game. You have ruined your chances with a fish that wanted the fly.

With bigger fish such as tarpon, or with any fish that has a hard mouth, striking with the rod does a poor job of setting the hook. You might feel the fish for a second,

STEPHEN FERNÁNDEZ

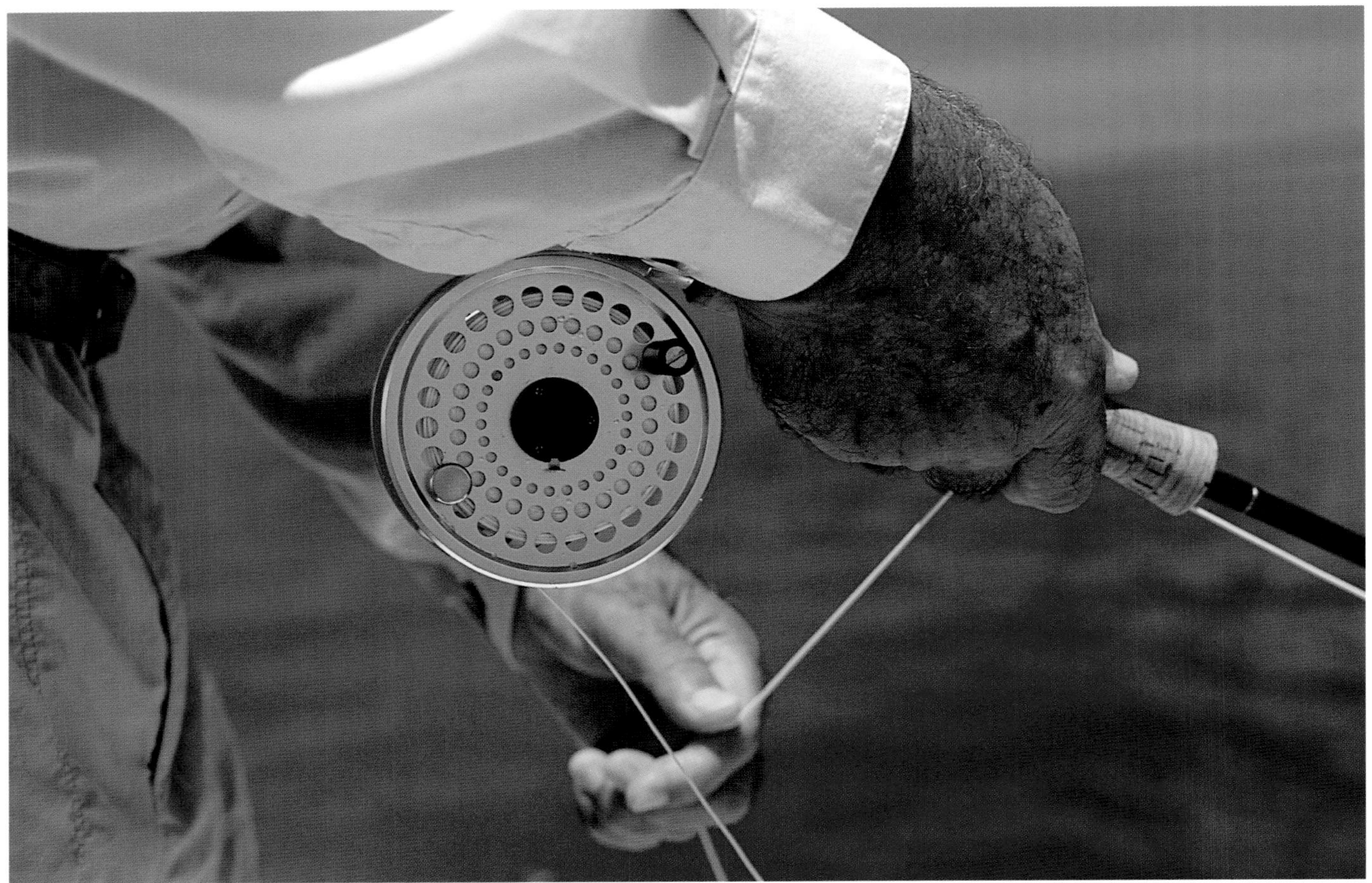

Even when you are not actively retrieving, make sure you are "tight" to the fly—that is, no slack.

but the rod simply doesn't transmit enough force to drive the hook home.

You are much better off using the strip-strike method. This is accomplished by stripping line, much as you do when retrieving a fly, but faster and harder. It's more like a pull than a strip. It's also lightning fast. As you strip-strike, you can lift the rod a little, but only a little; nearly all the force of the strike comes from your line hand. Strip-striking is one of the essential skills for flats fishing.

The length of the strip strike varies according to the amount of slack in the line. It may be a foot or a yard. Generally, the strip is shorter if you felt the fish pick up the fly, and a bit longer if you detected the bite only by the fish's body movement or were directed to strike by your guide.

Because you are pulling straight back with the line and without using the rod, this method produces a lot of force. Without much effort at all, you will easily drive the small hook into the bonefish's mouth. When you try to set the hook with the rod, the fish has all the advantage of the 9-foot lever in your hand. With a strip strike, you're pulling directly on the hook.

The strip-strike method has another great advantage if you miss. Unlike striking and missing with the rod, which yanks the fly many yards away from the fish, strip-striking moves the fly only a foot or two. The movement even looks natural, like that of a shrimp or minnow darting for cover, and it's unlikely to spook the bonefish. You are still in the game. Quite often, the bonefish will rush the fly and grab it again. If the fish doesn't charge immediately, resume the retrieve.

Sometimes a bonefish loses interest in the fly—or simply loses sight of it—after you strip-strike and miss. He's not spooked; indeed, he's still looking for food. Let him swim a few feet, maybe a few yards, and then quietly slide the line off the water to make another cast. This presentation should be easy. You have practically all the line you need outside the tip of the rod, and the bonefish is roughly the same distance from you. Since you don't have to shoot a lot of line, you should have no trouble making a very accurate second presentation.

Planting the hook in the fish's mouth does not complete the strike. Once you have made the strip-strike and felt a solid hookup, you need some cushion so that you don't break the tippet. After all, at the instant of the strike, you have a straight, tight line between you and the fish. Lift the rod to about a 45-degree angle as soon as you set the hook. The rod will bend a little, and that bend provides the cushion you need when the fish figures out that something is terribly wrong with the shrimp he just ate.

A good angler strip-strikes, sets the hook, and lifts the rod in a smooth, continuous movement. The entire event takes part of a second. It's the only way to strike a saltwater fish.

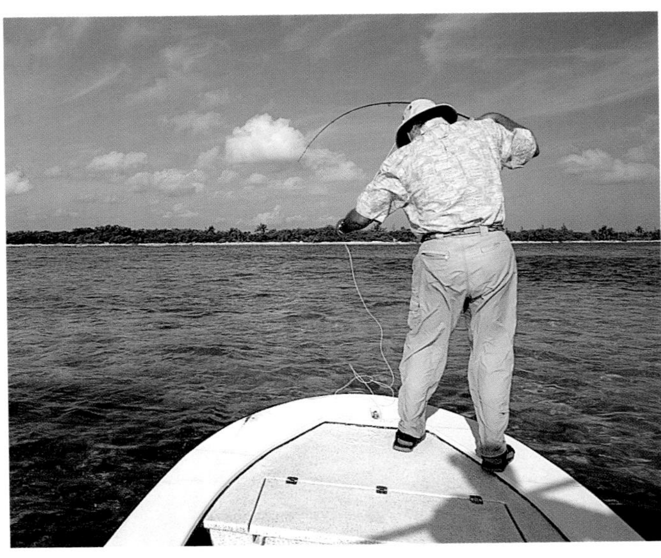

STEPHEN FERNÁNDEZ

I know it's hard, but don't look at the bonefish as it begins its first run. Look down at the fly line until you've cleared all of it.

CLEARING LINE

Congratulations. The fish found the retrieve satisfactory, you executed a perfect strip-strike and instantly raised the rod to 45 degrees, and now you have a hooked bonefish at the end of your tippet. A hooked bone may or may not react immediately to the pressure of the hook; sometimes a fish responds with a few seconds of surprise and confusion. Within no more than a few seconds, however, that fish will begin a very fast run away from the flat and toward the deepest water he can find.

Meanwhile, you have a lot of loose fly line at your feet. If the fish followed the fly for a good distance before making up his mind, you might have a great deal of loose line on the deck. When the fish starts his run—and even a very confused bonefish will have started by the time your heart has beat twice—all that loose line has to go through the rod guides without tangling, without catching on one of your feet, without wrapping about the rod's fighting butt. Getting the loose fly line off the deck, through the guides, and out of the tip-top without a mishap is called clearing the line.

To clear the fly line at your feet as the bonefish takes off at high speed, you must again do something that is not intuitive: you must take your eyes off the fish and look at your feet. I know it's hard to do. You want to look at the bonefish you just hooked, but it is essential that you don't.

Separate your hands. Your rod hand should keep the fighting butt against your wrist so that the line cannot loop around the butt, which is a very common way to break off a running bonefish. Don't keep the angle of the rod too high while clearing line. Too high an angle tends to make the rod throb back and forth. This movement makes it harder to clear line smoothly and creates slack that allows the fish to slip the hook. Hold the rod at a lower angle and keep it steady as you feed line out.

Your line hand should be lower than your rod hand. Apply almost no pressure as the line flies out through the guides—maintain just enough tension so that the line isn't running loose. This slight pressure gives you control. But don't hold the line too tightly. If you do, two things will happen, neither of them good. A tightly held fly line can burn your hand, and it will come through your hand in a series of sharp, erratic jerks, bouncing the rod, creating slack, and making the loose line still in the boat jump all over the place until it tangles on something.

I have heard of anglers who make an O with the thumb and index finger and let the fly line run freely through that hole. In my experience, a completely loose line will create more tangles than a lightly held line during the clearing process.

Once the fish has taken all but a yard or two of the loose line, you might think that you can relax and let go of the last little bit. You figure a few feet of fly line can't get caught on anything—it's too short. Big mistake. If you let go of the last portion of fast-clearing fly line, chances are good that that little loop of line will wrap around the first stripping guide. When that happens, the least disastrous outcome is a broken tippet. Many fish are lost this way. The biggest permit that I have ever hooked, a fish that probably weighed over 40 pounds, was lost to this mistake. It happened a long time ago, but I still remember that fish and the sick feeling I had as the last bit of loose fly line made a neat half-hitch around the stripping guide.

Keep control of the fly line as the fish begins his run. Maintain light pressure on it, watch the line at your feet, and as the last of the loose fly line comes off the deck, follow it with your hand toward the stripping guide and watch it disappear. You are not through clearing line until the reel starts to sing.

THE BAFFLED BONEFISH

From time to time you'll hook a bonefish that does not run, at least right away. He may keep coming your way or swim around in circles or do something else other than make the classic run away from you. But you still have a lot of line to clear.

I generally keep stripping line as he approaches the boat or circles around, but I make sure that I keep a tight line with absolutely no slack. I monitor the fly line at my feet, untangle anything that needs it, and basically get ready for the long run that is coming. And believe me, it's coming.

Sooner or later, the fish get his wits about him, heads for deep water as he should, and things go back to normal. Just remember not to give him any slack while he's swimming around in confusion.

Sometimes a bone will not run right away. While he's making up his mind, make sure that you do not give him any slack.

STEPHEN FERNÁNDEZ

SUSTAINING THE LONG RUN

"Keep the rod high!" was the usual advice years ago, and some anglers still live by it. You were supposed to raise both your hands well over your head with the fly rod way up high. The idea was that you would keep the fly line away from sea fans, coral, and other obstructions, but this generally is not true. Besides, to hold a fly rod so high while a fish makes a long run takes a lot of effort. And it's an unnecessary effort; it does nothing for you.

Lifting the tip of the rod as high as you can will raise only a few extra feet of fly line off the water. The rest of the line remains on the surface. You accomplish nothing by lifting the rod over your head, except to make yourself very tired.

Better to keep the fighting butt near your belt and the rod at an angle of 45 degrees or so, and let him run. There's nothing else to do for the time being. Enjoy your fish—this astonishing run is the reason you traveled thousands of miles to stand on a small boat under a blazing sun.

The one exception is when you hook a bonefish on a flat with small mangrove shoots. You may be able to clear some of these shoots by raising the rod, but only if they are very close to you. Lifting the rod is not going to help you clear a mangrove shoot 30 yards away.

As a fish runs, the diameter of the line remaining on the spool shrinks. That reduced diameter amounts to a shorter lever arm against the resistance of the reel's brake, which means that drag pressure increases as a fish takes line. How much the drag increases depends on the design and proportions of the reel; a small, wide reel will increase drag pressure considerably as a fish takes line, whereas a large-arbor model maintains more consistent resistance. In any case, you shouldn't need to adjust the mechanical drag during the first run because you should have started with a relatively light drag. As the fish runs, you can easily apply extra drag with your hands if you feel that you need it. That's why your reel has an exposed rim on the spool.

If you do feel the drag increasing to the danger point as the fish runs, you started with too much. Back off on the adjustment a little to avoid breaking the tippet or pulling the hook out. Of course, many anglers don't realize that they had set their drags too tight until it's too late. Besides, adjusting the drag during a long, fast run is another chance for something to go wrong—what if you turn it the wrong way or loosen it so much that the spool overruns?

Remember to start with a light drag. You need enough to keep the spool from overrunning, but not a great deal more. If you need to put more pressure on the fish, feather the spool.

DURING THE FIGHT

Eventually, he'll stop, though there are times when you wonder if he ever will. By then, the fish might be 50 or more than 100 yards away, if he happens to be a large fish. Now the fight begins; you have to regain all that line.

For starters, try to keep a tight line during the fight. A slack line gives the fish a better chance to dislodge the hook. Avoid slack as much as possible.

Your next big goal is to get the fly line back inside the rod. This is where you want to fight all fish, if

STEPHEN FERNÁNDEZ

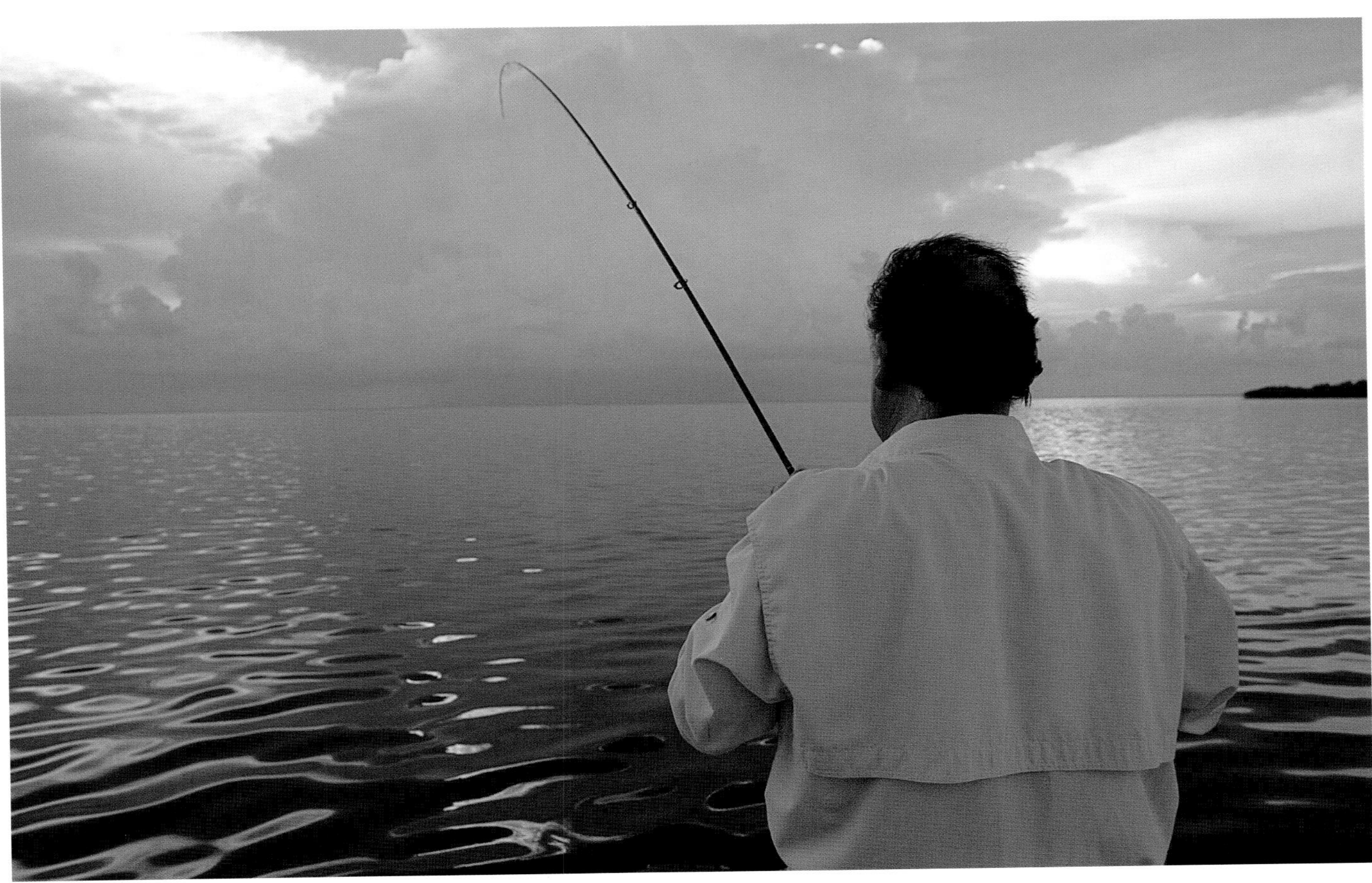

After the long run, make sure to keep a tight line. A large-arbor reel helps a lot in this situation.

possible. Your guide will pole after the fish as you reel in line (this is one time when you will really appreciate a large-arbor reel). If you're wading, you could chase the fish to regain line. With a 3-pound bonefish that gets a little into your backing, don't bother running across the flat—just stand there and enjoy him.

From time to time, a bonefish will start to run back toward you, creating a big belly of slack. Naturally, you must try to retrieve that slack as fast as possible. But do not bring the rod back in an effort to pick up some slack because you'll be in danger of wrapping the line around the tip of the rod. Instead, keep the rod tip ahead of you. If you want it not to wobble too much as you frantically crank the reel (this, too, can cause a loop of backing to wrap around the rod), keep the tip in the water. This works very well.

Stay as close to the fish as possible during the fight. The closer you are, the more the pressure of your rod will affect him. You'll simply have more control of events. Ask any experienced tarpon angler.

When a hooked fish manages to tangle some loose grass on the fly line or leader, try to get rid of the grass. You do not want heavy grass hanging from your line during a fight; the strain of dragging a bulky wad of vegetation through the water can break a light bonefish tippet even if your drag is set lightly. To get rid of the grass, lift the fly line as high as you can so that the clinging grass is off the water. Now shake the grass from side to side while it is in the air. With luck, all or most of it should drop off the line.

When a bonefish makes a long run and tangles your line or leader on a mangrove shoot, do not pull. Instead, give him some slack and then carefully approach the fish. As you get closer, you can see how the line is tangled and solve the problem before the fish takes off again. Chances are that the fish will not move much as long as you don't pull or make a big commotion as you approach him; he is usually tired after that first long run. I have saved many bonefish catches this way.

Toward the end of the fight, when the fish is close to you, keep a low rod angle. Apply pressure against his ever-changing direction of pull—if he pulls to the right, then you pull directly against him to the left, and so forth. By fighting this way, you'll land him sooner and release him in much better condition, which is what you want.

Try to keep a bonefish that is close to the skiff from going under it.

MARKUS HAUGG

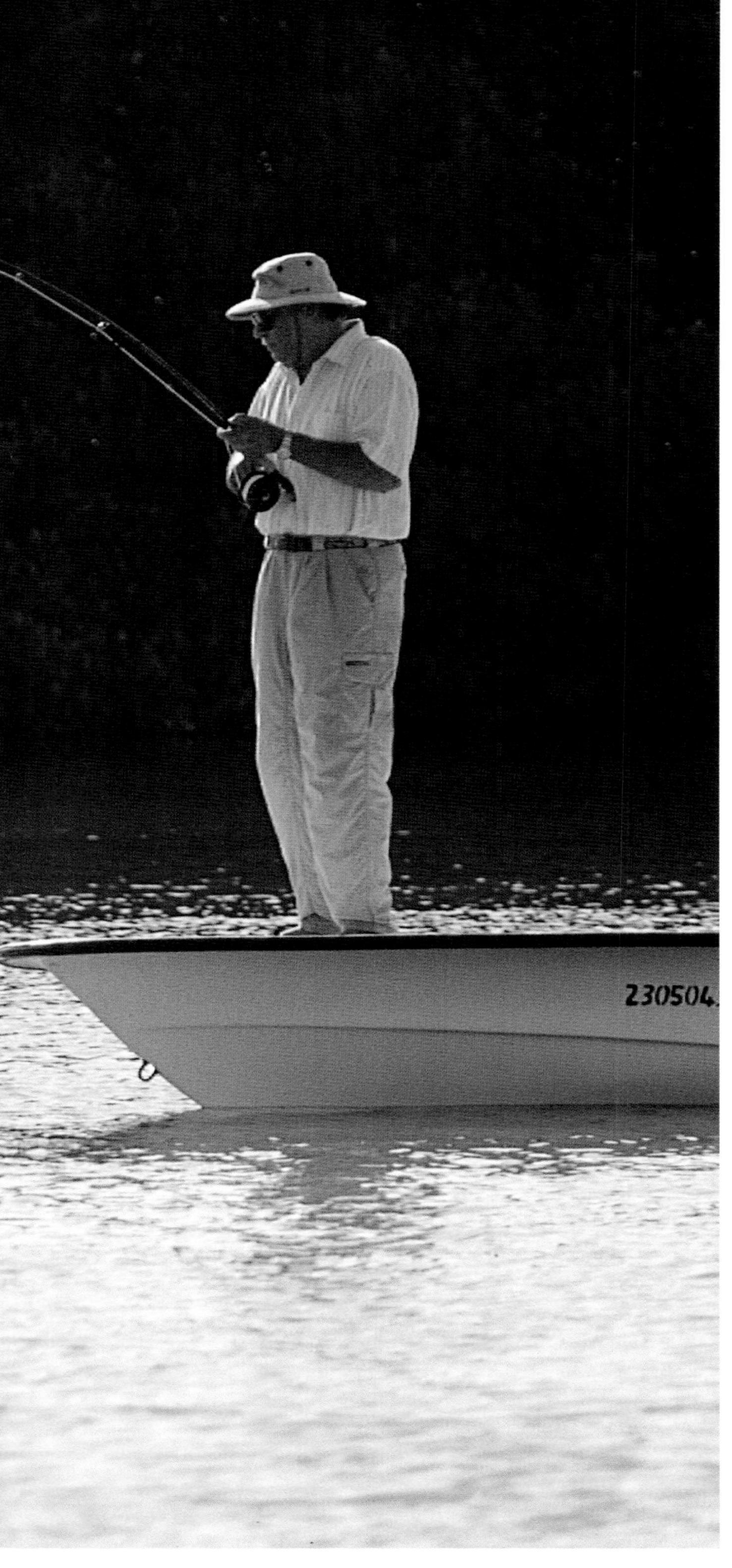

Once the fish is close to you or the skiff, be prepared for one or two final dashes. The fish might run only a few feet, but he can do it with enough strength to break the tippet if he catches you off guard. Besides, as you bring a bonefish close to the boat, a good part of your long leader comes inside the rod. A sudden lunge by the fish will pull the leader knot back out of the rod, clicking and slamming against every guide. Here again, a low rod angle helps by letting the leader slide freely through the guides. This is also when you find out why it's good to trim the tag ends of knots as close as possible.

At the end of the fight, a bonefish often pulls one of his most dangerous maneuvers, the "dive under the boat trick." Many fish break tippets this way, and some break fly rods.

When a fish dives under the skiff, do not keep the rod tip up—this is the worst possible time for high-sticking. The rod bends double and eventually breaks. Don't try to pull the fish back under the boat when he is already on the other side. Dip the tip of the rod, maybe a foot or more of it if the depth allows, into the water. Make sure that neither the line nor the rod is touching the boat. Then, with the rod tip in the water, move the line around one end of the boat, preferably the bow, and clear the fly line again. Now you are fighting the fish on the other side of the boat, free and clear.

If the boat is drifting toward the fish at the end of the fight, the bonefish will probably run under the skiff. The ideal (though not always possible) arrangement is to have the wind or current moving the boat away from the fish as you fight him.

One last item about pressure. If you are using a size 4 or smaller fly and a 10-pound tippet, remember that excessive pressure can straighten a small hook. A stainless-steel hook is rarely as stiff as a carbon-steel model made of equally thick wire. I've straightened a few size 4 and size 6 hooks with 10-pound tippets, but very few with 8-pound tippets. And I never use anything heavier than 10-pound-test material with a size 4 or smaller fly.

Chapter 17

Landing and Releasing Bonefish

A typical 9-foot fly rod is an awkward tool with which to bring a bonefish close enough to a skiff for you to land him. The rod's length keeps the fish out of your reach and gives him all the leverage. It's even harder to land a fish by yourself while wading a flat, which generally has no shore where you can beach your catch. Like everything else in bonefishing, the final act requires some thought and skill.

FROM A SKIFF

Your guide or another angler can help you land a tired bonefish, but you have to bring the fish to him. Stand at one end of the skiff and steer the fish toward the middle or the last third of the boat, where your guide or friend, who is down at gunwale level, can grab the fish or the leader. You can also stand behind your guide or friend as he kneels against the side of the boat and lead the fish to him. Whatever you do, don't bring the rod up and back in an attempt to raise the fish to your feet. You'll break the rod.

Some anglers still use landing nets, but I feel that a net removes too much of a bonefish's protective slime. I use a net with other species on the rare occasions when I want to keep a fish to eat, but I land all my bones by hand. If you do use a net (and it can simplify boating a fish), always bring the fish toward the net, not the net toward the fish.

Once the fish is in your hands, handle him carefully. If possible, keep a bonefish in the water while you remove the hook. Take him out of the water only if you have trouble removing the hook, want a photo, or want to weigh or measure him.

Don't raise the rod at the end of the fight. This is high enough.

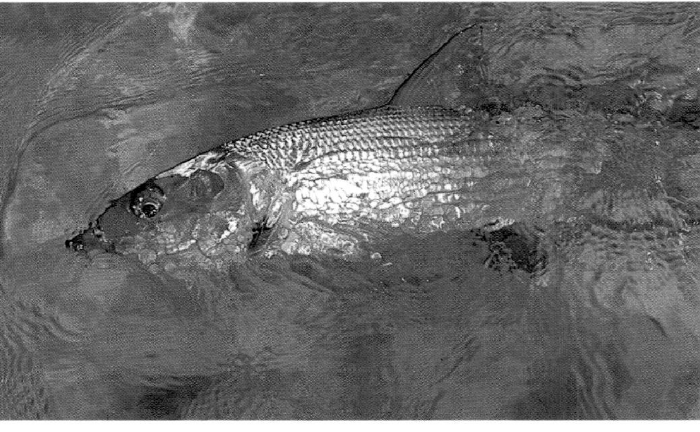

A bonefish ready to be landed

MARKUS HAUGG

gamefish on the flats. The loop-to-loop connection on the leader of your heavy outfit lets you switch from a rigged permit crab to a rigged shark fly in no time at all.

Chances are that you won't need quite that many rigs. Your guide will tell you which other gamefish he has been seeing lately. Maybe he hasn't run across many barracudas lately, and the jacks have been few and small, but he has seen some good permit and an occasional big shark. If you'd like to fish for those two species if the opportunities arise, prepare the appropriate loop-to-loop outfits. If your guide reports seeing a lot of 'cudas or big jacks, rig for those fish. I've been fishing this way for years, and I've taken some big fish simply because I was ready.

On most trips, I have a bonefish rod with a weighted fly for deeper water, a second bonefish outfit with a small, unweighted fly for tailing fish, and one or two 9- or 10-weight rods with loops in their butt sections. The heavy outfits are rigged for whatever species the guide thinks we're likely to find that day. The loop-to-loop leader comes in very handy when a selective barracuda rejects my fly. Without tying any knots, I can quickly replace the entire tippet and switch to another style or color of fly. That often does the trick. And if I break a rod, I have spares.

Bonefish are your primary targets, but they're not the only worthwhile targets on the flats. Why not add to the fun by catching other species?

A tailing permit is one of the great fly-fishing challenges.

PERMIT: THE KING

I first cast to a permit in the late 1950s on one of the many flats around the Island of Pines (Isla de Pinos), which lies south of Cuba about half an hour by air from Havana. It happened while I was wading for bonefish. Several long, dark fins came out of the water at the edge of the flat, and I immediately knew what they were. I had never caught a permit on any type of tackle, nor had I ever seen one in person, but I knew.

There were three fish, and they were probably close to 30 pounds each. A few years later, I learned that this area was known for very large permit. But by then it was too late: I was already living in Miami.

I waded toward the fish with my light bamboo rod, Medalist reel, and bonefish fly. In those days there was no such thing as a permit fly. All I remember of the fly is that it was white, tied on a Z-nickel size 1 hook, and unweighted. It could not have been a worse choice for a bottom feeder like the permit, but I didn't know that.

The permit kept tailing and moving, and it was hard for me to keep up with them as I tried to present the fly. This went on for quite a while, until the pod of fish reached the end of the flat and disappeared into deeper water unmolested. They never knew I was there. But I was so excited that I could hardly breathe when I got back to the skiff, where my guide was having lunch.

It would be years before I finally took a permit with a fly rod on the flats, with a white marabou fly weighted with a brass bead. Years.

Not long after, one of my heroes, Al McClane, wrote an article for *Field & Stream* about fly fishing for permit. The article had a photo of Al holding a permit that was almost 30 pounds in one hand and a bamboo saltwater fly rod in the other. Al caught the permit on the same bonefish flat I had fished near the Island of Pines in Cuba. If I recall correctly, he called the article "King Permit." It made the greatest impression on me. Years later, when I got to know Al fairly well, I told him that I had fished that same flat and seen some of those big permit. We both grinned.

There is something about a permit—the way it moves across the flats, its power, the stiletto-like fin showing high out of the water when it tails, the tall, flat

Every permit on fly is special; one never catches too many of them.

body that seems so improbable on the shallow flats, the way it projects wariness and intelligence—that makes this fish incredibly charismatic and desirable. The best casters lose their loop control when they see a permit. The most patient of anglers make hurried, desperate attempts. It's hard to approach a tailing permit and stay cool.

To be a good fly fisher for permit, you have to like to hunt more than you like to catch fish. You have to be above merely catching. Most good permit anglers have landed enough other fish that they no longer have to catch fish every time they go fishing; they don't need to return to the dock with stories.

To catch a permit, you have to hunt in areas a bit deeper than most bonefish water, places where it is harder to see fish and harder to pole a skiff. It's all about the thrill of the hunt—with a permit thrown in as a bonus from time to time if you are good, or if you are lucky.

"What did you catch?"

"Nothing."

"Nothing?"

"Nothing."

"Not even a nibble?"

"No," with a smile.

"Had a good time?"

"Oh yeah."

I've heard that dialogue a thousand times.

In the context of fly fishing, I think of the permit as a cult fish, and I like that, probably because I also like cult cars, cult music, and cult movies. You have to be a bit special to understand the subtleties. And when you do, you find yourself belonging to a very small society that speaks a different language. It's cool.

Or was cool. Because, slowly, it's all changing. It used to be, forty years ago, that catching a permit on the flats with a fly rod was almost magical. It really was that hard. We did not know that we needed flies that dove to the bottom when we stopped stripping. We did not know about crab flies and how to fish them. We would spend a year casting to permit during bonefish trips and have a few follows and a couple of flashes or boils at our flies, but no takes. For a whole year!

I remember a friend who loved to cook fish telling me, after losing his patience with one more story about follows and boils, "You can't fry a boil." I did not tell him that I intended to release the fish if I did catch it. It wouldn't have gone over well.

Today, however, with the invention and development of crab flies, and the constant refinement of how to present the fly and how to swim it or not swim it, permit fishing with a fly has become almost common. Sandy Moret, one of the great permit anglers (he has taken

MARKUS HAUGG

I release every permit I take in the flats, big or small.

more than 100 of them on flies), described the current state of fly fishing for permit by saying, "Given a very good angler and guide, with good tides and weather conditions, one can almost expect a permit a day."

A decent angler who fishes hard in ideal weather for a week can expect to take a few permit. Isn't that incredible? It is to those of us who struggled for years—no, decades—to catch a very few of these fish. But it's true. If you pay your dues, you *can* take permit on flies these days. But it's not easy, and it's still one of the greatest angling thrills.

Of course, we're talking about fishing for permit on the flats and without using chum. Deep-water anglers catch many permit by anchoring off a wreck and chumming the permit to the boat. In deeper water, the fish are not as spooky or as hard to hook. Quite often, the game requires no casting skill.

That kind of fishing can be a lot of fun, but it has nothing to do with the intense hunting that goes on when you look for permit on the shallow flats and the skills required to present and then manipulate the fly so that it looks like the real thing to a wise old permit. *That* is special.

The Atlantic permit is a member of the jack family. Scientifically, he is *Trachinotus falcatus*, and he goes by several other common names. Because of their very round shape, juvenile permit are called round pompano. They are very hard to distinguish from regular pompano. In Spanish-speaking countries, the permit is the *palometa*. You should know this name when you fish with a Spanish-speaking guide to better communicate with him during the search. But do not confuse the permit with the true palometa, *Trachinotus goodie*.

Unlike pompano, which seldom grow over 5 or 6 pounds, permit can get big. Several permit over 50

STEPHEN FERNÁNDEZ

Its deep body helps a permit during the fight.

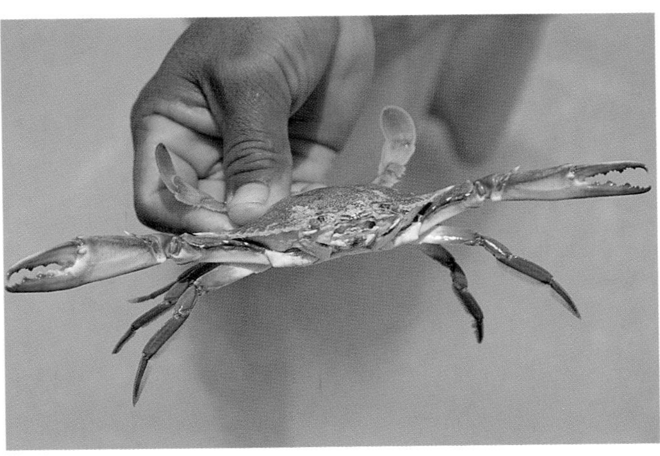

A blue crab is one of the permit's favorite meals.

pounds have been landed on rod and reel, and a few over 40 have been taken on fly tackle. A permit that lived in the Miami Sea Aquarium was known to weigh more than 70 pounds. Permit over 20 and even 30 pounds are taken all the time in the Florida Keys, the Bahamas, the Yucatan, Honduras, and other places.

The permit's range extends from Brazil to Massachusetts, and they can appear on any bonefish flat in the Atlantic. In general, the hotter the better. They seem to tolerate warmer temperatures better than bonefish do.

Because permit have deep bodies, their average feeding depth on the flats is a bit deeper than the bonefish's range. However, there is a big overlap, and you will often see permit while bonefishing. They frequent both inside and ocean-side flats. A hard-bottomed, ocean-side flat with an incoming tide is ideal.

At most tropical destinations, the permit fishing improves as the weather gets hotter. In the Florida Keys, we can be more specific about the best times. February and March can be great months if the weather is warm enough. The permit fishing in the Keys is very good, and often at its best, in July, August, September, and October, until the weather turns cool. July is the favorite month of two of the great permit guides, Capt. Dale Perez and Capt. Rick Ruoff.

The crab flies that work best are heavy and hard to cast, even in still air. But you don't cast them in still air; you need some wind to fish for permit. On a flat-calm day, they are so spooky and hard to approach that hardly anyone fly fishes for them. Ideally, winds from 12 to 18 mph will let you approach within casting range of permit while letting you cast comfortably. Fishing in winds just over 20 mph is not uncommon. That much wind makes for tough casting, but it also allows a very close approach, so I usually don't mind the wind.

Even a big permit can be tough to see at times, particularly in the windy conditions that create good fishing. You need to stay focused and hunt hard, scanning the water constantly. When you do spot one, you have to be fairly aggressive. Don't lead him too much. Take advantage of the breeze and hit him close. I know it's nerve-racking, but believe me, it's effective. You'll spook some, but you will also hook some. While permit can be very spooky, especially on calm days, they are probably not as easily spooked as a bonefish.

When they feed in a strong current, permit wait for crabs to drift their way. So, if the tide is really running, you may want to cast four or five feet ahead of the fish and let the fly drift.

Now we come to the core of the whole game: the retrieve. Casting a heavy crab fly in the wind might be difficult, but it's still easier than the retrieve.

You must interact with the fish. That is, watch his reaction to the fly from the moment it plops onto the water until the permit takes it. Sandy Moret's way of putting it is, "A permit requires that you *read* him, more than any other fish." I agree, and so do most other knowledgeable permit anglers.

As a rule, you will cast close enough so that the permit sees the fly as soon as it enters the water. If the fish reacts to the fly, let the crab drop to the bottom and see if he takes it. If the cast is not exactly on target, or if the fish does not see the fly, then retrieve it slowly and let it drop, or retrieve it slowly and evenly until the fish reacts to it, and then let it drop.

I am a great believer that the crab should not drop straight down, but rather descend at about a 45-degree angle. That's the angle at which I see crabs dive for safety.

Remember that you are trying to imitate a crab, a creature that does not dart or streak through the water

The assortment of flies in my permit box always seems to be changing.

like a baitfish does. Capt. Dale Perez, one of the great experts on fly fishing for permit, has this advice: "When he finally sees it, don't move the fly, especially if he is looking at it on the bottom. And if you must move it, move it very slowly."

Capt. Rick Ruoff, another permit expert, says, "When the fly is down, don't drag it on the bottom. It may spook him."

Yet Sandy Moret, long a member of the "cast, drop, and don't move it" school, is changing his technique a little after taking more than 100 permit on flies. "I have been going to a very slow retrieve, mixing it up a little," Sandy says. "Pull it. Then swim it."

Capt. Tom Rowland, who has done a world of fly fishing for permit around Key West, advocates the cast-and-drop technique for crab flies. But he adds this: "When I fish a shrimp pattern for permit, however, I feel the fly must be fished differently than the crab. It must be moved more as you read the fish. I tap the fly once or twice, and if he seems excited, then I continue that type of retrieve. Also, I fish small permit a bit differently. I like to cast in front of a school of small fish and let them approach the fly, and then I strip it, then stop, making the strips fluid, not jerky. I tap, tap, tap the fly, then maybe a long strip, and usually one of them has it."

When the fly is on the bottom, you often have to make a long, slow strip to see if the permit actually has it. If he does have it, you will feel him, and then you continue the long strip into a strip-strike. It's very exciting when that moment comes and the rod bends deep into the butt. But do not use sharp or abrupt strips, because these movements usually make a permit shy away from the fly.

All advice is relative, of course, and often it does not work. That's permit fishing. Still, the percentages are with the advice of the experts. I'd heed it if I were you.

Although my friends' advice is as state-of-the-art as we can get in permit fishing, they're talking mostly about the permit from Miami through the Florida Keys and into Key West. Anglers in other parts of the world might use slightly different retrieves.

While fishing out of the famous Casa Blanca fishing camp in Ascension Bay on the Yucatan Peninsula, my son and I learned that anglers there generally retrieve crab flies a bit faster, sometimes moving them almost as fast as they would a streamer or a shrimp imitation. Indeed, we even caught permit on Clouser Minnows—but crab flies were still better.

The area around Punta Gorda in southern Belize is another great permit destination. My friend John Oster has fished the area several times. John is one of the fanatics who belong to the very small society of serious permit hunters. Describing the retrieve for permit in that part of the world, John says, "As you know, in southern Belize the 'classic' cast and drop does not always work well. On the coral flats inside the reef, I have had results with a variation of the classic method. Cast and make fairly long strips until the fish sees it, and then let it sink. If he shows interest, I'll twitch it a time or two. In the mud-bottomed lagoons, where I've had the most success, I tend to keep the fly moving most of the time. But often I let it sit if a fish approaches the fly. As you know, you try to feel the fish's intention as you work the fly."

That's exactly what makes permit fishing so special: you do indeed try to *feel* the fish's intention. It can make every other kind of fishing seem simple.

When you fight a permit, even a big one, do not apply excessive pressure. This is not like tarpon fishing. The hook can easily tear out of the fish's relatively soft mouth. Medium-hard, steady pressure can subdue any permit, even a 40-pounder. Make sure that your guide stays with the fish so that you fight him with the fly line inside the rod most of the time. Any long run requires that you pole after the fish; you want to keep him close to you during the fight. Good permit guides earn every penny of their tips.

Permit on Dry Flies?

Over the last few years, Capt. Steve Huff has found a situation in which he can fish for permit with a floating crab fly. "Often in the summer," he says, "I find sort of a hatch of small crabs moving on the surface with the tide. The crabs are usually light tan on the back and pure white on the bottom, with blue tips on the legs. Their carapace is about half an inch in length and the whole crab maybe an inch. They are small. But permit know when it happens, and they are looking for them. You can often hear them taking the crabs on the surface. They just make a big wake and take them."

Steve says that in these situations he uses a matching crab fly made with closed-cell foam that floats. A good cast anywhere in front of a permit usually results in a hookup. These situations don't happen often, but they happen often enough that Steve always carries his floating crabs with him.

Permit on top. Now *that* is cool. And Steve, if you can't find anyone to go with you the next time the permit are feeding on the surface, give me a call. I'll go. Heck, I'll even pole you.

Tackle for Permit

The standard tackle for casting the awkward, heavy permit flies is a 9-foot, 9- or 10-weight rod with a floating line made for the hot tropical weather. Usually, a line with a braided-monofilament core is best. In the spring and late fall, when the weather in the Keys is less hot and humid, regular saltwater fly lines work fine, though the specialized bonefish and tarpon lines are still good. I don't care for sinking lines or slow-sinking clear tips for this type of fishing. One often has to pick up the line and make a second presentation as quietly and inconspicuously as possible. Give me a floating line, period.

A smooth reel with room for the fly line and 200 yards of 20-pound backing is more than enough. Permit usually don't make long runs. They are related to jacks, not to bonefish. Besides, any good guide is going to be poling after a running permit soon after the hookup. The rumors you hear about needing 400 yards of backing are just that—rumors. However, I do like a large-arbor reel because its fast retrieve helps me maintain contact with the fish throughout the fight.

Depending on the wind and your own ability to cast a heavy crab fly, your leader should measure between 9 and 14 feet. Mine is generally 12 feet long, of which half is butt section. The best all-around tippet is 12-pound test. Keep in mind that materials of nominally identical strength can differ in diameter and stiffness. A tippet that's too heavy or stiff impairs the crab fly's ability to dive and look natural. Use the 12-pound-test suggestion as a guideline rather than an absolute rule.

Before you go permit fishing, practice casting a crab fly. It's not like throwing a bonefish fly. And when you spot a permit, try to stay cool.

MUTTON SNAPPERS: THE SELDOM-SEEN SNAPPERS

I had been fishing for mutton snapper on shallow reefs most of my life, usually with spinning or bait-casting equipment and jigs. I figured that I understood them pretty well. In the mid-1960s, though, I learned that mutton snappers sometimes came up onto the same Key West flats frequented by permit. I was stunned. My friend Norman Duncan, creator of the Duncan loop, told me that an old fishing guide was fishing for them on the flats, where mutton snappers would tail like bones and permit, often following a working stingray just as permit and bonefish do.

Soon we were fishing for them with spinning gear and flat-headed jigs and with fly rods. The late John "Little John" Emery took an 18-pounder that was tailing behind a ray. We all took muttons over 10 pounds and maybe up to 15 or so with our fly rods.

A mutton snapper tailing in shallow water with its pink, translucent tail backlit by the late-afternoon sun is one of the most beautiful and remarkable sights one can ever witness on the bonefish flats. If you do see it, you will never forget it.

But muttons are much more sensitive to fishing pressure on the flats than bones and permit. As pressure in the Keys increased over the years, mutton snappers became scarce. Besides, there is always commercial fishing pressure on them because they are great to eat. In the last thirty years I have managed to land only a few of them on the flats, but I cherish the memory of every one of those catches.

A couple of years ago, my son Stephen and I went fishing on the west side of Andros with Capt. Joel Moxey. The day started well with a couple of nice bones and a good barracuda taken with a popper. We were poling on the lee side of an island looking for permit when Joel spotted a school of large fish moving right along the shore. He could not make out what they were. They looked like big jacks to Stephen and me, but Joel was not so sure.

They turned out to be a school of eighteen or twenty mutton snappers. I could not believe it. It was the first time in my life I had ever seen such a sight, since muttons are usually spotted on the flats as singles. Seeing three fish together is unusual.

They came by the skiff too fast for us to make a cast. I was upset at losing a once in a lifetime opportunity. But Joel did not give up. He cranked up the skiff, ran way around the school, which was still swimming parallel to the shore, and staked out 100 feet from shore. Then we waited for the school to come to us. I felt that we had no chance, but I was wrong.

A few minutes went by and here came the school of muttons, often tailing as they covered ground. When they came within range, I cast a Clouser Minnow in front of a tailing fish and he took the fly. After a long run and a hard fight, I landed an 11-pound mutton. What a great moment!

Interestingly enough, as great a gamefish as the mutton is on the flats, very few bonefish guides have ever heard of such a thing as a mutton snapper feeding and tailing in shallow water. Many bonefish destinations around the world have mutton snappers that visit the flats to feed, but the guides have never taken notice of them. They know about muttons on the reefs, of course, but

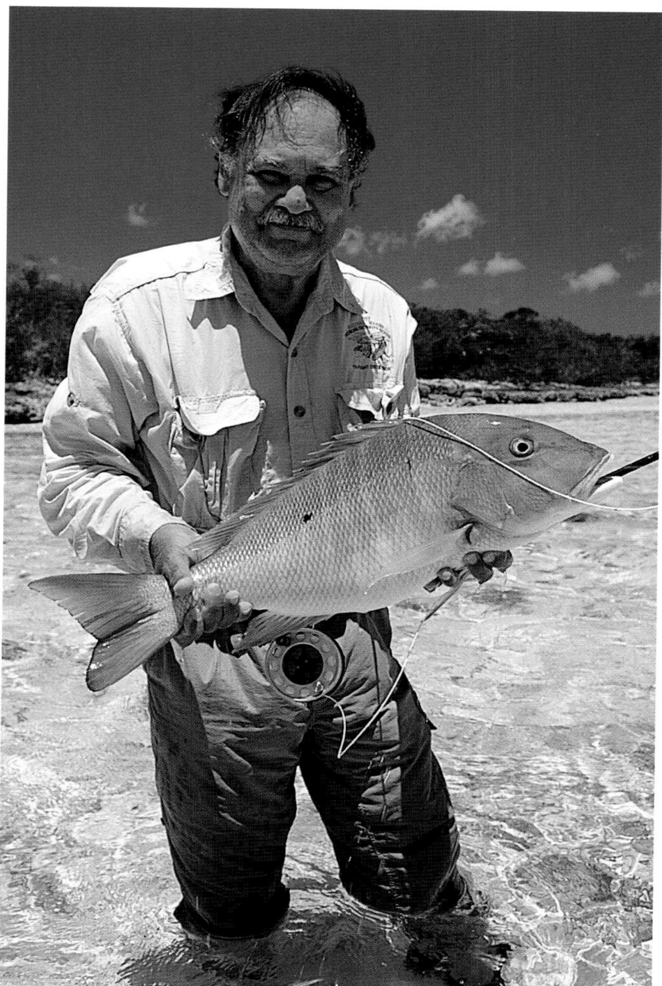

I caught this nice mutton snapper on an 8-foot, 8-inch, 7-weight rod.

when I ask about fishing for them in shallow water, the guides give me strange looks. Sometimes, though, one guide will later tell me that he knows about them. That is the guide I want to fish with the next day.

In my book, the mutton snapper is probably the grand prize of the bonefish world. Rare, hard fighting, and elusive, he has the stuff that makes fly fishermen dream.

You will find them on outside flats in much the same depth as you do tailing permit or big bonefish. Spring is probably the best time of year to find them. They will take permit crabs well, but unlike permit, mutton snappers also like baitfish, making a streamer a good choice. If you fish a crab fly, move it faster than you would for a permit. I have even taken muttons on poppers in four to eight feet of water over patch reefs.

Capt. Rick Ruoff, who shares my love for this species, feels that the best color for muttons is orange. He also likes a fly that does not sink quite as fast as a permit

STEPHEN FERNÁNDEZ

A mutton snapper in his typical outside-flat environment.

fly. But since most mutton snappers are spotted while an angler is permit fishing, most are caught on permit flies. Tarpon anglers take some with tarpon flies.

They fight very hard, but like the permit, they are not long-distance runners. The same tackle that you use for permit will do just fine for muttons. A 9- or 10-weight rod, a floating line with a 12-pound tippet, and 200 yards of backing are all you need.

Now for some good news. After twenty years of absence from Key West, the muttons seem to be making a very slow comeback. Over the last couple of springs, anglers report seeing some on the flats. Most were following stingrays, but a few were tailing. Seeing a mutton snapper near Key West is still a rare event, but perhaps it will become less rare. I hope so; you would enjoy fishing for them.

BIG JACKS: THE WRESTLERS

The bonefish flats and their surroundings can harbor several species of big jacks. In the Atlantic, the most common are the jack crevalle and the Atlantic horse-eye jack. The trevally is the big jack in the Pacific. These heavyweight wrestlers often cruise the flats or the edges of flats looking for food. Their diet consists mostly of smaller fishes, but they'll eat almost anything.

My first encounter with a really big jack on a fly rod happened around 1960, while I was still using bamboo fly rods. At that time, Biscayne Bay had millions and millions of mullet. It was not unusual to see school after school, each covering an acre or more, swimming undisturbed all day long. The only time their peace was certain to be disturbed was at daybreak. Then all hell would break loose, and one could often see an entire school of mullet in the air trying to escape pods of big jacks. The easiest fishing was at dawn, when the jacks would pin the mullet against shorelines and sea walls.

During this particular week, schools of mullet had been running along a stretch of sandy beach on one of the islands between Miami and Key Biscayne. And the jacks had been waiting for them every morning. Knowing this, I had been there several days in a row to enjoy the festivities. Getting up at dark and arriving just before dawn, I had landed several jacks weighing more than 10 pounds. As soon as sun broke over the horizon and the light increased just a tad, they were gone, and the mullet were mostly left in peace until the next morning.

On the third or fourth morning, the action started while it was still dark. When I heard the crashes, I cast a big, crude, yellow popper that I had made myself, and was immediately hooked up. In the dark, the strike seemed no more powerful than usual, but I quickly realized that I could not stop the fish. A minute later, most of my backing was gone.

I fought the fish well into the morning, putting on all the pressure I felt the bamboo could stand, which by today's standards was very little. It seemed to take half the morning to get the fly line back to the rod, and by then I was expecting a 6-foot fish. I just knew that whatever it was, it was huge. I was not thinking about jacks.

It must have been 9 o'clock when I finally saw the fish, and it looked only a yard long. I was so disappointed. Eventually I landed a jack that I estimated was over 20 pounds, but not 25 pounds. I was dead tired, but the fish still wrestled with me when I tried to take the hook out. And I do mean just the hook: the fly was destroyed. I went home a bit disappointed that such a small fish had given me such a fight.

These days, I'd go home elated after catching such a fish. Jacks are the strongest inshore fish I know. There's no reason to feel bad about landing a "mere" jack crevalle.

Twenty years later, I was fly fishing around the Palm Beach Inlet for the big jacks that come there during the mullet run in the fall. Using the heavy tarpon rods that were already available then, my buddy and I had each taken a fish over 30 pounds, and we were feeling pretty good. Jacks were all around us.

All of a sudden, the few big jacks that were around the boat disappeared. That's usually a sign of sharks in the area, but not this time. A pod of four *really* big jack crevalle showed up. They looked closely at everything around them and seemed aware of everything, almost like humans. They looked at the boat, and then one of them looked directly at me. It made me feel funny.

They were a different animal than any big jack I had ever experienced. After watching them for a little while, I cast a fly a few feet in front of them, not sure that I wanted a strike. The largest fish, which I judged to be well over 50 pounds, came up to the popper and did something strange. As the popper lay still, he turned sideways with his left eye inches from the popper, looking at it intensely for a couple of seconds like an expert fly tier examining someone else's crude fly. I don't think he had the slightest desire to eat it, or even thought it was food. Maybe he was just curious. Then, as quickly as they had appeared, they were gone. I have never forgotten them, or that big eye against the popper.

I can't think of a stronger inshore fish pound for pound than a big jack crevalle hooked on a bonefish outfit. When you hook one, you invariably think that you have a much larger fish. They are incredible.

Yet many anglers look down on them, mainly because they are so abundant and the smaller jacks are so easy to catch. But they are great fun. Don't let the purists keep you away from them! A big jack, one over 20 pounds, is one of the truly exciting fish in the salt, eager to attack a fly on the surface and uncommonly powerful and determined once hooked.

Because jacks appear in such a large range of sizes around the flats, no single outfit is right for all of them. If I am going to blind-cast a lot with a big fly, I usually choose a shorter rod, one under 9 feet. It makes prolonged casting easier on me. And when I do hook a nice fish, the shorter rod is better for the tough fight ahead. Rods from 9- through 11-weight work well for bigger jacks.

For a leader, I use a 6-foot butt section with a loop and 3 feet of tippet with a shock tippet. The class tippet is usually 12- or 16-pound line, depending on the size of the fly and the size of the fish I hope to catch. The shock tippet ranges from 30- to 50-pound mono, again depending on the fly and the fish. I use a 40-pound shock tippet most often. It casts well and I have yet to lose a jack because the shock tippet frayed and broke.

Pound for pound, a jack is probably the strongest inshore gamefish. Don't underestimate him; a big jack is worth your time.

Use a floating line to cast a popper. For blind-casting a streamer, try a clear, intermediate line; it casts farther and doesn't spook the big fish.

Streamers that imitate mullet and other baitfish will always catch jacks, but poppers and sliders are also excellent. A muddler with a big head like a mullet's is a great fly for jacks.

In the bonefish's world, the areas most likely to hold big jacks are channels between the flats. The fishing is best on a strong outgoing tide that forces baitfish and crustaceans into the channels. When you find a school of bait, you can expect a few big jacks to be nearby. A fast-moving fly, preferably a baitfish pattern with some flash, should get their attention. Choose a fly that seems just a bit too large for the size of the fish; they like a big mouthful.

When they come up onto the flats, jacks can become spooky and nervous. In shallow water, keep your distance from a jack and make a long cast well in front of the fish.

Really big jacks behave differently. They show more savvy and more maturity, almost like they're a different species. They're much harder to fool, too. Look for them in deeper water or along steep drop-offs next to flats. Big jacks are always looking for large quantities of food. An area with schools of mullet is a good place, and a large school of very small bonefish often attracts big jacks.

Besides flats, many bonefish destinations also have a lot of small islands separated by channels. The current moves swiftly through these channels, carrying bait with it. These are very good places to find big jacks. If you fish a good-looking spot for a little while without a bite, try blind-casting with the best of all dinner bells, a popper. Make a few casts in every direction. If there are any jacks within a few hundred feet, they'll come running.

A popper works beautifully when you're trying to chase a school of jacks. The fish move so fast, almost running into themselves, that you have to get their attention quickly, before they vanish. They might not see a streamer, but they will hear a big popper. Besides, the strike alone makes a popper a good choice.

Take your time when releasing a jack. Yes, they're very tough fish, but too many anglers just swing them overboard. After a long fight, a jack might be too tired to escape a shark. Rest and revive a jack as you would any other fish. A big jack is one of the great gamefish, a heavyweight wrestler that deserves your respect. They certainly have mine.

This horse-eye jack was taken from a large school that was cruising by the edge of a bonefish flat.

THE TOOTHY GUYS

The next two gamefish, barracudas and sharks, have sharp teeth that can easily cut your tippet on the strike or during the fight. It's not unusual to get a hit from a small barracuda while fishing for bones. The little 'cuda cuts the plain tippet so quickly that you never even feel the strike. You keep stripping, wondering why the bonefish hasn't seen your fly. Then you pick up the line to make another cast and realize that you no longer have anything at the end of the leader.

You need wire bite tippets to catch the toothy guys, which means that you have to learn to rig wire and cast it. But sharks and big barracudas are thrilling fly-rod fish, and you will never regret taking the time to prepare the special leaders that they require.

Leaders for 'Cudas and Sharks

Casting a large barracuda or shark fly attached to a few inches of wire is not easy, particularly in the wind. The shortest leader you can get away with is best. I use 9-foot leaders and have no problem turning over the fly to make a good presentation. A 9-footer is just long enough not to spook a 'cuda or shark, but short enough to make casting fairly easy, if it's designed right.

With a 9- or 10-weight outfit, use five feet of 40-pound butt section and a foot of 30-pound midsection. Make a loop at the end at the midsection. You could use just a butt section and tippet, but I think that the foot of midsection makes the leader cast and turn over more smoothly.

Make the class tippet with 12- to 15-pound mono and the bite tippet with 25- to 50-pound wire, depending on the size of the fish that you're looking for. The finished leader should have 6 to 8 inches of wire between the monofilament and the fly. If you use less than that, a shark or 'cuda might eat the entire bite tippet and instantly cut the mono behind it. A foot of wire is too heavy to cast. The complete tippet section should measure about three feet. A Bimini loop on the back end lets you attach it to the main part of the leader.

Constructing one of these tippets is neither quick nor easy. Use a haywire twist to make a narrow loop in one end of the wire. Tie a Bimini twist in the class-tippet material to produce a length of double line. With the double line, tie an Albright special to the loop on the end of the wire.

Tie another Bimini twist in the other end of the monofilament to produce a couple of feet of double line. Fold the double line and tie a surgeon's loop with all four strands, making a loop at the back end of the tippet section big enough to pass over the fly. Attach the barracuda or shark fly to the wire with a haywire twist. Remember that the finished bite tippet should be six to eight inches long.

It's easier to show someone how to make one of these leaders than it is to write about it. Learning how to do it from written instructions, even those with illustrations, is difficult. The best and easiest way to learn is to have someone show you. A good fly shop can help. Some shops run knot-tying seminars; if a store in your area conducts such classes, it would behoove you to attend them.

Of course, you can also buy saltwater tippets that have loops and wire. Companies such as Scientific Anglers and Rio make them. All you need to add is the fly. But you really should learn how to make your own. By doing your own rigging, you can make no end of variations to accommodate different outfits, larger or smaller flies, and even the wind. You might, for instance, make a 'cuda tippet with barely six inches of light wire and a fly tied on a size 2 hook for fishing on a windy day, and another with seven inches of slightly heavier wire and a longer fly for casting to very large barracudas. If you have a variety of rigged flies, you can quickly adjust to conditions.

When it's time to remove the hook from a 'cuda or shark, I use long forceps to make the operation as safe as possible. Even so, there are occasions when a shark seems too dangerous to mess with, or when a shark is hooked in a place from which removing the hook would entail jeopardizing my hands. In those cases, I cut or break the tippet. Since my hooks are barbless, the fish get rid of them in short order.

Large Barracudas: The Cheetahs

One of the most exciting gamefish on the flats is still an unsung hero among most anglers: *Sphyraena barracuda*, the

Top: *A size 1/0, small barracuda fly, mainly for fish under 15 pounds.* Middle: *An 11-inch, braided, chartreuse barracuda fly for the big guys.* Bottom: *An orange muddler shark fly on a size 4/0 hook, tied by Capt. Scott Hamilton. The small size 4 Bonefish Special provides size comparision.*

great barracuda. Everyone knows about them, but because 'cudas have a bad reputation among conventional-tackle anglers, they get no respect. And that's too bad. On the flats, a barracuda is even faster than a bonefish. The small individuals do not match a bone's stamina, but barracudas grow much bigger, and a large one, say over 20 pounds, can run much faster than a bonefish and just as far, if not farther. Add a big barracuda's ability to make one of the most spectacular jumps you will ever see, maybe six feet high and well over twenty feet long—while your reel is spinning at a million rpm—and you have a magnificent gamefish.

The extent of barracuda habitat is roughly from Florida to Brazil. Within that range, they can be found at almost any depth from the extremely shallow water of a bonefish flat to the open ocean. I have taken them in a foot of water with a fly rod and a surface slider while trolling for marlin with 50-pound tackle in blue water, right on the bottom in 200 feet of water while deep jigging for groupers and snappers, and with sinking fly lines in 100 feet of water over a wreck. They go anywhere they please while looking for food.

They grow large. Some have been known to reach over 100 pounds and close to 6 feet in length, but these days a fish over 40 is very large, and on the flats one over 20 pounds is a nice fish. The largest I have ever seen on a scale weighed 49 pounds.

Generally, the most likely time to see a big 'cuda on the flats is during the winter months, when the water is cooler. Some of my best memories on the flats were days when it got too cold to bonefish and we had to fish for 'cudas.

My most memorable 'cuda catch, if not the largest, occurred during a trip with a group of fly fishers to Los Roques, Venezuela, in the late 1980s. On the last day of the trip, six of us, riding on a 24-foot panga, arrived at a flat with a very steep drop-off at one end. Everyone got out and started wading right away because schools of bonefish were everywhere. I stayed on the panga eating half a sandwich while standing as high as I could on the tip end of the bow. All the anglers were soon hooked up amid schools of bones racing everywhere as far as I could see. It was enjoyable to watch.

In mid-sandwich, I saw a big, dark fish in the distance following and harassing a very large school of bonefish. It was either a shark or a very large 'cuda. I bet on the 'cuda. I grabbed my 9-weight rod that had an old Seamaster Mark II reel and a then-experimental Bonefish Taper line rigged with a 10-pound tippet, No. 4 wire, and a long, skinny barracuda fly. I don't remember what I did with the sandwich or soda, but I do remember wading for a long time after the fish, which turned out to be a large 'cuda.

I managed to position myself upwind from the fish and made a roughly 70-foot cast. The fly landed a couple of yards away from the 'cuda. He chased it for more than 20 feet and finally took it. He then ran 30 yards or so in no time at all and made a jump that had to be well over 6 feet high and 25 feet long. Never slowing down, he headed for deep water, taking another 50 to 75 yards of line. Fortunately, he had run in the direction of the panga. When he jumped again, he was well over 100 yards away and still running.

Two of my friends and the guide ran to the panga, lifted the anchor, and started to push the boat across the flat toward me. By the time they reached me, the fish had taken almost all of the 200 yards of backing on my reel and was still moving, though he had slowed down a bit.

My friends lifted me by the elbows and sat me on the gunwale while the guide poled to the drop-off and then started the engine. There were only a few turns of line left on the reel; I could see the arbor. We eventually caught up with the fish, which then sounded. He finally got tired, and we boated him. The scale read 34 pounds. While that's a large barracuda on a fly rod, a fish that size should never have run that far, even on a relatively light tippet. I don't know what got into him, but I do know that I will never forget him.

Nor will I forget a much bigger barracuda that I did not catch. I was fishing at the very southern end of Turneffe Island in Belize, wading after a giant school of small bonefish holding in less than a foot of water inside a shallow reef. Practically captive, the school stayed within a few yards of me and my guide, who was carrying my 'cuda outfit, just in case. In such an easy situation, it was not hard to land fish after fish from the school. Even after I'd caught a bunch, they would not go away. Finally, perhaps sick and tired of the big creature that was annoying them, the school moved about 100 feet away from me to the edge of the flat. Immediately, we saw why they refused to leave the shallows.

Pushing a big wake, the school of bonefish ran back toward us, some of the smaller fish half out of the water as they ran for their lives. Many of them swam right past us and even between our legs. Then, out of the deeper,

This 34-pound 'cuda came from a flat in Venezuela. Note the extra-large, braided needlefish fly.

dark green water at the edge of the flat, came a giant barracuda, his black back out of the water as he chased the small bones. He soon got one of the bonefish, only a few feet from me. The 'cuda was swimming so fast when he hit the small bone that a puff of silver scales formed a cloud in the water as he turned around and headed back toward the edge of the flat. The scales dropped like bright confetti to the bottom. I could still see part of the bonefish in the 'cuda's mouth as he swam away.

For the next few minutes, this enormous barracuda repeated his attacks on the bonefish school, taking a fish every few sorties. The guide and I moved to safer ground, lest we find ourselves between the 'cuda and his prey. We stood in less than six inches of water and watched the carnage taking place only a few yards away.

Finally, the attacks ceased. The school of bonefish stayed in the skinny water against the beach, and all was quiet. Then my guide pointed at a dark thing hovering in a yard of water, something that looked like a log. And sure enough, the big 'cuda was lying just under the surface less than 100 feet away. He was looking our way.

The guide looked at me very seriously and handed me the 9-weight 'cuda outfit and took away the bonefish rod. I really had no choice.

Slowly, I waded across the flat and into three feet of water, until I was within fifty feet of the 'cuda. As I started to false-cast the big fly, I noticed that the fish was still looking at me. I did not like that. I continued to false-cast, but the 'cuda started moving closer and closer to me, until he was maybe thirty feet away. I stopped false-casting. We held our positions for what seemed like half an eternity, not moving. Then, slowly, I picked up the rod and cast the fly in front of the fish, then swept the rod to move the big fly a yard from his nose. He did not move. I did it again. He did not move. I stopped casting. And again we stood still.

Then it occurred to me that perhaps he wasn't at all interested in the fly, and that maybe I shouldn't be there with him in the yard-deep water. I started to back up toward the flat and the beach, moving slowly. The 'cuda followed me. That made me nervous. I kept telling myself that the fish was just curious. But he looked mean, really mean.

It seemed to take forever to reach the edge of the flat. The 'cuda did not follow me onto the shallow, sandy flat, but stayed at the edge, still looking, while I kept backing up. Then, ever so slowly, he turned around and disappeared. He actually intimidated me.

It is my honest opinion that this barracuda weighed over 70 pounds and was well over 5 feet in length. He was so fat and dark on the top that, except for the pointed shape of his head, any experienced angler would have mistaken him for a good-sized shark.

I have been back to that area since, but I never saw that fish again. I still think about him.

I often look for large 'cudas in places that have big schools of small bonefish, such as the Bahamas and Belize. In areas like the Florida Keys, you are more likely to see a barracuda swimming alone, hunting anything from bonefish to needlefish.

A large 'cuda doesn't act like most other gamefish on the flats. On the one hand, he is spooky enough that you are going to need a very long cast to get him to take the fly. Thirty-foot casts will not do for barracudas, though they often suffice for bones and tarpon. Yet once he sees you, a 'cuda often does not spook like other fish. He will hang around or leave slowly, showing no fear of you.

Another reason for the long cast is that a large 'cuda often follows the fly for a long time before he takes it. While a seventy-five-foot cast may take the fish at thirty-five feet, a thirty-five-foot cast probably won't get a hit because the 'cuda will see the skiff long before he has made up his mind to take the fly. I like to approach from upwind so that the breeze can help me make the long cast with the big fly and wire bite tippet.

As fishing pressure increases, barracudas become more wary. It is essential that the skiff and its occupants make no noise at all. A 'cuda that has figured out that something strange is going on might not spook, but he won't eat the fly, either.

The classic "strip as fast as you can" retrieve works quite often. Other times, a steady, smooth retrieve is best. I like the fly to travel as close to the surface as possible. If the fly swims deep, the fish seems to be aware of the whole rig. You don't seem to get as many hits—a lot of follows, and an occasional nip at the tail of the fly, but no takes.

Fish a big fly for barracudas. This nice 'cuda took a 7-inch-long fly.

You need a big fly to take big barracudas. Small flies take plenty of fish under 5 pounds, but you'll need a big fly for the larger 'cudas. If the fly imitates a baitfish such as a shad, blue runner, or mullet, I like it to be 5 inches or longer. But if it is one of the many long, skinny needlefish imitations, then I prefer it to be well over 7 inches, and sometimes as long as 10 inches.

For smaller flies, white with a green top and flash on the sides is a good color scheme. Chartreuse is the favorite color for the long, skinny flies that imitate needlefish, followed by fluorescent red or orange. Hooks in sizes 1, 1/0, and 2/0 will hold any 'cuda. Although a size 2/0 hook might seem to make the most sense for a really big barracuda, remember that a large hook is harder to cast far, particularly with wire in front of it. Long poppers and sliders can work well for barracudas, but they are usually hard to cast far.

I prefer 9- and 10-weight outfits for 'cuda fishing. They are heavy enough to carry a big fly and wire a long distance, but not so heavy that they tire me out. A 7- or 8-weight is usually too light to carry the large fly and wire any distance.

After many years of looking for large barracudas on flats all over the world, my best advice is this: be completely rigged and ready. Have a rod rigged with wire and an appropriate fly with a very sharp hook. When you spot a barracuda, all you have to do is put the bonefish or permit rod down, pull the 'cuda outfit out of the rod holder, and start stripping line on deck. This is no time to start fabricating a leader with a wire bite tippet. Before you have the first haywire twist finished, the opportunity will be gone.

I've learned to carry several different flies, each rigged and ready. If the 'cuda doesn't like my first fly, I can quickly switch to another. That often does the trick.

A large shark, finally tired after a twenty-minute fight against a 10 weight. The bright orange fly that fooled him is easily visible on his jaw.

When you bring a big 'cuda to the boat, be very careful handling him, for he can cut you to ribbons. When in doubt, let the guide handle him, particularly if you have little or no experience with these fish.

My advice comes mostly from experiences I have had out of the country. To stay in touch with what's happening in the Keys and Key West, which is a great 'cuda destination, I called my friend Capt. Tom Roland.

"'Cuda fishing is good throughout the winter months, but December, January, and February are best," Tom says. "Barracudas from 12 to 15 pounds are plentiful in Key West, but fish over 20 pounds are trophy fish. Occasionally, we may see a fish over 30 pounds."

Tom and I use the same kinds of tackle for barracudas, but he adds something about flies, saying that he prefers "a big fly in orange or in orange, red, and yellow. I like it better than the chartreuse you like, Chico, because I can see it better in the water, so I am better able to tell my client what to do."

Tom tells me that the great majority of 'cudas caught around Key West are released, and that's great. That's not always the case in other countries. Please insist on releasing a big barracuda, even if your guide wants to keep him. Any given area cannot support very many big 'cudas, and any local population is easy to deplete.

Practice your long casts and learn to rig wire. You won't be sorry.

Sharks: The Quintessential Predators

Few anglers fish for sharks on the flats, and those who do seem to specialize in the stop-chum-wait style of fishing. While that type of fishing for sharks can be fun and productive, there's a lot to be said for simply poling a skiff and casting to a shark that is hunting on the flats. For starters, the strike of a 50- or 100-pound shark taking a popper is almost scary. When you add the fact that some species often make several jumps, you have quite a gamefish. I highly recommend them.

Sharks are a very old group of fishes that have learned, probably better than most others, how to survive in a great variety of conditions. One of their distinguishing characteristics is a skeleton made of cartilage rather than bone, which makes a shark very flexible both in the water and out. When you see a shark coming straight toward you across a flat, you'll notice its body waving in the water, like a snake's. A barracuda or bonefish will look perfectly straight. Later, if you manage to boat a shark and foolishly hold him out of the water, the fish can easily twist around and bite you.

A great variety of sharks ranging from only a few pounds to several hundred frequent the bonefish flats. Smaller sharks eat many of the same creatures consumed by bonefish. Larger sharks feed on 'cudas, a variety of baitfish, and, of course, bonefish.

A few species stand out as regulars on the flats. One of the most common is the lemon shark, *Negaprion brevirostris*, a species distinguished by its yellowish brown coloration and two dorsal fins of almost equal size. Individuals over 10 feet long are not uncommon. With a range from North Carolina to Brazil, lemon sharks can turn up on almost any bonefish flat in the Atlantic. I have seen them throughout most of the year, but they seem more numerous in spring and summer. On occasion, a lemon shark can be dangerous to a wading angler. A 50-pound lemon will give you a good fight on an 8- or 9-weight outfit, though you will probably win. They are great fun.

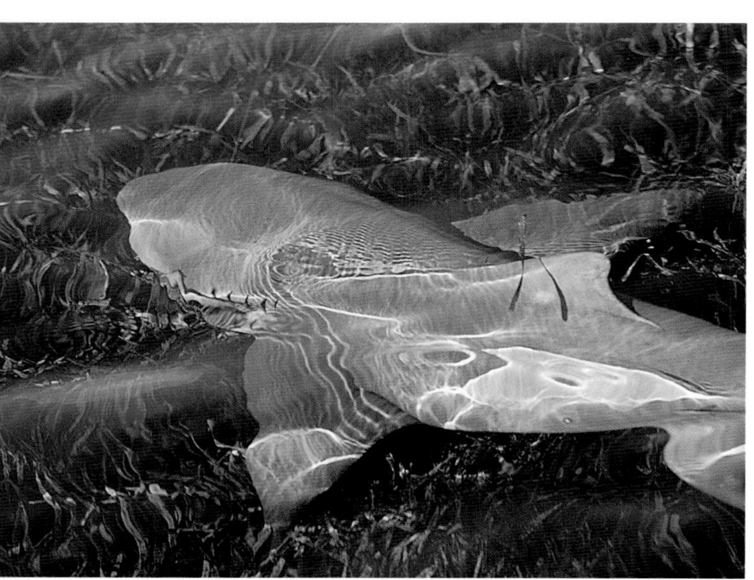

This big lemon shark took an orange fly.

Another common species is the blacktip shark, *Carcharhinus limbatus*, which derives its common name from the black tips at the end of the fins, particularly the pectoral fins. The blacktip looks much like its larger relative, the spinner shark, but has larger eyes. Blacktips can grow to over 5 feet, but most of those on the flats are closer to 3 feet in length. They are stocky and strong.

The blacktip moves faster than the lemon shark and makes great jumps, often while spinning in the air. A hooked blacktip can ruin a leader in a few seconds and fray any part of it. This is another great gamefish.

The blacktip's larger brother, the spinner shark (*Carcharhinus maculipinnis*), can easily grow to 8 feet. This species also sports black tips on its fins, but has smaller eyes than the blacktip. A spinner shark's coloration is similar to a blacktip's—dark gray with white bellow—but without the yellow or bluish cast that many blacktips display. I find these species hard to tell apart while fishing, though I will cast to either if the fish is the right size. South Florida is probably one of the best places to fly fish for them.

Once hooked, a spinner shark fights like an industrial-size blacktip. Many guides will tell you that pound for pound, a spinner will fight as strongly as a tarpon. A 100-pound spinner can be almost impossible to land with a regular leader and 12-pound tippet. This fish's spectacular spinning jumps, which quickly fray the leader against the shark's sandpaper skin, are followed by long, powerful runs. You won't win many fights with these fish, but you'll have fun losing.

I hooked my most recent big spinner against a sandy beach, using a 12-weight rod and 20-pound tippet. Three big jumps and one minute later, the shark had won. I got back a third of my 9-foot leader; the shark's skin had worn through the heavy butt section. Even some of my fly line was severely frayed. But I'm ready to hook another one.

Other species of large sharks can also be found on the flats if you or your guide knows where and when to look. Two that come to mind are the bull shark, *Carcharhinus leucas*, and the tiger shark, *Galeocerdo cuvieri*. The bull, a cousin of the great white shark with more human attacks to its credit, is a formidable adversary on a fly rod, though a few have been landed by fly fishers.

Tigers have also been taken with fly-fishing tackle, but they don't often appear on bonefish flats. If you see one smaller than 200 pounds or so, you'll have no trouble making out the characteristic bars on the body. A tiger is an uncommonly beautiful shark.

A few years ago, while fishing for bonefish out of Peace and Plenty in the Bahamas, I saw one cruising a sandy flat. He was probably 6 feet long, and the tiger bars on his sides were very pronounced. I took my barracuda outfit and started stripping line on deck while the guide poled hard after the fish. But we couldn't keep up with him, and after a few minutes the shark disappeared. What a fish! I would have loved to hook him.

The bonnethead shark, *Sphyrna tiburo*, belongs to the hammerhead family. Bonnetheads can attain almost 6 feet, but usually average 24 to 42 inches on tropical flats. I usually don't mess with these guys, but they are fun to see on a bonefish flat, and their presence indicates that the flat is in an active cycle. When you see bonnetheads, you're likely to see bonefish, too.

When I cast to a shark, I try to keep the fly just ahead of him and on one side so he can see it. If he decides to take it, he will accelerate and strike. Sharks are usually slower to hit flies in very clear water than in water that's been clouded a little by wind or current. Work the fly slower for lemons and a bit faster for the super-hyper blacktips and spinners.

For fishing in clear water, Capt. Dale Perez likes a white baitfish imitation with a darker top. In slightly off-color water, he prefers an orange fly.

Capt. Rick Ruoff has spent a lot of time fishing for sharks and has learned how they react to flies. "A shark likes a fly that stays suspended," Rick says, "one that does not sink head first. Even one that comes up instead of down as it's retrieved. A shark does not mind coming up for something, like a tarpon will, but going down is hard and unnatural for him. Also, don't let the shark bump the fly with his nose. If he does, he will know it is not real and now he will be really hard to talk into a strike."

Rick likes a fly with extra motion. He favors marabou and rabbit strips to get that type of action.

Don't hit a shark too quickly. "It's best to feel them before you strike them," says Capt. Tom Rowland. He's right, but most anglers, excited by the bite (I don't blame them), strike back too quickly and miss the fish.

When trying to remove the hook from a shark, be very careful about holding him too far behind the head. Remember, a shark's cartilage skeleton gives the fish exceptional flexibility. If you hold him too far behind the head, he can easily bend around and bite you. Even when you grab a shark right behind the head, he is still incredibly strong. A small, 20-pound shark will out-muscle you as you try to hold him still. This is one reason for always using barbless hooks when shark fishing. Getting a barbless hook out is hard enough; trying to remove a hook with a high barb increases your risk of finishing the day with a shark bite.

OTHER, SMALLER SPECIES: THE REST OF THE PARTY

As you can imagine, an environment as rich in food as the bonefish flats attracts many fishes besides the glamorous species. A great variety of smaller fishes feed on the same flats. Some of these will become much larger and eventually leave the flats. Although most of these smaller fishes grow to only a couple of pounds (or less), they are part of this unique environment. And I feel that knowing about them, hooking some on a light bonefish outfit, and seeing how they fit in the whole ecosystem can only add to your understanding and appreciation of the bonefish's world.

A small, bonefish-size crab fly fooled this yellow jack.

Besides, it's simply fun to know about many of the little guys. Even if you don't cast to them, and I often don't, you do see and recognize them as you glide by hunting for bigger game. There's more to bonefishing than catching a bonefish. Enjoying the unique world of the flats is a big part of the experience, at least for me.

Many types of jacks inhabit bonefish flats. In the Atlantic, the bar jack (*Caranx rubber*) and the yellow jack (*Caranx bartholomaei*), two of the largest, both grow to well over 12 pounds. I took yellow jacks up to 16 pounds in the lower Keys during the 1960s. In recent years, the biggest bar jacks and yellow jacks that I have seen were more like 6 pounds.

On the flats, these jacks will follow feeding stingrays, mix with schools of mudding bonefish, or simply cruise in schools or small pods. Both species fight hard, like any jack does. One over 2 pounds will run into your backing, and a 5-pounder can keep you busy for a while. A bar jack will frequently jump during the fight.

A variety of snappers live on the flats, frequenting potholes, small structures, and drop-offs. The gray or mangrove snapper (*Lutjanus griseus*), schoolmaster snapper (*Lutjanus apodus*), and small mutton snappers (*Lutjanus analis*), among many other species, often take bonefish or permit flies.

Larger potholes and drop-offs harbor many species of groupers, including some pretty good-sized ones, that readily take flies. I've taken many groupers up to about 5 pounds on fly tackle. Larger groupers have eaten my flies, but they all headed to the bottom and cut me off on a piece of coral or some other structure. My favorite is the Nassau grouper, *Epinephelus striatus*.

Nassau groupers tend to like shrimp-colored flies. This one took a Snapping Shrimp.

Other species will tail in very shallow water with small bonefish, often confusing an angler who thinks that he is casting to a tailing bonefish. Two of the species most often seen on the bonefish flats are the yellowfin mojarra (*Gerres cinereus*) and the scrawled cowfish (*Lactophrys quadricornis*). The yellowfin mojarra has a mouth that extends downward for feeding on the bottom. I have taken many, mostly by mistake, while casting to smaller bones tailing in very shallow water. Sometimes it's hard to know whether you're casting to bonefish or yellowfins. They prefer size 6 and smaller flies. Yellowfins can grow to well over a pound, but the average is smaller.

The scrawled cowfish is a member of the boxfish family, a name that derives from the hard, rigid, boxlike shells that cover the bodies of these fish. A cowfish can move only its fins, eyes, and mouth. This species can reach 18 inches long. They are surprisingly strong fish, and a good-sized adult can run well into your backing.

Chapter 19

Traveling for Bonefish

Getting to remote areas and fishing camps has always been a bit more of a challenge than normal travel. And now, after September 11, this is more true than ever, partly because fishermen go to out-of-the-way destinations, but also because our equipment and extra clothing are more likely to prompt security searches. Furthermore, there is still no consistency in rules from airline to airline, from country to country, and even from day to day.

As of autumn 2003, I can sometimes carry my fly rods (travel models, of course) onto a plane, but other times I have to check them. We do have to check our fly reels, fly boxes, pliers, and pretty much everything else needed for fishing the flats. That's the way it is and probably the way it will be for a long time. I do wish that things were better organized and travel rules were more consistent, but otherwise I have no complaints. Actually, we are lucky. Travel could be much more difficult.

Before you even think of going to any destination, make a bonefish-trip list or tropical-fishing list and keep it in your computer. I have lists for bluewater fly fishing, Alaska trips, canoe fly-fishing trips, and so forth. I consider these lists not merely helpful, but absolutely necessary. Forget your sunglasses on a week-long trip to the tropics, and you're toast. Or forget your favorite file on a week's trip to the Yucatan, and you are going to spend the week unconsciously trying to set the hook harder to compensate for a dull point. It won't work, incidentally. I bring spare glasses, spare files, and lots of other spares. I have never regretted it.

After you book the trip, do as much homework on the area as you can. A good camp gives you plenty of information about what to bring and what's there. You can often learn more from a good fly shop, the Internet, or magazine articles. The more you know, the more likely you are to bring what you need and to leave what you don't need. I've seen anglers come to a camp loaded down with gear, only to discover halfway through the week that they were missing a few important items or their equipment was a bit light or heavy for the area.

All reels should be rigged to the tippet before you pack them. Don't wait until you get to camp to rig. You

STEPHEN FERNÁNDEZ

A lush and healthy turtle-grass flat in the Yucatan has plenty of bonefish food on every tide.

might arrive in time to fish for a few hours that same afternoon, but only if you've already rigged all your tackle.

If you bought new equipment for the salt and it's heavier than the gear to which you are accustomed, practice with it for at least a few weeks before your trip. If one of your new outfits has a problem, you want to have time to go back to the fly shop. You also need all the practice time you can get, particularly if you're a newcomer to the salt.

Packing for a fishing trip might not seem like something that requires a lot of thought. But it does. For many years, I have traveled to many parts of the world not only to fish, but also to act as host and instructor for groups of anglers. I also travel frequently to teach fly-fishing classes and schools. Thanks to my hundreds of trips with tackle, I've had lots of practice at this. Perhaps I can save you some trouble and exertion.

THE CARRY-ON BAG

Before the September 11 attacks changed air travel, I always tried to carry my rods, reels, pliers, fly boxes, forceps, and other essential gear onto the plane so that I could go fishing even if my checked luggage did not arrive with me. Now, of course, I do things differently.

Most airlines allow at least one carry-on bag and one smaller personal bag such as a purse or laptop-computer case. My main carry-on item is my tackle bag (which, for air travel, contains no tackle), and my small bag is usually a waterproof camera case. Sometimes I'm allowed to carry my fly rods, too. All my luggage, carry-on or not, has luggage tags.

My carry-on bag always contains certain items:

My toiletry kit, which also holds any medications I might need. If my checked bags disappear for a day or two, I can still groom, to look good, and have my medicines, to feel good.

My fishing hat, sunglasses, and reading glasses. Spares of all three are in the checked luggage.

A fishing shirt or a long-sleeved T-shirt. It's always good to have an extra shirt in the tropics.

Two books. Sooner or later, you are going to get stuck in an airport for many hours or in your cabin

The Chico Fernández Adventure Travel Word Processor, a bandana, and the IGFA Yearbook accompany me on every trip.

because a storm keeps you off the water. I usually bring at least two books on a trip—one light read, such as a thriller or mystery novel, and something more serious or technical.

Besides those items, you should bring something with which you can take notes. A laptop computer will work, but it's too heavy and businesslike for a bonefish trip. I carry the Chico Fernández Adventure Travel Word Processor. It always works (in any language, no less), it's easy to use, it costs very little, it cannot accidentally lose or delete anything, it's waterproof, and it even floats. It might be the ultimate writing tool for travelers. I'd recommend it even if I hadn't invented it.

Here's how to build one. Start with a 5-by-7 note pad—small enough to carry easily, but big enough for writing a movie script if you are so inspired. Add two pencils, one sharpened at both ends and another with an eraser for the rare occasions on which you make a mistake. If you like, add a ballpoint pen or even a crayon. I used to carry a small knife to sharpen the pencils, but the airlines won't allow that anymore.

Put all the parts in a heavy-duty Ziploc freezer bag and seal it. If a pencil point breaks, you have spares. The plastic bag is waterproof, so you can take it in the skiff. Sealed, it will float. It's flat and easy to carry. Nothing to program or download. PC and Mac compatible. And it is guaranteed not to crash.

Once you complete your Adventure Travel Word Processor and it is running well for you, please send a dollar to defray the expense of my endless R&D program. Messrs. Jobs and Gates, look out.

All kidding aside, I find keeping notes on a trip to be both enjoyable and helpful. Interesting or strange events, items that you wish you'd brought, gear that you brought but didn't need, the phone numbers and e-mail addresses of new friends, new flies that you learned about—every trip has many things worth recording. I take some notes while fishing and spend a few minutes every night to complete the day's news. If I look at my notes as I'm flying home at the end of the week, at least a third of them refer to things I'd already started to forget. Don't entrust a bonefish trip entirely to your memory.

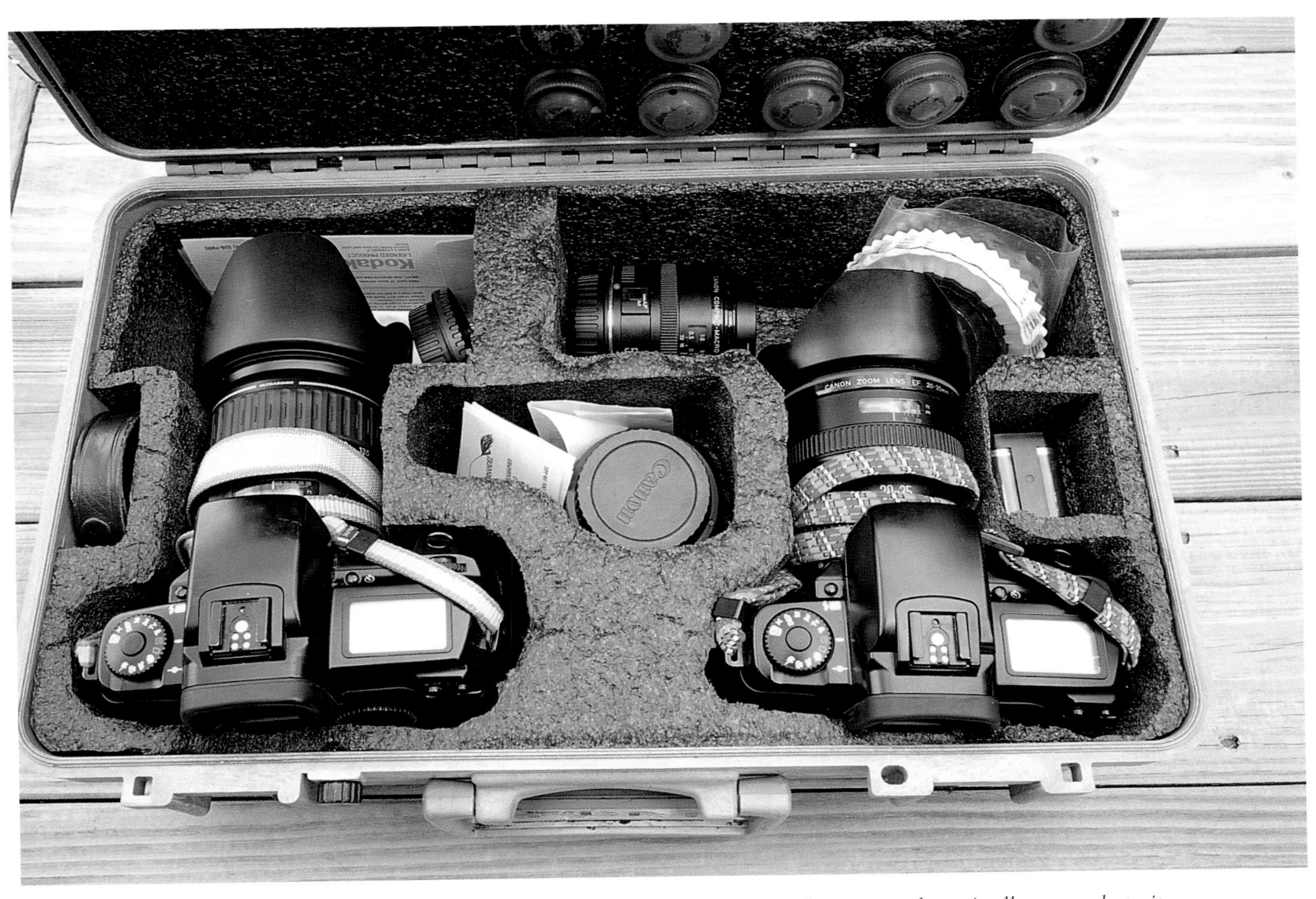

One of my traveling camera cases with two bodies, two zooms, a fish-eye lens, and a macro, plus miscellaneous photo items.

If my checked luggage doesn't arrive with me, my carry-on bag has enough to keep me reasonably comfortable and amused for a while. With my toiletry kit, medicines, hat, glasses, spare shirt, books, and note pad, I can survive until my bags show up.

CAMERA BAG

Not only do I love photography, both black and white and color, for its own sake, but I also need to shoot photos for my magazine articles and slide shows. I take several cameras and many rolls of film on every trip. Soon, I guess, I'll go digital and no longer carry film.

Even if you are not crazy about photography, I still urge you to bring a camera, even a point-and-shoot or an inexpensive digital. A camera records not only the fish you caught, but also the place, friends you met or shared a boat with, a special fishing guide, a beautiful sunset, a dilapidated shack at the edge of the water, and all sorts of other memories. It helps you bring the entire experience home. A few years later, some of the photos will be priceless to you.

If you use a camera with interchangeable lenses, a wide-angle 24- or 28-mm lens, a macro lens, and a telephoto of about 100 mm are all you need. With a digital camera that has different focal-length factors, choose the appropriate equivalent focal length. A lens with too long a focal length can make hand-held photography very difficult, especially in a skiff.

Many of the best opportunities to shoot great photos occur early or late in the day, during storms, on overcast or rainy days, or while banking in a small airplane as you approach camp. At noon on a clear, calm day, the tropical sun creates harsh shadows and no end of exposure problems; eating lunch is a more profitable midday activity than taking pictures.

Still, you should be prepared to use your camera at any time. No guts, no glory. But you also want to protect your camera from rain and salt spray. A hard, foam-lined case with an O-ring seal will safeguard a camera and lenses while you travel and protect it from rain and spray in the field.

Bring enough film. Even a moderately enthusiastic photographer can go through four to six rolls in a week. If you enjoy photography, you'll probably average more than a roll a day.

For traveling, I remove all my film from the boxes and carry the rolls in a heavy-duty Ziploc bag. At the airport, the security agent can inspect it and see that it is just film. If security personnel refuse to hand-check my film, they'll put it through the X-ray machine for carry-on bags, which shouldn't harm film with an ASA speed of 200 or less. Checked luggage can be subjected to a much more powerful X-ray machine that can damage some films. So far, I haven't lost any photos to X-rays, partly because I shoot only 50- or 100-speed film.

FLY-ROD CASE

I try to hand-carry my fly rods, but since I sometimes can't, I pack them so that they can travel either with me or in the baggage compartment. If I'm bringing four rods on a trip, I remove them from their aluminum tubes (but

A flat-calm day on a Bahamian bonefish flat (this one is near the North Riding Point Club) offers good photo opportunities if you can tear yourself away from the fly rod.

Finally, after much practice and preparation, the hookup, the main reason we travel to the bonefish destination, occurs. Life is good.

MARKUS HAUGG

leave them in their cloth bags) and bundle them together with two handles at one end of the bundle and two at the other. A few rubber bands keep the bundle together. Then all four rods go into a cloth-covered PVC fly-rod case, of which there are many on the market. Naturally, the case gets a luggage tag.

Packed this way, travel rods will fit in an overhead compartment. If someone at the airport decides that the case is too long or that it simply looks dangerous, then I check the case. Either way, my rods are protected.

A TOY

Bring a toy to camp. By "toy," I mean an outfit that is much lighter than the target species (bonefish, in this case) requires. Why? The weather or some other circumstance might make bonefish unavailable during part of your trip. When that happens, you can have a lot of fun catching saltwater panfish with an ultralight outfit. Or, if the fishing is very good and you've landed more small bonefish than you expected by midweek, you can try them on lighter tackle. Small bonefish are great fun on a 5- or 6-weight outfit, as long as you can cast well enough to use such an outfit on the flats. Practice, practice, practice.

SINKING LINES ON THE FLATS?

Regardless of the destination, I always carry some sinking lines. I am always prepared to fish deep. Why would I do that on a bonefish trip? Because even the best destinations don't always have great bonefishing. With a few sinking lines, I can salvage the slow days by fishing for other species. In many places, other species are much more than just a backup plan. The Bahamas, Belize, the Yucatan, and other destinations have many deep channels between flats and lots of patch reefs just outside flats that face the open ocean. These deeper spots hold snappers, groupers, jacks, mackerel, and others, all waiting for a fly. They can be lots of fun.

Sight-casting to bonefish is very exciting, but so is hooking a big fish while blind-casting in deeper water. Something wallops the fly and then peels line off your reel at great speed, and you don't know what it is. For me, that has always been one of the great thrills of saltwater fishing, and it is available just a short boat ride from many bonefish flats.

TACKLE BAG

When I reach my destination, I take all the gear that traveled in my checked luggage and put it in my tackle bag. I have put more thought into what to carry and what not to carry in my soft tackle bag (the one that goes in the skiff with me) than probably any other piece of luggage. I can't help it; as I get older I want to carry less but still have everything I need.

Avoid the temptation to throw everything and anything in your tackle bag, figuring that if you throw in enough stuff, you'll be fine. Unless you make a plan, you will forget something important. Good packing requires hard thinking, but it pays off in smaller, lighter loads.

Besides, a huge, overstuffed tackle bag won't fit in a typical bonefish skiff.

My tackle bag contains bonefish- and permit-fly boxes; a miscellaneous-fly box with large flies for barracudas, big jacks, and sharks, and weighted flies for snappers and groupers; a rigging kit for making leaders or repairing fly lines; hook files; 6- and 10-inch forceps; two clippers; line dressing; light and dark polarizing glasses; close-up glasses; glasses cleaner; rain gear; my hat; sunscreen and lip balm; Chico's Adventure Travel Word Processor; a bandana; a measuring tape; extra reels with different or sinking lines; spare leaders and tippet material; binoculars; and a few other miscellaneous items.

No matter how careful I am about the tackle that I allow into my bag, things multiply inside it. After a few months, my bag starts to gain weight and finding things becomes more and more difficult. So I put it on a diet. Every six months or so, I take *everything* out of the bag and put back only what I feel is necessary. I always find some surprises.

Don't let your tackle bag get too heavy. If you do, you will carry things that you don't need all over the world.

WADING BAG

About halfway through a hosted bonefishing trip, it was my turn to fish with an angler who turned out to be a very good caster. We took turns catching bones all morning. After lunch, the guide found an area with a few small schools of tailing, very active bones. We were deciding which school to tackle next when the guide spotted a huge school directly behind us. It must have had a thousand bonefish, he said. And it looked it.

For a minute or two we stood there trying to decide what to do and joking about what a great problem we had. Finally, trying to get the most out of the situation, the guide suggested that he and my client go for the big school, since they were both more excited than I was about its size. I could get off the boat and work the many small schools in front of us. They looked at me like two kids waiting to go to the candy store. "Sure," I said.

Knowing that they were eager to head for the big school, I grabbed my fly rod and jumped off the skiff. The guide poled a hundred yards or so to the nearest channel, fired up the engine and ran for a few minutes, and then stopped and resumed poling. Soon, the skiff and its occupants were barely visible. But my attention was on the many pods of bones feeding on the incoming tide. I felt that I could easily take several before the tide got too high.

The first pod, a mix of tailing and mudding fish, was feeding eagerly. I cast a lightly dressed, size 4 Bonefish Special, one of my favorite flies for sandy areas, but the fly landed a bit off target and the bones paid no attention to it. I started to pick up the line for another cast. Just as the fly was about to become airborne, a small barracuda, about a foot long, took it and instantly cut the tippet.

A fraction of a second later, I became painfully aware that I had left my wading bag, with more than fifty flies, safe in the skiff, which was, by my estimation, two hours' walking distance from me. I was frustrated. I was mad at myself. And I suffered greatly as I watched the many pods of bonefish feeding all around me. But my suffering had barely started.

Since there was nothing to do but walk back to the skiff, I reeled in my naked leader and started walking. For the next hour or so, I encountered countless bonefish. Schools, pairs, singles. They were doing it on purpose. I'm convinced of that. Every now and then, I would drop to my knees and let some fish come as close as possible. One school must have come within fifteen feet before mildly spooking, and then continued to feed. They knew I had no fly.

By the time I got to the skiff, well over an hour later, I had cleared several flats of bonefish. My client, on the other hand, had taken several bones out of that big school and found other, smaller schools of willing bonefish. He was very happy.

I had several gin and tonics that evening, and have not forgotten my wading bag ever since. I have learned that several of my friends have had similar experiences.

The wading bag: don't leave the skiff without it.

Some anglers seem to have a casual approach to wading. They'll drop a couple of flies in their pockets (a good way to get hooked) or stick them on the brims of their hats. If they feel ambitious, maybe they'll grab a small fly box and a few yards of tippet—better, but not ideal. They'll be sorry.

Anytime you intend to wade away from your big tackle bag, you need a wading bag, or belt pack. You need to be self sufficient.

Since this is a bonefish bag that will be used in hot weather, do not get a black or very dark one. Both of mine are sand colored or tan.

Obviously, a belt pack cannot hold everything that fits in your regular tackle bag. You want to carry only what you might need while wading, and not one item more. Here's what I carry. First, I find a fly box that fits vertically inside the wading bag; this leaves room for other items. The box contains some bonefish and permit flies and a couple of big streamers or poppers in case I run across a big jack or another large fish. Naturally, I'll need a hook file, forceps (or pliers), and clippers. I carry a couple of knotless leaders, some tippet material, and a

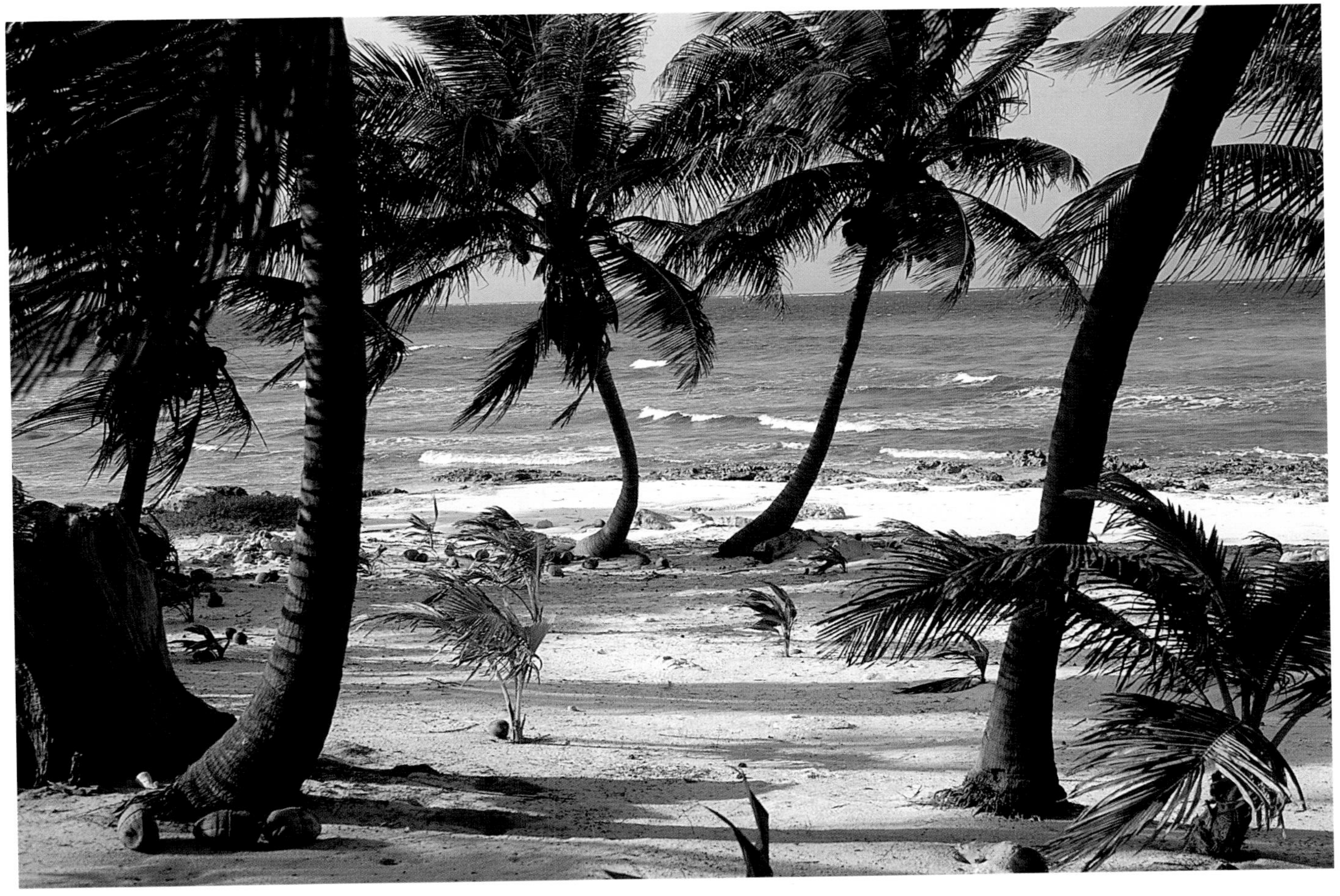

Casa Blanca in Ascension Bay on the Yucatan Peninsula. My room had a great view.

loop-to-loop tippet rigged with wire or a heavy monofilament shock tippet and a 'cuda or jack fly.

Rather than wade with one of my full-size, expensive cameras, I carry a quality point-and-shoot camera stored in a heavy Ziploc bag, and an extra roll of film. This might seem like unnecessary weight, but you never know what you will catch or see while wading. It would be a shame not to have a photo of a big bonefish that you caught when you and your guide spent half a morning away from the skiff.

Some of my friends and clients carry water when they leave the skiff. It makes sense to do so in the tropics, and many wading bags have holders for water bottles. I usually don't carry water unless I anticipate wading for a long time.

I also carry a measuring tape. If you'd rather guesstimate the lengths and weights of your fish, I understand.

The last item I carry, and one that you probably will not want, is a small note pad and pencil. Even while wading, I take notes. Besides, one looks very professional standing on a bonefish flat next to a remote key, taking notes with the fly rod tucked under one arm. You should try it.

Rigging a Wading Bag

Don't just throw everything in your wading bag. When you need something, you won't have a table on which to empty the bag so that you can find what you want. Spend a minute organizing and rigging your belt pack.

Attach a cord or retractor to the bag and place your clippers, forceps or pliers, and hook file on it. Pieces of old fly line work fine. If you drop any of these items, even in a foot of gin-clear water on a bonefish flat, it can be next to impossible to find. When you bring a fish to hand, you won't have to open the bag and fumble around inside it for your forceps. After removing the hook, you won't have to think about putting the forceps back; just drop them and let them swing on the cord.

Finally, dedicate a place in the bag to a rigged, loop-to-loop tippet with a popper or barracuda fly. When you need that fly, you'll need it in a hurry. If you can't grab, attach, and cast that fly in a hurry, don't bother bringing it.

Fishing with a Wading Bag

The type of bag that has proved most practical on the flats is the belt or fanny pack. I wear mine on the right side, low and slightly to the rear. It's out of the way while I am fishing, but easy to pull around when I need something. I cannot cast or fish comfortably with a bag designed to hang in front of my chest. But that's just me. A belt pack is so comfortable that sometimes I forget it's there until I sit down to eat a sandwich.

Once a year, whether you think you need to or not, empty the bag and see how many things have accumulated that you no longer need, and how many things you rediscover that you had forgotten about. Then vacuum or clean the bag and put the tackle back.

If you take your wading bag off while in the field, don't leave it on a background that's the same color. For instance, don't lay a sand-colored bag on a beach and then walk away. I did that once and practically had to organize a search party to find my wading bag.

THE BIG BAG

I'm done carrying big bags across parking lots and through airports. If I'm going to check it, it's got wheels. Rolling beats carrying.

Quite a few fishing bags these days have hard-plastic bottom compartments for storing multipiece fly rods. When I know that I am going to check my rods, this kind of luggage is great. Everything travels in one bag that rolls easily no matter how big or heavy it is. I don't use duffels anymore.

Good fishing luggage is a good investment. It protects your gear, lets you organize things, and makes traveling less strenuous and stressful. Leave the long duffel bags with shoulder straps to the young guys with big muscles.

AFTER ARRIVING

When I get to camp, I try to find out who will guide me the next day. Then I find out the guide's favorite drink; the cook always knows this. I go down to the dock with two drinks, the guide's favorite and mine. We chat for a while, and I find out how the fishing has been, whether the guide and his clients have been catching fish other than the target species, what he expects the next day, and much more. With this information, I can arrive at the dock rigged and ready the next morning. Over the years, these drinks and conversations have led to some of the best fish I've caught.

Finally, be sure to pack your tight loops and accuracy before leaving home. You don't buy those, of course—you earn them through practice. Lots of practice. But believe me: you will forget about all the hours casting on the lawn under a hot sun when you make a good presentation to a bonefish, watch him pounce on your fly, and then hear your reel make great music as he makes one of those runs that only a bonefish can make.

Chapter 20

Giving Back

A gamefish is too valuable to be caught only once. —*Lee Wulff*

Not too long ago, releasing bonefish was enough. Or at least we thought it was enough. But today, at the beginning of the twenty-first century, we fly fishers need to do more than merely let bonefish go after we have enjoyed them. We have to give back, in money and time, if we are to leave a better environment for our children and grandchildren, and if there is to be a future for our sport.

Sure, we can go to many great fishing camps and see relatively good fishing and good-looking environments. For now, that is. In too many places, however, there is trouble in the bonefish's world. Bad guys are netting and poaching. Bonefish are being consumed in many parts of the Caribbean and Central America, to name just a couple of areas. They often show up in fish markets (along with tarpon, incidentally). Large numbers of bonefish are taken as bycatches by bait fisherman, who often keep them. We must even consider the increasing pressure from anglers like you and me who want to participate in this wonderful sport.

Please join and support one or more conservation organizations to help preserve the world of the bonefish and the fly-fishing environment in general. The minimum annual dues of most organizations are generally less than the price of a fly line. If you want to give a larger amount, remember that it is tax deductible.

At the local, state, national, and international levels, conservation groups do the work that will preserve bonefish angling and all other facets of our sport for future generations. This is important—no, *essential*—work, and I am proud to belong to a number of organizations. Among them are Bonefish & Tarpon Unlimited (BTU), of which I am a lifetime member and chairman of the Bonefish Research Committee; the International Game Fish Association (IGFA), to which I have belonged for many years; the Federation of Fly Fishers (FFF), of which I am a lifetime member; the Snook Foundation, for which I serve as a member of the advisory council; and the Coastal Conservation Association. These and other organizations exist to save what you and I love so much, so that our children and grandchildren can enjoy a fly fisher's world.

Instead of describing various organizations or merely listing their addresses, I thought it would be better to let each group speak directly to you. What follows, then, are messages from several leading conservation and education groups, unfiltered by me. Please support them. The fish deserve it—and so does the next generation of fly fishers.

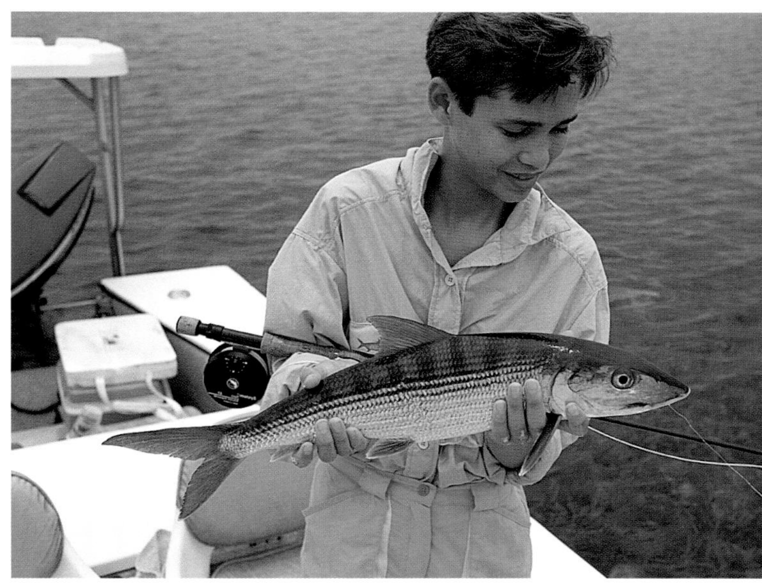

Stephen Fernández with one of his first bonefish on a fly. I want my future grandson or granddaughter to experience the bonefish flats as I have.

BONEFISH & TARPON UNLIMITED

I was very pleased to receive Chico Fernández's request to write a word or two about Bonefish & Tarpon Unlimited for two reasons. First, I am always pleased to beat the drum about BTU and explain our mission and purpose. Second, it is a special pleasure to contribute to Chico's book because Chico was one of the original founders and directors of BTU and has been intently involved in our bonefish research efforts. He currently is the chairman of the Bonefish Research Program.

Bonefish & Tarpon Unlimited (BTU) was formed by several like-minded, active, and long-standing saltwater flats fishermen who shared a concern about the future of bonefish, tarpon, and permit fisheries worldwide.

BTU's mission is to preserve, nurture, and enhance the bonefish, tarpon, and permit fisheries through research, education, and regulation to provide information and opportunities to our members to make their fishing experience more rewarding.

Flats fishing is a large, rapidly growing sport worldwide. Twenty-five years ago, there were only a handful of skiffs with poling platforms to be seen poling their way around the Florida Keys flats and those of the Bahamas. Today, they dot the horizon in every direction in most shallow saltwater areas of the world. Despite this popularity, very little is known about the life cycles and behavior of these three species.

Such basic knowledge as where they spawn, where the juveniles grow up, how often the same fish is caught, the effects of fishing pressure, and what factors limit the population size were all unknown when BTU was formed. BTU has been a proactive instigator and supporter of research to capture this knowledge with the end objective at least to sustain our sport and, we hope, enhance it.

With the significant increase in shallow-water fishing pressure and other environmental changes that are impacting the fishery, it is highly probable that the quality of our sport will decline rapidly. There are many areas of the world where these fish are killed regularly as part of the daily food supply.

These concerns are evidenced by such examples as the Port Aransas, Texas, experience. Port Aransas was the self-proclaimed Tarpon Fishing Capital of the World as recently as 1960, but today a tarpon sighting there is a rare event.

At present, we support research by the University of Miami, Mote Marine Institute, Pfleuger Institute of Environmental Research, and other individual researchers. Geographically, there are research programs under way in the Florida Keys, the Bahamas, and selected Gulf of Mexico coastal areas.

We need your help in this pursuit. Research costs money, and meaningful research requires a long-term financial commitment. We can do this only through sustained member dues and special multi-year research pledges.

If you are not a BTU member, we would welcome you. You can join through our web site (www.tarbone.org), by fax (305-367-3546), or by e-mail (tarbone@bellsouth.net). If you are already a member, we encourage you to consider becoming a member of the Tarbone 40 club by making a four-year research pledge.

As a member, you will receive your initial membership package of a newsletter, decal, and special awards based on your level of support. You will also receive regular updates on current research findings.

BTU's founding and sustaining members include the famous names of saltwater fishing and serious flats fishermen worldwide. If you are not already a member, we look forward to welcoming you soon.

Tom Davidson
Chairman, Bonefish & Tarpon Unlimited

BONEFISH AND IGFA: MUCH MORE THAN RECORDS

In addition to being a lifelong angler, Chico has also been a member and supporter of the International Game Fish Association for over twenty years. We could not be more pleased that he has given us this opportunity to talk about IGFA and what it represents to anglers worldwide.

You probably know that the IGFA houses fly-fishing records for bonefish and other popular recreational species of fish. In fact, IGFA has been administering world records for fly fishing since 1979. However, IGFA is much more than just a repository for world records.

Since its inception in 1939, IGFA has been an organization dedicated to the conservation of fish species and their environment. IGFA staff represents recreational angling interests on numerous national and international fisheries-management panels. We encourage research projects for recreational species and also serve as a mechanism to disseminate this information to the fishing community. A great example of this was IGFA's involvement as the host and co-convener for the first International Tarpon and Bonefish Symposium.

The IGFA Fishing Hall of Fame and Museum located in Dania Beach, Florida, is the epicenter of all that is fishing. This state-of-the-art, 60,000-square-foot facility houses the most complete fishing and interactive educational exhibits in the world. The E. K. Harry Library of Fishes, located on the second floor of the museum, is recognized as having the most extensive and comprehensive recreational fishing collection in the world. The library's unique database can help you locate periodicals, books, and even videos and DVDs relating to fly fishing for bonefish, or whatever you choose, instantly. By the way, we have more books written on fly fishing than any other type of fishing.

By becoming a member of IGFA, you help support an organization dedicated to fisheries conservation and the preservation of recreational angling's rich history. And yes, we're also the people to talk to when you catch the next world-record bonefish on a fly. For more information, give us a call at 954-927-2628 or visit us on the web at www.igfa.org.

Good tides.

Jason Schratwieser
Fishing and Science Director
International Game Fish Association

FEDERATION OF FLY FISHERS

Chico Fernández ranks in the very top echelon of saltwater fly-fishing experts. Fly fishing in salt water is the ultimate challenge. Tarpon, marlin, snook, tuna—big fish, heavy flies, rugged tackle, muscle-fatiguing fights. Bonefish, barracudas—spot and stalk, stealthy approaches, delicate casts, gin-clear water, torpedo-like runs. Saltwater fly fishing presents the angler with a tremendous variety of fish and fishing situations requiring encyclopedic knowledge. No saltwater fly fisher is better equipped to perform successfully than Chico, and no one is better able to teach novice and experienced saltwater fly fishers how to improve their skills and thereby get maximum pleasure from this sport.

The Federation of Fly Fishers was founded nearly four decades ago to advance the sport of fly fishing. We promote fly fishing for two reasons. It is a challenging, effective, and fun way to catch all species of fish, from trout to bass, from bonefish to zander. Our motto is "All fish, all waters." FFF's educational programs and our dedicated members have taught hundreds of thousands of people how to fly fish. Second, we believe that fly fishers become passionate and effective proponents for the conservation of our sport fisheries. We want more fly fishers because we want more stewards who will protect our aquatic resources. Education and conservation—these are FFF's core competencies.

We are proud to count Chico as one of our life members, and prouder still that he is an emeritus member of our Casting Board of Governors. His life membership in FFF signifies a special status, a special dedication to the principles for which FFF stands: catch and release, native fish, ethical angling behavior. There is no doubt about Chico's commitment to conservation. He has been a tireless advocate for the protection and restoration of saltwater gamefish. And he excels as a teacher of the sport. FFF's Casting Instructor Certification Program has provided tremendous value to the fly-fishing consumer who wants to learn to cast. The CICP was established to create a pool of casting instructors who are schooled and certified to rigorous standards established by the FFF's Casting Board of Governors. Chico's involvement with the CICP from its inception has earned him Governor Emeritus status.

If you'd like to join Chico in the federation's education and conservation work, call 406-585-7592, visit www.fedflyfishers.org, or write to the Federation of Fly Fishers, P.O. Box 1595, Bozeman, MT 59771.

Jim Rainey
Executive Director
Federation of Fly Fishers

A pristine bonefish flat early in the morning is an experience all its own. And it's up to us, the fly fishers, to lend help and financial support to the many organizations that are fighting to keep it that way.

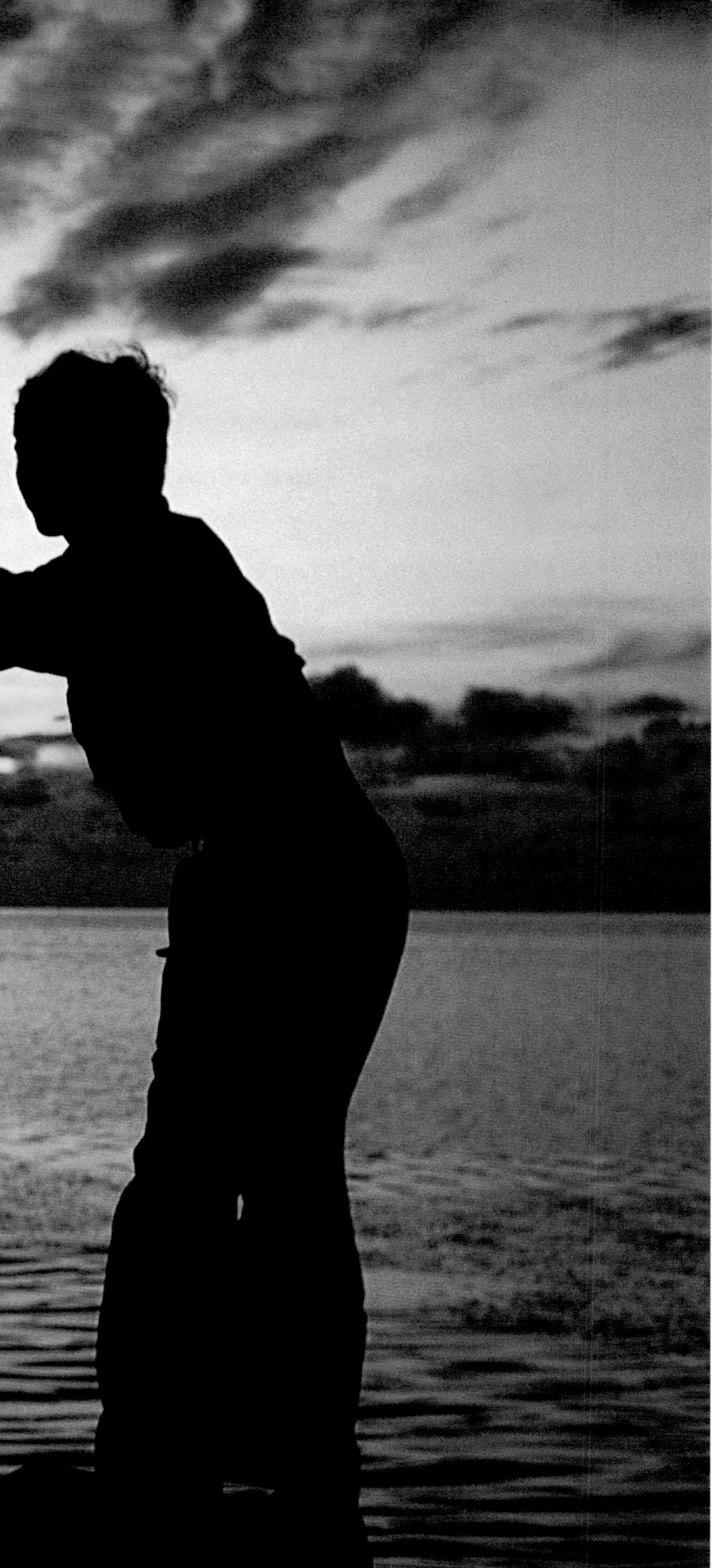

COASTAL CONSERVATION ASSOCIATION: UNITED IN CONSERVATION

Anglers are optimistic by nature. We are great believers in what is possible every time we cast a fly or lure. We are driven to prepare and practice and plan every last detail. We may not catch a single fish, but great hope rides on every effort; a fervent belief that something good is about to happen accompanies every cast. This combination of diligence and optimism is what makes recreational anglers such effective stewards of our marine resources.

In 1977, hope for conservation was a little hard to find on the Texas coast, even among recreational fishermen. Years of intense commercial pressure had driven two of the state's premier sport fish to the brink. A group of fourteen anglers met in a Houston tackle shop and decided that something had to be done to improve not just the management of those two species, but also attitudes toward marine resources in general.

After years of fighting ineffective state management processes, Coastal Conservation Association successfully established gamefish status for both species, removed gill nets, and empowered recreational anglers to make a difference in the conservation of coastal resources.

As American jurist Oliver Wendell Holmes once said, "Greatness is not in where we stand, but in what direction we are moving. We must sail sometimes with the wind, and sometimes against it, but sail we must, and not drift, nor lie at anchor." That statement effectively sums up the evolution of CCA into the national, grassroots organization that it is today. The battle against wasteful commercial fishing practices in Texas suddenly cast a harsh light on many others. Our message of the wise, sustainable use of marine resources appealed to tens of thousands of anglers in states all along the Gulf and Atlantic coasts.

Today, CCA is highly regarded and respected around the nation and the world. Our ability to focus on specific goals and achieve results has made us a role model for recreational fishermen everywhere.

That CCA is such an effective organization is due entirely to the relentless effort and commitment of our members. Becoming a member of CCA does not end with the mailing of a check. CCA members fuel the conservation agenda for their states by organizing banquets and other fundraisers. The funds they raise stay in their states, and are ultimately used to enhance and improve the condition of local marine resources and expand fishing opportunities.

CCA relies on its members' knowledge, skills, and commitment to conservation, and the results have been amazing. Dedicated CCA volunteers are on the front lines of most major fisheries-management debates on two coasts. They have successfully banned gill nets in several states, won gamefish status for key fish species in the Gulf of Mexico and in the Atlantic, established bycatch-reduction guidelines for the shrimp industry, and won a complete commercial net ban in Florida.

We could paint a glowing picture of how far we have come in little more than a quarter century, but more important is what lies over the horizon. Our oceans, bays, and estuaries face new threats every day, and we will have to protect our gains with vigilance. But we should not lose sight of the fact that we also live in a world of great opportunity. CCA will continue to fight for the health and conservation of our marine resources for future generations, and we will do so with diligence and optimism.

At CCA, united in conservation, we always believe that we can make good things happen. To learn more about us, you can call 1-800-201-FISH, visit www.joincca.org, or write to the Coastal Conservation Association at 6919 Portwest, Suite 100, Houston, TX 77024.

Ted Venker
Communications Director
Coastal Conservation Association

The fish you release is your gift to another angler, and remember, it may have been someone's similar gift to you. —*Lee Wulff*

Bibliography

Richards, Bruce W. *Modern Fly Lines*. Birmingham, AL: Odysseus Editions, 1994.

Ritz, Charles. *A Fly Fisher's Life*. New York: Crown Publishers, Inc, 1972.

Roberts, George V. *Fly-Fisher's Guide to Saltwater Naturals and Their Imitations*. Camden, ME: Ragged Mountain Press, 1994.

Stokes, Joseph F. *Divers and Snorkelers Guide to the Fishes and Sea Life of the Caribbean, Florida, Bahamas and Bermuda*. The Academy of Natural Sciences of Philadelphia, 1984.

Voss, Gilbert L. *Seashore Life of Florida and the Caribbean*. Miami: Banyan Books, Inc, 1976.

Wulff, Lee. *Lee Wulff on Flies*. Mechanicsburg, PA: Stackpole Books, 1980.

Zeiller, Warren. *Tropical Marine Invertebrates of Southern Florida and the Bahama Islands*. New York: Wiley-Interscience Publications, 1974.

Index

Page numbers in italics indicate illustrations.